The
Journal Reader

Anthony C. Winkler   **Jo Ray McCuen**

Glendale College

Harcourt Brace College Publishers

Fort Worth Philadelphia San Diego New York Orlando Austin San Antonio
Toronto Montreal London Sydney Tokyo

Publisher	Ted Buchholz
Acquisitions Editor	Stephen T. Jordan
Developmental Editor	Tia Black
Senior Project Editor	Katherine Vardy Lincoln
Production Manager	Erin Gregg/Wendy Temple
Art Director	Jim Dodson
Compositor	G&S Typesetting

Library of Congress Cataloging-in-Publication Number: 93-77718

ISBN: 0-15-500868-4

Photo and Literary Credits in the back of the book.

Copyright © 1993 by Harcourt Brace & Company

All rights reserved. No part of this publication may be reproduced or transmitted in any form or by any means, electronic or mechanical, including photocopy, recording, or any information storage and retrieval system, without permission in writing from the publisher.

Requests for permission to make copies of any part of the work should be mailed to: Permissions Department, Harcourt Brace & Company, 8th floor, Orlando, FL 32887.

Address for editorial correspondence: Harcourt Brace College Publishers, 301 Commerce Street, Suite 3700, Fort Worth, Texas 76102

Address for orders: Harcourt Brace & Company, 6277 Sea Harbor Drive, Orlando, FL 32887 / Tel: 1-800-782-4479, or 1-800-443-0001 (in Florida)

Printed in the United States of America

3 4 5 6 7 8 9 0 1   0 5 9   9 8 7 6 5 4 3 2 1

The
Journal Reader

For Hazel McCuen, who has been more helpful to us than she will ever know, with admiration and gratitude.

Preface

All English instructors know that students find personal writing the easiest to do and the most fun to read. Yet we are also aware that the grimmer business of objective writing must be taught as well. That is exactly what *The Journal Reader* attempts to do, using diary and journal entries as practical models for rhetorical patterns.

And what rhetorical models do journal entries make! No one is ever aloof in the pages of a personal diary, and even writers who carefully tailor a public persona for the world's sake quickly abandon it when they scribble down their thoughts in a quiet room at the end of the day. Here the heart whispers its most intimate secrets and the words are apt to flow with a compelling honesty. Here, also, writers are just as likely to organize their thoughts into the habitual patterns of coherence that a rhetorical reader should teach.

Our apparatus is brief and to the point. We open with an overview essay that acquaints students with the rhetorical patterns the book teaches and with the usefulness of journal keeping to all writers, veteran or beginner. We discuss what we think are the four primary benefits to students of keeping a journal: namely, learning to write freely without fear of criticism; developing a natural style; discovering what they really think about a topic; and practicing the craft of writing.

The readings are then grouped into chapters organized to model the nine most commonly taught rhetorical patterns: Narration, Description, Causal Analysis, Process, Classification, Definition, Comparison/Contrast, Examples, and Argument. Every reading is prefaced with a headnote that introduces the entry and sets a context for understanding it. Every entry is followed by questions grouped under the heading "Speculations" and by two writing assignments. Each chapter ends with a student journal entry following the rhetorical mode of each chapter.

These writing assignments, in nearly every case, use the diary entry as the springboard for an objective essay. For example, after the excerpt from the diary of Etty Hillesum, a Dutch Jew who perished in Auschwitz and who wrote in her diary that she would help God by her exemplary behavior, one of the writing assignments asks students to discuss this question in an argumentative essay: "What is the duty of one who is confronted with oppression and evil?"

Similarly, after the entry by Amelia Stewart Knight, a pioneer mother who trekked across the prairies in a covered wagon, fretting in her diary about Indian raids and the safety of her frolicsome children, an assignment asks students to reconstruct, by textual inference, the diarist's personality.

In sum, *The Journal Reader* is a unique collection of journal entries organized by rhetorical type. It is based on what we think is a simple truth: personal writing, while being more fun to read than impersonal writing, can also be just as effectively used to model and teach rhetorical strategy.

Anthony C. Winkler & Jo Ray McCuen

Table of Contents

Keeping a Journal and the Writing Process

1. Narration   9

Winter, 1920. "I killed a sea otter today. I killed him with the ax, dragged him home, and skinned him." The diary of a pregnant woman marooned by an avalanche in Alaska.
                                                         Martha Martin.   11

April 27, 1862. "We were aroused this morning at one o'clock by the firing of guns and yelling of Indians, answered by our men." A Pioneer Woman's diary.
                                             Jane Gould Tourtillott.   21

February 14, 1865. "What a panic the whole town is in!" The burning of Columbia, South Carolina, by Sherman's troops.
                                             Emma Florence LeConte.   34

May 21, 1660. "All afternoon the King walked here and there, up and down (quite contrary to what I thought him to have been), very active and stirring." The restoration of Charles II.
                                                        Samuel Pepys.   44

Narration – Student Journal   48

2. Description   51

2nd September, 1666. "This fatal night, about ten, began the deplorable fire, near Fleet Street, in London." The Great Fire of London.
                                                        John Evelyn.   54

11th November, 1728. "His legs are very thick and very short, and his hoofs exceedingly broad." A Young Buffalo at Sugar-Tree Creek.
                                                       William Byrd.   61

November, 1945. "At the end of his life, he was still playing bit parts (utility men, as theater people call them). . . ." The death of an old actor.
                                                        Albert Camus.   64

27 October, 1862. *"Of all doleful, dismal, desperate experiences seasickness is certainly the dolefulest, dismalist, and desperate-est!" A 19th-century sea voyage.*
                                        Charlotte Forten Grimke.   68

Description–Student Journal   73

3. Causal Analysis   **75**

January 1, 1869. *"It was then that I left you, my two precious eldest children. I did it and would do it again at any moment, and yet I miss you both and think of you day and night." Why she left her husband and children for Richard Wagner, and the price she paid for doing so.*
                                        Cosima Wagner.   79

November 24, 1918. *"I take some aspirin to help me sleep. But the pain awakens me in the middle of the night, and I think I am going mad." A chronicle of the distressing effect of his homosexual affairs on his marriage.*
                                        André Gide.   82

August, 1932. *"My Lover is in my husband's bed." Duplicity in romance.*
                                        Anaïs Nin.   88

11th July, 1942. *"Many accuse me of indifference and passivity when I refuse to go into hiding." Why she refused to hide from the Nazis.*
                                        Etty Hillesum.   94

Causal Analysis–Student Journal   100

4. Process   **103**

April 9, 1853. *"Started from home at about 11 o'clock and traveled 8 miles and camped in an old house; night cold and frosty." The process of travelling across the plains in a covered wagon.*
                                        Amelia Steward Knight.   106

July, 1943. *"I believe that the Führer will carry the thing through to a successful end." The Battle of Stalingrad as seen by an anonymous German soldier.*
                                        Anonymous.   122

July 12, 1955. "Here I am, in the Passevant Hospital, for a three-day check-up." The process of a physical.
Noël Coward. 128

February 16th, 1964. "I was nervous, fearing the baby would have pain." The process involved in a Jewish briss or circumcision ceremony.
Frances Karlen Santamaria. 133

Process–Student Journal 137

5. Division and Classification 141

August 26, 1805. "The Shoshonees are a small tribe of the nation called Snake Indians. . . ." Classification of the Shoshone Indians.
Meriwether Lewis. 144

January, 1839. "And here it may be well to inform you that the slaves on this plantation are divided into fieldhands and mechanics or artisans." Kinds of slaves on an antebellum Southern plantation.
Fanny Kemble. 151

July 22, 1903. "Next came Hardy—Tess of the D'Ubervilles, which is of a very different type." The kinds of books she enjoyed reading in the country.
Virginia Woolf. 154

March 12, 1865. "In the afternoon Chaplain Lovering came up and held forth. . . ." Types of Civil War Chaplains.
Private John W. Haley, 17th Maine Regiment. 158

Division and Classification–Student Journal 160

6. Definition 163

January 13, 1901. "I have attained an egotism that is rare indeed." Definition of herself.
Mary MacLane. 166

April 8, 1942. "It seems to me absurd to talk about 'happy' and 'unhappy' marriages. Real marriages are both at the same time." Her definition of marriage.
Anne Morrow Lindbergh. 172

July, 1960. "No one ever told me that grief felt so like fear." Defining the terrible grief he felt upon the death of his beloved wife.

C. S. Lewis. 176

October 30, 1973. "Which was more real, the waking or the dream?" An attempt to define reality.

Peter Matthiesson. 183

Definition–Student Journal 188

7. Comparison/Contrast 191

May 20, 1851. "There is, no doubt, a perfect analogy between the life of a human being and that of the vegetable. . . ." A comparison between humans and vegetables.

Henry David Thoreau. 194

October 25, 1914. "While waiting outside the Albert Hall, an extraordinarily weird contrast thrust itself before me. . . ." A contrast between two women seen on the streets of London.

W. N. P. Barbellion. 198

May 18, 1925. "I lunched today, here in Prescott, at the Palace restaurant which in bygone days, twenty years ago, was the Palace Saloon. . . ." A contrast between a famous saloon, then and now.

Henry Fountain Ashurst. 201

March 7, 1944. "If I think now of my life in 1942, it all seems so unreal." A comparison/contrast between the life she led when she was free and her life after going into hiding from the Nazis.

Anne Frank. 204

Comparison/Contrast–Student Journal 208

8. Examples 211

January 12, 1765. "I had eyed a singular lady some time. She was very debauched. But I took a fancy to her." Courting in Italy.

James Boswell. 215

January 14, 1808. *"Of all our acquaintances in Brunswick, the only really intelligent one is Jacobsohn." Examples of the kinds of people he met in Brunswick, Germany.*
Stendhal. 227

June 28, 1921. *"There's no doubt that certain incidents are symbolic." An extended example of a certain symbolic incident in his life.*
Siegfried Sassoon. 231

March 11, 1975. *"Everyone wants to go home." Examples of life in a nursing home.*
Joyce Mary Horner. 236

Examples – Student Journal 246

9. Argument 251

12th March, 1902. *"However much one loves this man whom people regard as a genius, to do nothing but bear and feed his children, sew, order dinner, apply compresses and enemas and silently sit there dully awaiting his demands for one's services, is sheer torture." A personal argument.*
Sophia Tolstoy. 256

27th June, 1940. *"France did not fight." An argument on why the French didn't and couldn't stop the German advance on Paris during World War II.*
William Shirer. 260

January 30, 1964. *"One thing I know for certain: Unlike most of the members of Hitler's intimate circle, I did not have a crippled psyche." Why he served Hitler.*
Albert Speer. 267

22nd November, 1980. *"The campaign is on, and I will be part of every part of it—and I will always be out of place." An argument for what the politician should be and do.*
Mario Cuomo. 271

Argument – Student Journal 278

Keeping a Journal and the Writing Process

The diary or journal is a personal record of experiences, ideas, and reflections and has been kept by the infamous as well as famous, by kings and commoners, by pioneers and the condemned. Ordinarily it begins as an intimate bedside companion, a private refuge for the burdened heart; frequently it ends as a treasure trove of history. For example, Samuel Pepys, a rather obscure London bureaucrat, kept a journal from January 1, 1660 to May 29, 1669, meticulously scribbling down at the end of the day his domestic problems, extramarital flirtations, special dinner engagements, and historical events in a mysterious, private shorthand of his own invention. Today Pepys's journal is regarded as the best of its kind in the English language and gives us some tantalizing glimpses into London society during the Restoration.

Other important English journals were kept by John Evelyn, who described the famous London fire; by the satirical writer Jonathan Swift, whose diary includes a famous description of his beloved "Stella"; by Fanny Burney, a novelist whose letters and diaries paint a fascinating view of upperclass English 18th-century society; by James Boswell, the most prolific and tireless diarist of all, who left behind an enormous journal numbering thousands of scribbled pages discovered decades after his death.

There are some famous American diarists as well. Samuel Sewall, a wealthy Bostonian judge, best known for having presided over the Salem witch trials, kept a journal whose three large volumes have become a priceless record of early provincial Massachusetts; Sarah K. Knight, a Boston schoolteacher, recorded her 1704 journey from Boston to New York, revealing some fascinating colonial customs. Another famous American diarist was William Byrd, one of the wealthiest men in the colonies, who lived the splendid life of an English country gentleman. His many trips into the backwoods of Virginia were meticulously recorded in a polished and witty style that later furnished material for three popular books on Southern life. Henry David Thoreau kept a journal whose scribbled notes frequently ended up in his essays or books.

In modern times, the journal has become the literary companion of travelers, statesmen, politicians, and others as a practical way of damming up on the page the relentless trickle of daily events in which they have had a

1

hand. These intensely private chronicles, when made public, provide extraordinary insights into the mind of an author and his or her sense of the times.

Of what use, however, is keeping a journal to the student who is bent on the pragmatic business of learning the nuts and bolts of writing? How can a journal be of any practical help to such a one?

It can in several ways. First, the journal provides a sanctuary for *writing freely without fear of criticism.* We all have within us an internal editor dispensing those practical rules and principles about writing that we have learned over the years. Although the useful function of this editor is to pass judgment over the style, grammar, and content of everything we write, sometimes it can become so faultfinding and severe as to impede creativity. Journal writing, because it has no audience, liberates us temporarily from this internalized editor and critic, allowing us to play with words without the usual accompanying carping. We write with an exhilarating freedom, for the sheer love and joy of it. Virginia Woolf, among the finest writers and novelists of this century, wrote this about keeping a diary:

> ... *I got out this diary and read, as one always does read one's own writing, with a kind of guilty intensity. I confess that the rough and random style of it, often so ungrammatical, and crying for a word altered, afflicted me somewhat. I am trying to tell whichever self it is that reads this hereafter that I can write very much better; and take no time over this; and forbid her to let the eye of man behold it. And now I may add my little compliment to the effect that it has a slapdash and vigour and sometimes hits an unexpected bull's eye. But what is more to the point is my belief that the habit of writing thus for my own eye is good practice. It loosens the ligaments. Never mind the misses and the stumbles. Going at such a pace as I do I must make the most direct and instant shots at my object, and thus have to lay hands on words, choose them and shoot them with no more pause than is needed to put my pen in the ink. I believe that during the past year I can trace some increase of ease in my professional writing which I attribute to my casual half hours after tea. Moreover there looms ahead of me the shadow of some kind of form which a diary might attain to. I might in the course of time learn what it is that one can make of this loose, drifting material of life; finding another use for it than the use I put it to, so much more consciously and scrupulously in fiction.*

Another practical use for the journal is this: keeping one will encourage you to develop a *natural style*, to learn to use and recognize your own particular voice. All writers modulate their words on the page to match their intended audience. If you are writing an academic assignment, you are likely to write in a formal voice. If you are writing to a maiden aunt, you will use the voice of a respectful nephew. But when you write a journal, you are writing only for yourself, and if you do it enough, sooner or later you will learn to recognize your natural voice, which in turn will help tell you when you have unconsciously lapsed into the stilted, put-on style composition teachers wearily call "collegese." With an ear for your own voice, you would automatically wince at this unmemorable sentence in a college essay: "In my transition years, from the age of thirteen to fifteen, I was of a highly pessimistic and rebellious bent towards legal systems that drew boundaries for my personal existence." You would learn to express the same idea more directly, like this: "In my teens I hated rules that cramped my freedom."

Journal writing will also allow you to *discover what you really think about a topic*. All writers are sometimes vague, biased, or befuddled about an issue until they put down their thoughts on paper. Students are no exception. For example, a young woman in one of our classes admitted that she had no firm opinion on the Equal Rights Amendment until after reading an article by Ellen Goodman, which caused her to think about the matter at length and to confide the following ideas to her journal: "Common sense tells me that unisex toilets and homosexual marriages will not make the sexes equal. Nor will switching men and women around in their social and economic roles do it. Real equality will come only when men and women evolve into true social equals, both spiritually and mentally." Sorting through her thoughts and putting them down on paper clarified for this student how she really felt about equal rights for men and women.

Finally, journal writing is useful because it will provide you with regular *writing practice*. Cultivation of good writing requires the same repetitive practice used to hone the physical skills of playing football or the violin. The more you practice writing, the better you will become at it. Eventually the discipline of keeping a journal and writing regularly will teach you how to prune deadwood, recast bulging or tortured passages, and infuse paragraphs with vivid yet concise details.

HOW TO KEEP A JOURNAL

The journal you keep for your English class will differ from an ordinary journal only in this: you may wish to use some of your entries as kernels for an essay to be submitted to your instructor. To this end, you will want to make your entries as coherent as possible. This does not mean that you should throttle any impulse towards spontaneity, merely that you should try to channel the flow coherently. Here are some suggestions for creating a useful journal.

Keep your journal available and ready.

The most practical medium for a journal is a notebook, which we recommend that you keep in the same place. We do not recommend that you carry it around with you everywhere in case something noteworthy should happen; doing so is likely to turn your journal writing into a frenzied, rather than a relaxed, exercise. Moreover, entries written after the fact are usually better and more balanced than those scribbled down during the heat of the moment.

Be honest in what you write.

This is not gratuitous advice; for some students writing is as formal and ceremonial an act as climbing into a pulpit and as likely to evoke an impulse towards sounding grand and proper. Abandon all idea of properness; what you are after is to put down in the journal how you feel, in your own words. Don't pose; don't shriek and rant and rave. But do express yourself honestly and openly. This entry was written in a diary by one of our students who agreed to let us publish it:

> *Normally I would never associate with Harry, my boss. Every inch of his person is covered with filth. Let's start with the fact that he doesn't bathe. Sitting in the closed cab of a diesel truck on a cold rainy day with Harry is like being shut up in a sewage plant. In fact, today the smell he emanated made my eyes water and my stomach gag. Harry's looks complement his smell, He is short and pudgy, with a beer belly that bulges then hangs out between his grimy, hole-ridden tee shirt and his muddy, rumpled work pants, the latter being held together by a safety pin because his zipper is broken. Harry's belly, a dirty bubble of blubber, hangs naked to the world and has as its high point a belly button packed with some of the richest top soil in the world. . . .*

This description is excessive and detailed, but it is honest and has the ring of sincerity. Although the language and expressions might be out of place in a research paper or formal essay, they do belong in a journal.

Write faithfully and regularly.

Some students feel tyrannized by the need to write in a journal every day. Others start off keeping their journals with a bang but abandon the effort around the middle of the term with a whimper. The middle ground is best: keep your journal regularly but don't become guilty and obsessive about it. Save your entries for impressions that have aroused, surprised, or in some other way excited you. Journal writing is apt to become especially tedious if it is allowed to dwindle into a transcription of tedium and trivia. Every meaningless act does not have to be recorded in your journal simply because it happened. You do not need to amass entries that read like this one:

> *I got up at six, ate some dry Cheerios, fed the cat, and went to my political science class to hear a dry lecture on government ownership and management of the means of production and distribution of goods.*

A journal is not supposed to be as faithful and picky as the minutes of a meeting. It isn't supposed to record all that happens to you, only all that you think really matters, Here is what one student wrote in her journal:

> *This morning I read in the paper that Fergie and Andrew, the Duchess and Duke of York, are getting a divorce. I can't tell you how sad this news made me feel. When these two famous people got married, I was caught up in their romance, feeling that their world was a magic, golden one that could rub off on my drab life. I expected their fairy-tale romance to last forever, but I guess the rich and famous are really not so different from the rest of us.*

Your best journal entries will be the result of your natural sense of wonder, your yearning for happiness, your despair over sorrow, your delight in gossip, your sense of satire, your petty jealousies, and any particular emotion that floods over you in a tidal surge of feeling. Later, when you reread your journal, its authenticity will spur you on to write as truthfully about more formal topics.

Keep your journal private.

Don't share your journal—not even with your closest friend or with your parents. Keep the entries private and utterly your own. If you make your journal public, you might begin to slip into the pose of a writer with an audience, in which case your writing might lose its spontaneity. Naturally, since you are keeping a journal for a class, your instructor might ask to look at it, but this check will be to ensure that you did the writing, not to analyze its quality or content.

Be as coherent as possible.

Journal writing is not brainstorming, which is the act of writing down anything at all that pops into your mind, regardless of whether or not it makes sense. Brainstorming is a useful technique for breaking the "blank page" syndrome because it helps loosen your thoughts and gets something down on paper when you feel thwarted and tongue-tied. Here is an example of brainstorming about an essay on cruelty to animals:

> *Cruelty toward animals is wrong.*
> *After all, they are living creatures like human beings.*
> *That's an important point; now what more is there to say?*
> *Can't really think of anything that would prove animals to be as important as people.*
> *Wouldn't it be worth killing a few thousand rats to find a cure for cancer or AIDS?*
> *I suppose so, or would it?*
> *Killing animals seems so barbaric.*
> *Hideous to imagine how they cut off the heads of rats in labs or knock cows senseless to butcher them.*

When you brainstorm you write without regard for grammar or structure, simply putting down what you think. Journal writing, on the other hand, requires more rhetorical discipline and form, and means putting down your thoughts in a purposeful focus. Thus, a journal entry about cruelty toward animals might read like this:

> *After listening to an argument in the college cafeteria during lunch today, I am convinced more than ever that cruelty toward animals is no different than cruelty toward human beings. In fact, it may be worse because animals are more defenseless. They do not have a League of Anti-Defamation or an NAACP or a Jewish Defense League to protect their civil rights, No constitutional amendment is pending to guarantee their safety. Yet, animals are human beings minus the highly developed brains that make humans self-conscious and able to plot and plan the future. Maybe they can't read or write, but neither can babies or mentally handicapped persons. Yet, we wouldn't dream of using babies or handicapped humans in scientific experimentation, no matter how noble the objectives. . . .*

The difference between the two kinds of writing is a matter of convention. In the first you don't care whether your points can be followed logically and whether your sentences are grammatical; in the second, you do care. Brainstorming is used to warm up a cold brain and get it ready for formal writing; on the other hand, the journal plants seeds that will, it is hoped, later sprout into complete essays. In writing your journal, you do not need to edit or rewrite, but you should put down your thoughts with enough clarity to use them later as the germ in a more formal writing assignment.

THE JOURNAL AND RHETORICAL PATTERNS

Excerpted in this book are entries from journals that conform to certain rhetorical patterns. These eight patterns are narration, description, causal analysis, process, classification. definition, comparison/contrast, examples, and argument. Rhetorical patterns are simply abstract patterns for organizing thoughts and ideas into readable presentations. Students are taught to use them as handy organizational tools, and sometimes assignments are tailored to one specific pattern or another. An instructor, for example, may ask you to compare and contrast your two best friends, or to specify the process involved in baking bread, or to argue for or against a proposition.

Journal writers, as a general rule, are not concerned with rhetorical form, but with simply expressing what they think or feel. Surprisingly enough, however, many diarists will automatically use an identifiable rhetorical pattern to express themselves simply because it provides a convenient organizational structure. The chapters in this book excerpt journal entries as examples of specific rhetorical patterns, and often the assignments that follow will ask you to write about a related topic in a similar pattern.

We do not, however, expect you to write your journal entries in specific patterns nor even to concern yourself with any particular form. But you should simply write your journal as if you were writing utterly to yourself, as if no one else on earth will ever read it. Doing so will encourage your spontaneity and freedom as a writer and will enable you to apply these qualities later to the writing you must do on more formal occasions.

1.

NARRATION.

Winter, 1920s. "I killed a sea otter today. I killed him with the ax, dragged him home, and skinned him." The diary of a pregnant woman marooned by an avalanche in Alaska. Martha Martin.

April 27, 1862. "We were aroused this morning at one o'clock by the firing of guns and yelling of Indians, answered by our men." A pioneer woman's diary. Jane Gould Tourtillott.

February 14, 1865. "What a panic the whole town is in!" The burning of Columbia, South Carolina, by Sherman's troops. Emma Florence LeConte.

May 21, 1660. "All afternoon the King walked here and there, up and down (quite contrary to what I thought him to have been), very active and stirring." The restoration of Charles II. Samuel Pepys.

CHAPTER 1

Narration

If any of the rhetorical modes by which this book is organized can be called natural, it is narration. All of us have occasionally heard someone described as a "natural storyteller"; on the other hand, few have ever heard anyone described as a "natural contraster" or a "natural definer." Storytelling or narration is the rhetorical pattern you will find yourself using the most often as you develop your own journal.

Narrative writing is nearly always sequential, not only in the mechanical sense of occurring in a fixed grammatical pattern, but also because it consists of details arranged to be climactic. The gifted storyteller begins simply, elaborates on the complication of events, and builds to a climax. In the process, characters are sketched, events intertwined, and a plot emerges. If the writer has mastered the storyteller's art, natural curiosity will rivet the reader's interest on the unfolding tale.

Our narration chapter begins with a remarkable chronicle by an anonymous pregnant woman who, separated from her husband in Alaska by an avalanche, gives birth unaided. Jane Gould Tourtillott, a pioneer who crossed the prairies in a covered wagon, recounts her terror of Indians while Emma Florence LeConte, an impassioned seventeen-year-old Southern belle, writes about invading Yankee troops with a patriot's disgust. And Samuel Pepys, the most renowned of all the diarists, describes the triumphant return of Charles II to the English throne after a long exile.

For diarists, whose daily transcriptions are usually driven as much by time as theme, narration is the inevitable outcome of any evening's recounting of the daily events. It is the way that children automatically write when they have first mastered the language. For the beginning journal writer, it is an ideal first exercise in developing a sense of self-expressiveness. Jotting down in your journal what happened in your daily life will teach you how to separate the meaningful detail from the trivial, and how to order events so that they will seem naturally climactic.

MARTHA MARTIN

The identity of Martha Martin, the pseudonym used by the author of this journal, is unknown. We know that she was the wife of a gold prospector in Alaska during a winter in the 1920s and became separated by an avalanche from her husband and his partner for whom she cooked and kept house. Her arm broken by the avalanche, she devised a makeshift splint for her injury and struggled to find her way back to her husband and civilization, eventually giving up as winter closed in. She was, at this time, not only injured but also pregnant. Alone and unaided, she gave birth to an infant daughter in the prospector's cabin; the child, whom she baptized "Donnas," later died after Martha and her husband were reunited. All this comes from a manuscript accidentally discovered by a Macmillan editor some thirty years after the events related here.

Remarkable as is this story of gritty survival, what is striking to a modern reader steeped in feminists' sentiments is the growing sense of self-confidence that Martha Martin recorded during her ordeal. We see her coping with the harsh environment, tanning an otter skin to be used as a blanket for her baby, feeding the wild animals over whom she ruled as self-appointed "Queen," and plotting survival techniques to withstand the brutal Alaskan winter. When she was finally "rescued" by the arrival of Indians on a fishing trip, she confessed to being bewildered and somewhat reluctant about leaving the wilderness, which may have trapped her, but which had also given her an exhilarating sense of her own self-sufficiency and power.

Winter, 1920s

I killed a sea otter today. I actually did kill a sea otter. I killed him with the ax, dragged him home, and skinned him. I took his liver out, and ate part of it. I'm going to eat the rest of it, and his heart, too. His liver was quite large, bigger than a deer's, and it had more lobes to it. It was a very good liver, and I enjoyed it.

Most of today was devoted to the sea otter; getting the hide off was a real task. It's a lovely skin, the softest, silkiest, thickest fur I have ever seen. I am going to make a robe for my baby out of the beautiful fur. My darling child may be born in a lowly cabin, but she shall be wrapped in one of the earth's most costly furs.

It was such a splendid piece of luck. Lucky in more ways than one. The otter might have killed me, although I have never heard of such a thing.

This morning I went to the woods to gather a load of limbs. As I was coming home with them, I saw the tide was nearly out, and I thought I'd walk over to the bar and take a look at the boat . . . I was going along, swinging the ax in my left hand, managing the crutch with the right hand, ... not thinking of anything in particular, when right beside me I heard a bark. It was like a dog bark; not a bow-wow bark, more of a yip. I looked around and saw a huge creature reared up on its haunches. I saw its white teeth.

5 Without thinking, I swung the ax at the side of its head, saw it hit, felt the jar in my arm, heard the thud. As I swung the ax, I turned and tried to run. I was so terrified the thing would nab me from behind that I could hardly move. I glanced over my shoulder to see how close it was. It hadn't budged from where it dropped ...

6 I got down on my knees and examined it from one end to the other. First off, I noticed the lovely fur. I took off my glove and ran my fingers through the nice silky coat. I decided right then I would have the skin. I saw it as a baby blanket ...

7 It is very much against the law to kill a sea otter. Right now I don't care a rap for law. I'd like to have a picture of a game warden who could arrest me now. I am safe enough from the law, and I think I always will be. Under the circumstances I doubt if any judge would send me to jail for what I have done ...

8 I dragged my kill home, and was a long time doing so. I'll bet the creature weighed a hundred pounds. I worked and worked, rested, pulled, and dragged, rested some more, and by and by I reached the cabin with my prize ...

9 I decided to skin it exactly the way the men do a deer. I have watched them many times, but I never helped or paid much attention. I didn't know very much about skinning a fur-bearing animal when I went to work on that creature. How I wished I had an Indian squaw to instruct and help me ...

10 The head was a mess, so I just cut the skin at the neck line and let the head fur go. I chopped off the feet and threw them in the stove. After I got the legs and sides skinned, I turned the otter on his belly and worked the skin off his back down to the tail. I had more trouble with that tail than I did with all the rest of the animal, I wanted it for a neckpiece, and I tried to get the bony tail out without slitting the skin. It can't be done ...

11 My hands got awful cold examining the innards, rather smelly, too. I had let the fire go down, and there wasn't enough hot water for me to scrub properly. I made up the fire, washed a little, and then sat down to rest and gloat over my wonderful sea-otter fur ...

    I woke up in the night, and felt rested, so I got up, lit the carbide lamp, and sat here writing all about my sea otter.

I had planned to work on my otter skin today, but when I looked out 12
this morning I saw Old Nick was flaunting a plume [a sign that a
cold wind was coming up] . . . I put all my energy into gathering
wood and left the skin alone . . .

Goodness, I have lots of work to do before I am ready for my little 13
darling. I must get the fur finished for her. I am determined my child
shall have a priceless gift . . .

I've begun scraping off the fat from my otter skin, and it's about half 14
done. I have learned a few things about scraping skins: they scrape
better when they are stretched tight over the end of a block of wood,
and the fat comes off easier when it is cold. Another thing, when a
skin looks scraped, it still has lots of fat on it. I know I'll have to go
over the whole hide at least twice . . .

At last I have finished scraping the otter skin. It is all very nicely 15
done, and not one single hole did I cut in it . . . I am going to scrub it
well in lots of warm soapy water . . .

Goodness me, I have more chores than a farmer . . .   16

Hurray! My otter skin is nailed to the door. It's the biggest thing— 17
much bigger than I thought it was. It nearly covers the whole door . . .

The wind still howls, swirls, and rages. It's awful cold, maybe ten 18
below. All the peaks look like volcanoes with their great trailing
plumes . . . I brought in some more wood today, but I didn't stay out
long. It was too cold and windy . . .

While I was out in the cold, my breasts ached. They drew up and the 19
nipples stuck out firm, and they ached. When I came in I examined
them, and found they were swelling and have water in them, not
milk, but clear water. Soon my child will be here, and I am not yet
ready to receive her. So much to do and so little time . . .

I have decided to burn the floor. I'll cut the part I have already taken 20
up, now, and save the rest for reserve. There are seven sills, all logs
ten to twelve inches through, under the floor, which is nailed to
them. If I can dig around them, saw them in two, pry them out, and
cut them into blocks, they'll make a lot of fine wood. They are yellow cedar, and so is the puncheon . . .

The otter skin is a disappointment. It's as hard as a board, and I'm 21
just sick about it. I might make it into a Robinson Crusoe umbrella,
but it can never become an infant's robe in its present stiff state. I remember reading or hearing that the Eskimoes chew skins to make

them soft. It would take a lot of chewing to make this big skin soft. I just can't chew it, and I won't even try.

22 The fur is lovely, and it smells clean. I put my face in it, and it's the softest thing I've ever touched. I do wish the skin wasn't so stiff. There must be some way I can fix it. Baby must have one present.

23 If we were home she would have many gifts—a ring, a silver cup with her name on it, a necklace, a silver spoon, a baby book, dresses with lace and ribbons, fine soft knitted things. Even in this northland she would have gifts if anyone knew we were here . . .

24 I believe I have found a way to soften the otter skin. I doubled over a corner of it, and it didn't break as I thought it might, so I folded it some more. No breaks. I kept on folding and creasing it, and now it is no longer board-like; but it's still a very long way from being as soft as I want it to be.

25 I washed a few clothes today. I want clean things for the coming of my child. Surely she will be here soon. I am getting things ready to receive her, and I have done a lot of sewing. Tomorrow I will bathe and make myself presentable for a newborn child . . .

26 I made a birth cloth today from one of Don's union suits. It is all wool and should serve nicely to wrap a newborn child in . . .

27 I plan to use string raveled from a flour sack to tie the cord. I boiled a piece to make sure it is clean . . .

28 I've worked again on the fur, and I'm pleased with the result. I used a different system—pulled it back and forth around the bunk pole. I admire the fur more and more, and I want so much to get it soft enough to use for my baby . . .

29 The milk case is pretty well filled with baby things. Don's shaving soap is in one of the pockets. Shaving soap should be good for baby. It seems right to bathe my child with her father's shaving soap . . .

30 Only a few more days now until I will have a child in my arms.

31 I have been working and working at the otter skin, and I am making progress . . . A dozen times a day I pick it up, rub a part of it between my hands, brush it, hold it to my face, hold it at arm's length to admire it . . .

32 The wind has died away. It is very much warmer, and a haze covers the sky. I went wood gathering and was delighted with my outing. I saw twenty-six deer, and I brought some boughs for the ones who

will pay me a friendly call . . . Two ravens came to eat the otter. I wonder how they knew it was there . . . Maybe they smelled it. My thrush never comes back, and I liked it so much. Those mean old jays—I really shouldn't feed them a crumb . . .

I baked bread, lots of it, far more than I need for myself. The deers are fond of bread, and I thought I'd have an extra amount on hand. Five of them came today to bum a handout, and I didn't disappoint them. I think all of them have been here several times before, but I can be sure of only one—Sammy with the mark on his throat. He is the tamest of the lot, and knows me. He even eats out of my hand . . .

I pounded up my cast and put it on the floor with the gravel. It was quite hard, much harder than I thought. If I had fallen, the cast would have given my arm good protection. Now that my arm is well, I haven't worn the cast for weeks. I don't use my crutch any more, either, but I'm not disposing of it yet . . .

I always think of the child as a girl. What if it's a boy? Oh, it couldn't be . . .

This awful deep snow and hard cold is going to kill off much of our wild life. Poor creatures, what a pity they can't all be like bears and sleep the winter through. But then, what would I do without my friendly bums to come around and ask for bread and lick their chops at me?

Since the baby came down to live in the lower part of my abdomen, I have been constipated, and I don't like it. I think it's the cause of my swollen ankles. I had absolutely nothing here to correct it, so I looked around to see what the wilderness might provide, and hit on the idea of eating seaweed. Certainly it can be called roughage . . . I went along the beach and gathered a mess . . . I picked it over well, washed it thoroughly, and ate quite a lot—ate it raw. It wasn't too awful, but I certainly don't like the stuff. It was very effective, almost more effective than I desired it to be. I was busy all day with the honey bucket . . .

The otter skin is getting to be as soft as I want it to be. I have invented another way to soften it. I made a small mallet and gently pound the folded fur over a block of wood . . .

The fur is finished, and it's exactly as I wished it to be. I am very proud of it. So soft and warm—such a lovely thing. I shall wrap my baby in it when she goes for her outings, and we will walk pridefully along the beach . . .

40 Snow seals every crack, so I only burn a little wood when there is no wind, and open the door for air.

41 I have bathed and washed my head. My hair has grown about three inches and is as curly as can be.[1] I like short hair because it's so easy to wash and dry. I think I may keep it short and never again be bothered with hairpins . . .

42 My body is heavy, and my movements are slow and not too definite. I am becoming clumsy and awkward. I don't like it. Maybe I should sit down and just twiddle my thumbs until Baby comes. I do hope she comes before I use up all this water and burn all my wood . . .

43 I brought a few branches and put a bouquet of cedar and hemlock boughs on my windowsill and placed the finest of Don's ore specimens on either side of it. The window has a nice look, as though a man and a woman lived here . . .

44 There was a little show of blood, and when I saw it I remembered my mother saying it was a sure sign that the child would be born soon . . .

45 I have never seen a child born. I always felt inadequate to help and was too modest to want to be a spectator. I have never seen anything born—not even a cat . . . I am no longer afraid, yet I do wish someone were with me to help me take care of the child . . .

[Martha's child was born after two days of labor, during which she cooked, cared for herself and wrote recollections of life with her husband to try "to order my thoughts, be calm, and not bother my head about all I don't know." Again, she found herself able to cope alone, to deliver the child, to rest, to tie the cord, cut it, and then deliver the afterbirth. And the next day she went on with her narrative.]

46 My darling little girl-child, after such a long and troublesome waiting I now have you in my arms. I am alone no more. I have my baby.

47 I went outside for a short walk on the beach today. It's the first time I've been out since the baby came. The tide was nearly low, and there were dozens of deer on the beach, maybe forty or fifty, maybe as many as a hundred . . . Poor things, they are starving . . . I just can't let all the deer starve. I can cut a little brush, maybe enough to keep some of them alive . . .

48 Several of them followed me back to the cabin and begged for food. I fed them a little, and promised more. I promised to bake lots of

---

[1] Martha had treated her scalp wounds with bacon grease, but mice nibbled at the grease while she slept and she cut her hair to the roots.

bread and make a feast ... It will be the christening feast for the baptism of Donnas. I'll invite the deer to come share our joy and gladness and our food ...

Yesterday was lovely. A beautiful late winter day with a bright sun and a warm southerly breeze. It was a perfect christening day ... When the deer saw me go for a little walk and heard me call to them, they came, and all went well.

Donnas was dressed in all her finery and wrapped in the otter robe, only her little face showing deep down in the fur ...

"Donnas Martin, I baptize thee in the name of the Father, and of the Son, and of the Holy Ghost. Amen."

I dipped the tips of my fingers in the water and signed my child with the sign of the cross. Then I threw more bread morsels to our guests, whose attention had begun to wander ...

I held my baby close, wrapped well in her fur robe, loved her and talked to her. It's wondrous good to talk. It's been so long since I've talked to anyone ... I told her all about us.

"I'm the queen," I told her, "and you are the little princess. The cabin is our palace. None are here to dare dispute our word."

I told her the deer are our helpers and our friends, our subjects and our comfort, and they will give us food and clothing according to our needs. I told her of the birds, the little ptarmigan, the geese, ducks, grouse, and the kindly owl; the prankish ravens and the lordly eagle. Told her of the fishes, the clams, and the mussels. Told her of the mink and the otter, and the great brown bear with his funny, furry cub. Told her of the forest and of the things it will give us; of roots, stems, leaves, and berries, and the fun of gathering them; of the majestic mountain uprising behind us with a vein of gold-bearing ore coming straight from its heart. Told her that all these things were ours to have and to rule over and care for ...

This afternoon I went out and cut brush for the deer. I left baby alone in the cabin, explaining that it was my duty as reigning queen to provide for my subjects. I told her famine was now on our land and I must go cut brush ...

When deer are hungry, they behave differently than when well fed. When a deer is feeling good, he will look up for his food, at least some of the time; but when he is weak with hunger he looks down all the time. There's lots of browse within reach if they would only stretch their necks to get it, but they act stupid, and don't seem to know anything about the food within their reach. Perhaps they are too weak to stretch up: maybe they get dizzy looking up . . .

58 Half and hour before dark seven gray arctic geese came in and settled on the beach almost in front of the cabin. They are either sick or exhausted, or maybe they're tame geese. I went out to look at them, being careful not to frighten them away. I was ready to duck back into the cabin at the first sign of alarm. They didn't seem alarmed, and I went quite close to them. I then gave them food, and they paid no attention to me. Why should wild geese act so? Has something happened to me since my baby came?

59 This is the last piece of usable paper. But that doesn't matter, for I no longer have such need to write. I have no problems to ponder through . . . I am not lonely any more; I have my baby for company . . .
   Soon someone will come and find us here . . .
   Maybe the Indians will come to their fish camp . . .

60 The Indians have come, good, good Indians. Shy, fat, smelly, friendly, kindhearted Indians.

61 Early this morning Donnas and I were out on the beach, she getting the benefit of the warm spring sun, and I putting the finishing touches on the bottom of my overturned dinghy. I looked up from my work and saw two Indian canoes near the far side of the Arm.

62 I rushed to the cabin, grabbed my gun, and fired call shots. I shouted and waved. The canoes turned and started toward my shore.

63 Hurriedly I made up the fire and set coffee water to boil. I brought out my baby's best clothes and got her into them in a jiffy. I ran outside and waved, saw I had time, rushed back and prettied myself up.

64 The cabin was already clean, and there were fresh blueberry blossoms on the windowsill and on the table. I shook out the otter skin to fluff the fur, wrapped Donnas in it, and went to the water's edge. There we awaited our guests.

65 Both canoes grounded at about the same time, and right in front of me. For a little while we just looked at each other. I was all trembly, and it was hard to behave with dignity. After what seemed a rather long time, I did manage to say, "Good morning."

66 "Hello." A breathing space, then another "Hello."
   "I'm glad to see you." That came a little easier.
   "You bet," was the reply, and following a pause, "By golly."
   There was a consultation in Siwash.

"Not dead?"
"No, not dead."

So the conversation went on until I had told my story. No one made a move to get out of the canoes, and it occurred to me they might be waiting politely for an invitation. I hastened to extend one, ending with, "And come see my baby." I held her out toward them.

They piled out, nineteen of them. They didn't seem to see the baby, or me either. All eyes were on the otter skin. There was much Siwash talk, then the spokesman fingered the fur. "Against law. You go jail."

They all laughed.
   "Where you get otter?"

I pointed to the spot on the beach where I had killed the animal, then I acted out the part. That seemed to loosen my tongue, and I talked a streak. The Indians laughed and laughed. They came and fingered the fur, stroked it, looked at the underside.

Then an old squaw said, "Pret-ty good." Splendid words of praise . . .

I knew these poor people needed all the fish they could catch, and I hated to ask them to take time out to do anything for me, yet I thought I had been here long enough, so I asked to be taken to Big Sleeve.

"You bet," was the quick answer. But the west wind was blowing, and it would increase until sundown. It would be better to go in the morning . . .

I was glad for a little more time in my cabin. I almost didn't want to leave at all, I was so mixed up. . . .

Speculations

1. Although we do not know from what part of the journal this excerpt comes, what can we infer about the writer from the episode with the sea otter? What part of the journal do you think this episode came from?
2. What three examples can you give from the journal that attest to the author's skillful adaptation to living alone in the wilderness?
3. In paragraph 23, the writer describes the gifts her baby would have had if she were home. What can you infer about the writer's attitude towards her daughter from the listing of these gifts?

4. In paragraph 54, the author says to her infant daughter: "I'm the queen, and you are the little princess. The cabin is our palace. None are here to dare dispute our word." What does this pronouncement tell you about her?

5. What elements of the writer's style do you think are typical of diary writing?

Spin-offs for writing

1. From your reading of the diary, write an essay reconstructing the author's personality and character. Make and support your intelligent guesses about her age, frame of mind, tastes, and disposition.

2. Write a narration about any wilderness or outdoor adventure you may have had.

3. What functions do Martha Martin's journal and preparing the sea otter skin serve in her life? Explore the benefits of an activity or object in your own experience that might play a similar role.

JANE GOULD TOURTILLOTT

In 1862 Jane Gould Tourtillott began keeping a diary of her family's westward migration in a wagon train from Mitchell, Iowa, to California. Twenty-nine years old at the time, she made the trip with two small sons and her then husband Albert Gould, who, dogged by bad health from the outset, died shortly after their trek ended. Jane soon remarried and bore her new husband, Levi Lancaster Tourtillott, five more children. Her descendants continue to live in California today.

Most of what we know about the early pioneers who crossed the prairies in wagon trains comes from movies and television shows. But other, perhaps more realistic accounts exist in journals and diaries kept by the pioneers themselves, many of whom were women. By the time the family of Jane Gould Tourtillott began the journey, the behavior of the Plains Indians had become unpredictable, even threatening. Some tribes begged from the pioneers, traded with them, and even helped them make river fordings. But others attacked the wagon trains and occasionally slaughtered the wayfarers. Jane Tourtillott's diary chronicles the drudgeries of the journey, which took five grueling months, and her fear and loathing of the Indians. Unlike the movies, her account depicts a real human being suffering hardships for the chance to begin life anew in a promised land.

1 **Sunday, April 27.** Left home this morning, traveled through sloughy prairie, found some hay in an old stack, nooned, and went on to camp four miles from Chickesaw. Camped in a grove near a house where we got grain and hay for our teams. The lady of the house offered us some milk but we had that, came sixteen miles.

2 **Monday, April 28...**

3 **Tuesday, April 29.** When we got up this morning found a white frost on everything. The weather is rather cool for camping yet. Having no stove it is rather unpleasant cooking. Our road is very good today.

4 **Wednesday, April 30.** It was raining this morning when we awoke. Had to get breakfast in the rain, having no tent....

5 **Thursday, May 1.** Took nearly an hour to build a fire this morning, the ground was very wet and the wind blew cold from the Northwest. Started late. Bought some hay during the forenoon, carried it in bundles. Nooned in a grove, camped for night near an old house which served as a wind breaker....

6 **Friday, May 2–Thursday, May 15...**

7 **Friday, May 16.** We are to stay some time to recruit our teams at this place. Most of the women of our company are washing. I am baking.

I made some yeast bread for the first time for three weeks, which tasted very good after eating hot biscuits for so long.

8 **Saturday, May 17.** Awoke this morning, found it raining hard as it could pour down. The men went out of the wagon, made some coffee and warmed some beans and brought the breakfast to the wagon, which we all crowded into. Used a trunk for a table and made out a very comfortable meal. After eating they put the dishes under the wagon where they remained till four o'clock, when the rain ceased and I left the shelter of the wagon for the first time today. It had grown very cold through the day, most of the men were wet through.

9 **Sunday, May 18.** The air was pure this morning but very cold. We were all shivering till about nine, when the sun shone out clear and made the air much warmer. I went out with the children to take a walk and gather flowers. We went in a path through the hazel bushes, saw some hazelnuts laying on the ground. We picked up some and cracked [them] and finding them good, gathered two quarts, which were quite a luxury this time of the year. Some of the women are washing. Sunday though it be. Two gents and ladies of our company went out horseback riding for their health.

10 **Tuesday, May 20.** The weather was fair this morning but towards noon it clouded up. Our company all left us to go on. We were detained waiting for a part of our company. While we were preparing our supper it began to rain so that by the time supper was ready we were slightly dampened and what was worse, we had to eat in the rain.

11 **Wednesday, May 21–Thursday, May 29** . . .

12 **Friday, May 30** . . . Lou[1] and I shot at a mark with a revolver. The boys said we did first rate for new beginners. . . .

13 **Saturday, May 31** . . . Gus[2] was fiddling in the evening and two ladies and one gent came over. Albert played some. They wished us to come up to the house and have a little dance but Albert, feeling rather indisposed, we decline the invitation.

14 **Sunday, June 1** . . .

15 **Monday, June 2** . . . Albert went fishing and caught two fish about as long as one's finger. I cooked one for him. His appetite is rather capricious, he not being well.

---

[1] Lou—The author's sister-in-law.
[2] Gus—The Gould's hired hand and friend.

Tuesday, June 3 . . . In the afternoon we passed a lonely nameless grave on the prairie. It had a headboard. It called up a sad train of thoughts, to my mind, it seems so sad to think of being buried and left alone in so wild a country with no one to plant a flower or shed a tear o'er one's grave. . . .

Wednesday, June 4. Had an early start this morning. A beautiful morning it was too. Clear, bright and warm. We traveled nearly ten miles. I should think, nooned on the Platte banks. The boys waded across on to an island and brought some chips in a sack which were sufficient to get our supper with. . . .

June 5–June 10 . . .

Wednesday, June 11 . . . Lou and I went calling on a new neighbor who has a sick child. . . .

Thursday, June 12 . . .

Friday, June 13 . . . A lady on our train was thrown from her horse and injured quite severely. They sent on ahead a mile for Doctor, who was in the next train.

Saturday, June 14–Sunday, June 22 . . .

Monday, June 23. 'Twas somewhat cloudy this morning when we arose. Had a rough road this forenoon. Stopped for noon near the Platte. It is filled with small islands. The boys have gone bathing. There is a grave of a woman near here. The tire of a wagon is bent up and put for a head and foot stone, her name and age is filed upon it. . . .

Tuesday, June 24. Were up rather late this morning, but had a choice breakfast of antelope meat, which was brought us by Mr. Bullwinkle, some that he bought of the Indians. He brought it for us to cook on shares. It was really delicious. We passed through a small Indian village (a temporary one) this forenoon. We saw that they had over a hundred ponies. There were sixteen wigwams. The road has been better today. Nooned on the Platte banks. While we were eating our lunch there was an Indian Chief rode up on a nice mule, his bridle was covered with silver plates, he had the Masonic emblems on it (he the Indian) was dressed in grand style. He had a looking glass and comb suspended by a string, had a fan and silver ornaments made of half dollars made into fancy shapes. I can't describe half the ornaments that he wore. He was real good looking for an Indian. He wore earrings as much as eight inches long. . . .

25 *Wednesday, June 25* ... The Indians came around, so many times that we hardly had a chance to get our dinners. They were very anxious to "swap" moccasins and lariats for money, powder and whiskey, but we had none to trade. Charley[3] traded a little iron tea-kettle for a lariat. Two of them shot at a mark with Albert's gun. He beat them. ...

26 *Thursday, June 26–Friday, June 27* ...

27 *Saturday, June 28.* Did not travel today. Stayed over to let the cattle have a chance to rest. Albert set the tire of his wagon wheels and set some shoes on the horses, which made a pretty hard days work for him. He also shortened the reach for his wagon. The smith here only charges ten dollars for shoeing a yoke of oxen. I did a large washing and Lucy did a large quantity of cooking. Made herself nearly sick working so hard. Gus and I took my clothes to the river to rinse them. Was a little island covered with wild bushes nearby. Gus tried to wade over to it—to hang the clothes but it was too deep so we were obliged to hang them on some low bushes close to the river.

28 *Sunday, June 29—Monday, June 30* ...

29 *Tuesday, July 1* ... In the night I heard Mrs. Wilson's baby crying very hard indeed, it had fallen from the wagon. It cried for nearly an hour, he struck his head. ...

30 *Wednesday, July 2—Thursday, July 3* ...

31 *Friday, July 4.* Today is the Fourth of July and here we are away off in the wilderness and can't even stay over a day to do any extra cooking. The men fired their guns. We wonder what the folks at home are doing and oh, how we wish we were there. Albert is not well today, so I drive. I have been in the habit of sleeping a while every forenoon, so naturally I was very sleepy driving. Went to sleep a multitude of times, to awaken with a start fancying we were running into gullies. After going a short distance we came in sight of a mail station, on the other side of the river there were several buildings. They are of adobe, I suppose. Nearly opposite on this side of the river we passed a little log hut which is used for a store. It was really a welcome sight after going four hundred miles without seeing a house of any kind. ...

32 *Saturday, July 5—Tuesday, July 8* ...

---

[3]Charley—Albert's brother and husband to Lou.

Wednesday, July 9 . . . We hear many stories of Indians depredations, but do not feel frightened yet. . . .   33

July 10 . . .   34

Friday, July 11 . . . There was a little child run over by a wagon in Walker's train, who are just ahead of us. The child was injured quite seriously. . . . They sent for a German physician that belongs to our train, to see the child that was injured. He said he thought it would get better.   35

July 12—July 19 . . .   36

Sunday, July 20 . . . The men had a ball-play towards night. Seemed to enjoy themselves very much, it seemed like old times.   37

Monday, July 21 . . . Our men went to work this morning to building a raft. Worked hard all day. Half of the men in the water, too. . . .   38

Tuesday, July 22 . . . Went to work this morning as early as possible to ferrying the wagons over. Had to take them apart and float the box and cover behind. The two boxes were fastened together by the rods, one before to tow in and the other to load. Worked till dark. We were the last but one to cross tonight. Got some of our groceries wet, some coffee, sugar dissolved.   39

July 24–July 25 . . .   40

Saturday, July 26 . . . Annie McMillen had lagged behind, walking, when we stopped. The whole train had crossed the creek before they thought of her. The creek was so deep that it ran into the wagon boxes, so she could not wade. A man on horseback went over for her, and another man on a mule went to help her on. The mules refused to go clear across, went where the water was very deep, threw the man off and almost trampled him, but he finally got out safe, only well wet and with the loss of a good hat, which is no trifling loss here.[4]   41

Sunday, July 27 . . .   42

---

[4]There are two versions of the diary entries between April 27 and July 26. One version, edited by Philip K. Lack, said to have been copied from the original diary by Jane Gould's mother, is published in the Annals of Iowa. See vol. 37, 37 (Fall 1964, and Winter, Spring and Summer, 1965), 460–76, 544–59, 623–40, 68–75. A copy of the manuscript is deposited with the Iowa State Historical Library. Another version of the first 89 days of travel is reprinted here with permission of Jane Gould Tourtillott's granddaughter, Mrs. Gertrude T. Bradley, Cupertino, California. A copy of this manuscript is deposited with the Bancroft Library, University of California, Berkeley. The Iowa and California branches of the family have lost touch with each other. It is difficult to establish which text is authentic.

43 **Monday, July 28** . . . Came past a camp of thirty six wagons who have been camped for some time here in the mountains. They have had their cattle stampeded four or five times. There was a woman died in this train yesterday. She left six children, one of them only two days old.[5] Poor little thing, it had better have died with its mother. They made a good picket fence around the grave.

44 **July 29–31, August 1–2** . . .

45 **Sunday, August 3** . . . We passed by the train I have just spoken of. They had just buried the babe of the woman who died days ago, and were just digging a grave for another woman that was run over by the cattle and wagons when they stampeded yesterday. She lived twenty-four hours, she gave birth to a child a short time before she died. The child was buried with her. She leaves a little two year old girl and a husband. They say he is nearly crazy with sorrow. . . .

46 **August 4** . . .

47 **Tuesday, August 5** . . . Did not start very early. Waited for a train to pass. It seems today as if I *must* go home to father's to see them all. I can't wait another minute. If I could only *hear* from them it would do some good, but I suppose I shall have to wait whether I am patient or not. . . .

48 **August 6–9** . . .

49 **Sunday, August 10** . . . Traveled five or six miles when we came to Snake River. We stayed till two o'clock then traveled till about four or five, when *we* from the back end of the train saw those on ahead all get out their guns. In a short time the word came back that a train six miles on had been attacked by the Indians, and some killed and that was cause enough for the arming. In a short time were met by two men. They wanted us to go a short distance from the road and bring two dead men to their camp, five miles ahead.

50 Albert unloaded his little wagon and sent Gus back with them and about forty armed men from both trains, to get them. We learned that a train of eleven wagons had been plundered of all that was in them and the teams taken and the men killed. One was Mr. Bullwinkle who left us the 25th of last month, at the crossing of Green River. He went on with this Adams train. Was intending to wait for us but we had not overtaken him yet. He was shot eight times. His

---

[5]Here Jane Gould's account, like those of other women diarists, avoids associating the woman's death with the mention of childbirth.

dog was shot four times before he would let them get to the wagon. They took all that he had in his wagon, except his trunks and books and papers. They broke open his trunks and took all that they contained. (He had six.) It is supposed that they took six thousand dollars from him, tore the cover from his wagon, it was oilcloth. He had four choice horses. They ran away when he was shot, the harnesses were found on the trail where it was cut from them when they went. It was a nice silver one. The Captain had a daughter shot and wounded severely. This happened yesterday. This morning a part of their train and a part of the Kennedy train went in pursuit of the stock. They were surrounded by Indians on ponies, two killed, several wounded and two supposed to be killed. They were never found. One of those killed was Capt. Adams' son, the other was a young man in the Kennedy train. Those that we carried to camp were those killed this morning. Mr. Bullwinkle and the two others were buried before we got to the camp. There were one hundred and fifty wagons there and thirty four of ours. Capt. Kennedy was severely wounded. Capt. Hunter of Iowa City train was killed likewise by an Indian. We camped near Snake River. We could not get George to ride after the news, he *would* walk and carry his loaded pistol to help.

Monday, August 11 . . . The two men we brought up were buried early this morning with the other three, so they laid five men side by side in this vast wilderness, killed by guns and arrows of the red demons. The chief appeared yesterday in a suit of Mr. Bullwinkle's on the battlefield. . . .

Tuesday, August 12. Capt. Adams' daughter died this morning from the effects of her wound. Was buried in a box made of a wagon box. Poor father and mother lost one son and one daughter, all of his teams, clothing and four thousand dollars. Is left dependent on the bounty of strangers. . . . In the evening we took in Mrs. Ellen Ives, one of the ladies of the plundered train. Her husband goes in the wagon just ahead of us. She was married the morning she started for California. Not a very pleasant wedding tour. . . .

Thursday, August 13 . . . After going up the canyon about four miles, we came to a wagon that had been stopped. There was a new harness, or parts of one, some collars and close by we saw the bodies of three dead men, top of the ground. They had been dead two or three weeks. Some one had been along and thrown a little earth over them, but they were mostly uncovered again. One had his head and face out, another his legs, a third, his hands and arms. Oh! it is a horrid thing. I wish all of the Indians in Christendom were exterminated. . . .

54 *Friday, August 15.* We were aroused this morning at one o'clock by the firing of guns and yelling of Indians, answered by our men. The Capt. calling, "come on you red devils." It did not take us long to dress, for once. I hurried for the children and had them dress and get into our wagon, put up a mattress and some beds and quilts on the exposed side of the wagon to protect us. The firing was from the willows and from the mouth of the corrall. There were two other trains with us. There are one hundred and eleven wagons of all and two hundred or more men. The firing did not continue long nor do any harm. Our men shot a good many balls into the willows but I presume they were not effectual. We sat and watched and waited till morning. Yoked the cattle and turned them out with a heavy guard and several scouts to clear the bushes. Cooked our breakfast and started. There were ball holes through two or three wagon covers. . . . We nooned in a little valley but kept our eyes open to all that might be hidden in the bushes and behind the rocks. . . . In the night we were all startled by the bark of the kiota [coyote], which sounded very much like the Indians when they attacked us last night. The alarm gun was fired, which awakened us all. After a while we concluded it was the wolves and went to bed. Most of the train slept under the wagons, dug a trench and blockaded on the outside of the wagon. Set up flour sacks and all manner of stuff. We hung up a cotton mattress and some quilts, and slept in the wagon. . . . It is not an enviable situation to be placed in, not to know at night when you go to bed, whether you will all be alive in the morning or not.

55 *August 16–20.* [Each night the emigrants dug trenches and kept anxious watch for Indians.]

56 *Thursday, August 21.* The road was rough some of the way. Some steep hills to pass over. We saw several Indians today for the first time. They were Snakes. One of them said that he was chief. Three of the men in the Newburn train burned their wigwams in their absence. They came on at noon, were very indignant about it and wanted us to pay for it. Capt. Walker told them who it was that burned them. They got quite a good deal of bread and bacon from different ones from our camp. After being in trouble with them for so long, we are glad to let them be friendly if they will. Albert, Lucy and I went a short way from the road and got our arms full of currant bushes laden with fruit, both red and white. We ate what we wished and had nearly two quarts to eat with sugar for supper. They were real refreshing.[6]

---

[6] Gathering berries was a chore usually assigned to the children, but after the Indian attack, only the adults risked moving any distance from the wagons.

Saturday, August 23 . . . Oh dear, I do so want to get there. It is now almost four months since we have slept in a house. If I could only be set down at home with all the folks I think there would be some talking as well as resting. Albert is so very miserable too, that I don't enjoy myself as well as I would if he was well. There have been Indians around today begging. We are glad to see them do so now, for all we are disgusted with the wretched creatures.

Sunday, August 24–Tuesday, August 26 . . .

Wednesday, August 27 The first thing I heard this morning was that Mr. McMillen was dead. Died at ten last night. He died quite suddenly. Was buried early this morning. They could not get boards to make a coffin. They dug his grave vault fashion made it just the right size for him, high enough for him to lay in, then wider to lay short boards over him. He was in his clothes with a sheet around him. It seems hard to have to bury ones friends in such a way. I do feel so sorry for the poor wife and daughter, strangers in a strange land. All of her relatives are in Ohio. . . . [Gus, the friend and hired man of the Goulds, took over the driving of Mrs. McMillen's team.]

Thursday, August 28 . . .

Friday, August 29 . . . We came to where there have been Indian depredations committed. There were feathers strewn around, a broken wagon, and a large grave with stones over it, a bloody piece of a shirt on it. It had probably two or more persons in it. There was a hat and a nightcap found near, also some small pieces of money. It had been done only a few days. We camped after dark on the Humboldt River for which we were very thankful. . . .

Saturday, August 30–Thursday, September 4 . . .

Friday, September 5 . . . Here we are obliged to separate some of the train go the Honey Lake Route and some the Carson River Route. We and 24 others go the latter one. The Capt. goes with the former. We seem like a family of children without a father. *We* think he is the best Capt. on the road. Some could hardly refrain from shedding tears at parting. Tears came into the Capt's. eyes as he bade them good-bye. . . .

Saturday, September 6 . . .

Sunday, September 7 . . . We hear such discouraging account of our road to Carson River, that the female portion of our little train are almost discouraged. We sat by moonlight and discussed matters till near eleven o'clock. Had quite a number of gentlemen visitors during the evening. They say there is no grass between here and Carson River. If not, I don't know what we can do.

66 *Monday, September 8* ... Some of the train had a dance, but we did not join them.

67 *Tuesday, September 9* ... When we arose the men told us that if we were in a hurry with our work we might have time to walk up to see [Humboldt] City. So we hurried. Lucy and I. Mrs. McMillen and Annie went to see. Found it a long walk, I should think all of the way up hill. There are some twenty-five buildings. Some of them rough stone and some adobe, some plastered and some not (on the outside) mostly covered with cotton cloth. We called to see a woman who has a sick husband. They are emigrants. Have only been here a week, are waiting for him to recover. He has the typhoid fever. They wished to cross the Nevada range this fall. Provisions are very high here. Flour is thirteen dollars per cwt., coffee 45 cts. per pound, sugar three pound for a dollar, bacon 35 cts per pound. Mrs. McMillen and Annie went into a house and stayed for a few minutes. When she came out she said she intended to stay there, and in the face of all the opposition we raised, she stayed. There were none of us that had any more than provisions enough to last through and some I fear, *not* enough, so Gus was obliged to stay too. I was sorry to leave him this side of Cal. as long as he started with us, and is an old acquaintance. I was sorry to leave Mrs. McMillen, it does not seem like a good place for a woman to stay, there are only four families here, the rest are single men. We came on six or eight miles and stopped without much grass for noon (I am just as homesick as I can be). I chanced to make this remark and Albert has written it down. ...

68 *Wednesday, September 10–Saturday, September 13* ...

69 *Sunday, September 14* ... Ellen and Will Jones got a chance to go to Virginia City free of charge for which we were very glad, on account of our heavy load. We are nearly out of provisions too. We have to pay five cts. per lb. for hay. Albert sold his wiffletree[7] and neck yoke for five and a half dollars. We had ten miles to go to get to the desert. ... Lou and I walked a great deal. The roads are literally lined with wagon irons and keg hoops and piles of bones every five rods. ...

---

[7] The wiffletree (or whiffletree) is the pivoted swinging bar to which the traces of a harness are fastened and by which the wagon is drawn.

Monday, September 15 . . . The road is the worst I ever saw. Lou and I walked the whole ten miles, till we came to within a mile of Ragtown. We saw the trees on Carson River and thought we were almost there but we kept going and going and it seemed as if I never could get there.

September 16–18. [They were now passing through the California mining camps.]

Friday, September 19 . . . Were quite surprised to find Ellen here. She had hired out for a month for twenty dollars. Her husband is at Virginia City working for fifty dollars per month. After coming five miles farther we come to another well and a tent for a station. Found Mrs. McMillen here, just ready to go. Went on together a mile and a half. Lou and I and she and Annie walked so as to visit. [Mrs. McMillen decided not to remain in Humboldt City, but came with Gus all the way to the coast, where the Goulds met her.]

September 20 . . .

Sunday, September 21 . . . There are houses and public wells all along on the road to Empire City, which is ten miles from Dayton. We stayed at Empire all night. This town is not as large as Dayton, but the streets are full of freight wagons. We see a great many fruit wagons here from Cal. There is a quartz mill here also. Money seems to be plenty. Buildings going up fast. Here is the place to make money, especially for a man without a family can get fifty dollars per month, and board, for most any kind of work and mechanics get more.

September 22–30 . . . [The party came through the Great Redwood Forest, where Jane found the Big Tree Hotel already a prosperous inn. She and Lou danced a "schottische" on the surface of a polished giant redwood.]

Wednesday, October 1. Our roads are rather rough. I walked on before the teams two miles or more, called at a farm for a drink and to rest. Had the pleasure of sitting in a large rocking chair, the first time in five months. They have plenty of fruit trees. Albert called for me and bought some fine grapes, and a pail of tomatoes. The lady of the house gave me some roses and verbenas, they were beautiful and fragrant too. . . .

Thursday, October 2 . . .

Friday, October 3 . . . Arrived at the first house in the settlement in the San Joaquin Valley on this road at ten o'clock. The moon shone brightly, we pitched our tent and got supper. In this part of the country all of the water is pumped by power of windmills. The orchards are not as they are in the States, they are so small and the trees so near together. Every garden and orchard has its windmill to irrigate it. . . .

79 *October 4–5* . . .

80 **Monday, October 6.** Lou washed today. The men went to town to see what was to be seen and done. Albert came home sick, went to bed and did not sit up but a few minutes, the rest of the day. . . .

81 *Tuesday, October 7.* Are still staying here. Albert seems to be no better. I have almost have the "blues" having to camp out and Albert sick too. . . . This day seems long, I can't set myself to sewing although I have so much to do.

82 *Wednesday, October 8.* Arose this morning with the intention of going to town. Lou and I went over a few minutes to call on Mrs. Burkett, she had a visitor from town, she regaled us with some very fine peaches. Went to town and pitched our tent. A lady called by the fence and told us of a house to rent, also gave us some green corn, the first we have had this year. Charlie went with her to the house, made a bargain, provided it pleased all around, which it did, we picked up and went right over. Slept in a house the first time for over five months. The house is one block east of the Lunatic Asylum. The block which intervenes is vacant. We are to board the owner of the house, Mr. Bray. The house is very convenient. We pay ten dollars per month rent. The house is over half a mile from the business part of town.

Farewell to the old Journal.

(Signed) Jane A. Gould

Speculations

1. What can you infer about the writer from the style of this diary?
2. What can you deduce about the division of labor between the sexes that prevailed on the wagon train?
3. Why do you think the writer observes such a strict day-by-day chronology in her diary? What is the major advantage and disadvantage of this method of diary writing?

4. Aside from the detailed chronological accounting rendered in this diary, how else do you think a pioneer crossing the prairies in a wagon train might have structured a diary to record the event?

5. How would you characterize the author's attitude towards the Indians before the attacks began?

Spin-offs for writing

1. Write an essay identifying those themes and preoccupations that, in your mind, identify the diarist as a woman.

2. Write an essay contrasting Jane Gould Tourtillott's depiction of a wagon train journey across the prairies with the portrayal of the event in any movie or television show you remember.

EMMA FLORENCE LECONTE

Emma Florence LeConte (1847–1932) was seventeen years old in 1865 when Sherman's troops attacked Columbia, South Carolina, the town where her father, Joseph LeConte, a renowned scientist, was a faculty member at the South Carolina State University. From December 1864 through August 1865 she kept a diary in which she faithfully chronicled the turbulence of the Civil War as seen through the eyes of a patriotic Southern young woman.

This diary is all the more remarkable when we remember its writer's youth. Her reactions are typically passionate and enthusiastic, as we would expect from someone so young, but her descriptions of the burning of "Poor old Columbia" sparkle with a vividness and liveliness that any veteran reporter would envy. She begins by saying that the family had decided to remain in Columbia as Sherman's troops approached but that her father would leave. What she does not tell us is that her father was a key scientist involved in producing powder for the Confederacy and would no doubt have been imprisoned by Sherman's troops had he been captured. The rest of the diary is an electrifying narrative of the excitement and terror that shook the family as they watched Sherman's victorious troops sweeping through Columbia.

Columbia, South Carolina

1 **February 14, 1865.** What a panic the whole town is in! I have not been out of the house myself, but Father says the intensest excitement prevails on the street. The Yankees are reported a few miles off on the other side of the river. How strong no one seems to know. It is decided if this be true that we will remain quietly here, father alone leaving. It is thought Columbia can hardly be taken by raid as we have the whole of Butler's cavalry here—and if they do we have to take the consequences. It is true some think Sherman will burn the town, but we can hardly believe that. Besides these buildings, though they are State property, yet the fact that they are used as a hospital will, it is thought, protect them. I have been busily making large pockets to wear under my hoopskirt—they will hardly search our persons. Still everything of any value is to be packed up to go with father. I do not feel half so frightened as I thought I would. Perhaps because I realize they are coming. I hope still this is a false report. Maggie Adams and her husband have promised to stay here during father's absence. She is a Yankee and may be some protection and help.... I look forward with terror, and yet with a kind of callousness to their approach....

2 **February 15.** Oh, how is it possible to write amid this excitement and confusion! We are too far off to hear and see much down here in

the Campus, but they tell me the streets in town are lined with panic-stricken crowds, trying to escape. All is confusion and turmoil. The Government is rapidly moving off stores—all day the trains have been running, whistles blowing and wagons rattling through the streets. All day we have been listening to the booming of cannon—receiving conflicting reports of the fighting. All day wagons and ambulances have been bringing in the wounded over the muddy streets and through the drizzling rain, with the dark clouds overhead. All day in our own household has confusion reigned too. The back parlor strewed with clothing etc., open trunks standing about, while a general feeling of misery and tension pervaded the atmosphere. Everything is to go that can be sent—house linen, blankets, clothing, silver, jewelry—even the wine—everything movable of any value. Hospital flags have been erected at the different gates of the Campus—we hope the fact of our living within the walls may be of some protection to us, but I fear not. I feel sure these buildings will be destroyed. I wish mother could have sent more furniture to different friends in town, but it is too late now. . . . I have destroyed most of my papers, but have a lot of letters still that I do not wish to burn, and yet I do not care to have them share the fate of Aunt Jane's and Cousin Ada's in Liberty Co., which were read and scattered along the roads. I will try to hide them. One of my bags is filled. The other I will pack tonight. Henry will stay with us, and vows he will stand by us through thick and thin—I believe he means it, but do not know how he will hold on. It is so cold and we have no wood. The country people will not venture in town lest their horses should be impressed. So we sit shivering and trying to coax a handful of wet pine to burn. Yonder come more wounded—poor fellows—indeed I can write no more.

Night. Nearer and nearer, clearer and more distinctly sound the cannon—Oh, it is heart-sickening to listen to it! . . . Just now as I stood on the piazza listening, the reports sounded so frightfully loud and near that I could not help shuddering at each one. And yet there is something exciting—sublime—in a cannonade. But the horrible uncertainty of what is before us! My great fear now is for father—Oh, if he were only gone—were only safe!

The alarm bell is ringing. Just now when I first heard it clang out my heart gave a leap, and I thought at once, "It's the Yankees." So nervous have I grown that the slightest unusual sound startles me. Of course I knew it was fire, yet it was with a beating heart I threw open the window to see the western horizon lit up with the glow of flames. Although we are composed, our souls are sick with anxiety. . . .

Later— They have passed our first line of breastworks. No firing tonight. Father and Uncle John leave tonight or tomorrow morning.

6 ***February 16.*** How can the terror and excitement of today be described! I feel a little quieter now and seize the opportunity to write a few lines. Last night, or rather early this morning, father left. After the last lines in my entry last evening, I went downstairs and found in the back parlor with father a man calling himself Davis. I had heard father speak of him before. He met him in Georgia while making his way back home with Sallie, and he was kind to them during that difficult journey. He calls himself a Confederate spy or scout and is an oddity. I only half trust him—he evidently is not what he pretends to be. He says he is a Kentuckian and is both coarse and uneducated, but wonderfully keen and penetrating. . . . He has taken an unaccountable fancy to father—as shown by his hunting him up—and he assures him again and again that he will have us protected during the presence of the Yankees here. He claims great influence with the Yankee officers and entire knowledge of the enemy's movements. All the evening he seemed exceedingly uneasy that Father should so long have deferred his departure and very impatient to get him off. He offered to lend him a horse if that would facilitate his leaving. Father is not uneasy, for our authorities assure him that all is right, but I do not like this man's evident anxiety. Can he know more than the Generals? About half-past twelve father took leave of us. Thus to part! Father starting on an uncertain journey—not knowing whether he may not be captured in his flight, and leaving us to the mercy of the inhuman beastly Yankees—I think it was the saddest moment of my life. Of course father feels very anxious about us, and the last words the man Davis said to him were to assure him that he might feel easy about us. I wonder if there is any confidence to be put in what he says! Hardly, I suppose. We said goodbye with heavy hearts and with many presentiments of evil.

7 After father was gone I sat up still, talking with Davis. I could not sleep, and besides I wanted to hear that father was safely off. We asked our guest how he thought Columbia would be treated—he said he would not tell us—it would alarm us too much. Does he really know all he pretends, or is he only guessing? It was three o'clock before I lay down and fell into a disturbing doze which lasted until seven. Davis stayed and slept on the ground floor, but was gone before we awoke.

8 The breakfast hour passed in comparative calm. About nine o'clock we were sitting in the dining room, having just returned from the piazza where we had been watching a brigade of cavalry passing to the front. "Wouldn't it be dreadful if they should shell the city?" someone said. "They would not do that," replied mother, "for they have not demanded its surrender." Scarcely had the words passed her lips when Jane, the nurse, rushed in crying out that they

were shelling. We ran to the front door just in time to hear a shell go whirring past. It fell and exploded not far off. This was so unexpected. I do not know why, but in all my list of anticipated horrors I somehow had not thought of a bombardment. I leaned against the door, fairly shivering, partly with cold, but chiefly from nervous excitement. After listening to them awhile this wore off and I became accustomed to the shells. They were shelling the town from the Lexington heights across the river, and from the Campus their troops could be seen drawn up on the hill-tops. Up the street this morning the Government stores were thrown open to the people and there was a general scramble. Our negroes were up there until frightened home by the shells. The shelling was discontinued for an hour or two and then renewed with so much fury that we unanimously resolved to adjourn to the basement and abandon the upper rooms. Sallie and I went up to our rooms to bring down our things. I was standing at my bureau with my arms full when I heard a loud report. The shell whistled right over my head and exploded. I stood breathless, really expecting to see it fall in the room. When it had passed I went into the hall and met Sallie, coming from her room, pale and trembling. "Oh Emma" she said, "this is dreadful!"

9 We went downstairs—mother stood in the hall looking very much frightened. "Did you hear—" "Yes indeed"—and at that instant another whistled close overhead. This was rather unpleasant and we retreated to the basement without further delay, where we sat listening as they fell now nearer, and now farther off. Sallie suffered most—she would not be left alone, and would not allow me to go to the outer door to look about, but would call me back in terror. The firing ceased about dinner time. . . .

10 During the afternoon a rapid cannonade was kept up and I do not think the forces could have been more than half a mile from here. Dr. Thomson says they are only skirmishing. Davis says we have received reinforcements, but he thinks we cannot hold the town as we have given up the strongest position. He was here this morning during the shelling and stood talking to me in the dining room for some time, giving me a picture of the confusion in town. Our soldiers had opened and plundered some of the stores. He brought me a present of a box of fancy feathers and one or two other little things he had picked up. He says the bridge will be burned and the towns evacuated tonight.

11 *10 o'clock P.M.*—They are in bed sleeping, or trying to sleep. I don't think I shall attempt it. Davis was here just now to tell the news—it is kind of him to come so often to keep us posted. I went up to see him—made Henry light the gas and sat talking to him in

the hall, while through the open door came the shouts of the soldiery drawn up along the streets ready to march out. Perhaps the Yankees may be in tonight—yet I do not feel as frightened as I thought I would. . . . We have moved into the back basement room. I opened the door which gives from our present sleeping room on the back yard just now, and the atmosphere was stifling with gun-powder smoke. Henry had to cut down a tree in the yard today for fuel. . . .

12 *February 17.* . . . At about 6 o'clock while it was still quite dark and all in the room were buried in profound slumber, we were suddenly awakened by a terrific explosion. The house shook—broken window panes clattered down, and we all sat up in bed, for a few seconds mute with terror. . . . We lit the candle, and mother sent Jane to inquire of Henry the cause. Of course he did not know. I went out of doors. The day was beginning to break murkily and the air was still heavy with smoke. All continuing quiet we concluded that the authorities had blown up some stores before evacuating. . . . After breakfast the cannon opened again and so near that every report shook the house. I think it must have been a cannonade to cover our retreat. It did not continue very long. The negroes all went uptown to see what they could get in the general pillage, for all the shops had been opened and provisions were scattered in all directions. Henry says that in some parts of Main Street corn and flour and sugar cover the ground. An hour or two ago they came running back declaring the Yankees were in town and that our troops were fighting them in the streets. This was not true, for at that time every soldier nearly had left town, but we did not know it then. . . . Mother is downright sick. She had been quite collected and calm until this news, but now she suddenly lost all self-control and exhibited the most lively terror—indeed I thought she would grow hysterical. . . . By-and-by the firing ceased and all was quiet again. It was denied that the Yankees had yet crossed the river or even completed their pontoon bridge, and most of the servants returned up town. They have brought back a considerable quantity of provisions—the negroes are very kind and faithful—they have supplied us with meat and Jane brought mother some rice and crushed sugar for Carrie, knowing that she had none. How times change! Those whom we have so long fed and cared for now help us. . . . A gentleman told us just now that the mayor had gone forward to surrender the town.

13 *One o'clock P.M.*— Well, they are here. I was sitting in the back parlor when I heard the shouting of the troops. I was at the front door in a moment. Jane came running and crying, "O Miss Emma, they've come at last!" She said they were marching down Main Street, before them flying a panic-stricken crowd of women and children who seemed crazy.

I ran upstairs to my bedroom window just in time to see the U.S. flag run up over the State House. O what a horrid sight! What a degradation! After four long bitter years of bloodshed and hatred, now to float there at last! That hateful symbol of despotism! I do not think I could possibly describe my feelings. I know I could not look at it. I left the window and went downstairs to mother. In a little while a guard arrived to protect the hospital. They have already fixed a shelter of boards against the wall near the gate—sentinels are stationed and they are cooking their dinner. The wind is very high today and blows their hats around. This is the first sight we have had of these fiends except as prisoners. The sight does not stir up very pleasant feelings in our hearts. We cannot look at them with anything but horror and hatred—loathing and disgust. The troops now in town is a brigade commanded by Col. Stone.[1] Everything is quiet and orderly. Guards have been placed to protect houses, and Sherman has promised not to disturb private property. . . .

Later— Gen. Sherman has *assured* the Mayor, "that he and all the citizens may sleep as securely and quietly tonight as if under Confederate rule. Private property shall be carefully respected. Some public buildings have to be destroyed, but he will wait until tomorrow when the wind shall have entirely subsided." . . .

February 18. What a night of horror, misery and agony! It even makes one sick to think of writing down such scenes. Until dinnertime we saw little of the Yankees, except the guard about the Campus, and the officers and men galloping up and down the street. . . . We could hear their shouts as they surged down Main Street and through the State House, but were too far off to see much of the tumult. . . . I hear they found a picture of President Davis in the Capitol which was set up as a target and shot at amid the jeers of the soldiery. From three o'clock till seven their army was passing down the street by the Campus, to encamp back of us in the woods. Two Corps entered the town—Howard's and Logan's[2]—one, the diabolical 15th which Sherman has hitherto never permitted to enter a city on account of their vile and desperate character. Slocum's Corps remained over the river, and I suppose Davis' also. The devils as they marched past looked strong and well clad in dark, dirty-looking blue. The wagon trains were immense. Night drew on. Of course we did not expect to sleep, but we looked forward to a tolerably tranquil night. . . . At about seven o'clock I was standing on the back piazza in the third story. Before me the whole southern horizon was lit up by camp-fires which dotted the woods. On one side the sky was

---
[1]Colonel George A. Stone, with men from Iowa.
[2]Major-General O.O. Howard and Major-General John A. Logan.

illuminated by the burning of Gen. Hampton's residence a few miles off in the country, on the other side by some blazing buildings near the river. Sumter Street was brightly lighted by a burning house so near our piazza that we could feel the heat. By the red glare we could watch the wretches walking—generally staggering—back and forth from the camp to the town—shouting—hurrahing—cursing South Carolina—swearing—blaspheming—singing ribald songs and using such obscene language that we were forced to go indoors. The fire on Main Street was now raging, and we anxiously watched its progress from the upper front windows. In a little while, however, the flames broke forth in every direction. . . . Guards were rarely of any assistance—most generally they assisted in the pillaging and the firing. The wretched people rushing from their burning homes were not allowed to keep even the few necessaries they gathered up in their flight—even blankets and food were taken from them and destroyed. The firemen attempted to use their engines, but the hose was cut to pieces and their lives threatened.

17 The wind blew a fearful gale, wafting the flames from house to house with frightful rapidity. By midnight the whole town (except the outskirts) was wrapped in one huge blaze. Still the flames had not approached sufficiently near us to threaten our immediate safety, and for some reason not a single Yankee soldier had entered our house. . . . Henry said the danger was over, sick of the dreadful scene, worn out with fatigue and excitement, we went downstairs to our room and tried to rest. I fell into a heavy kind of stupor from which I was presently roused by the bustle about me. Our neighbor Mrs. Caldwell and her two sisters stood before the fire wrapped in blankets and weeping. Their house was on fire, and the great sea of flame had again swept down our way to the very Campus walls. . . . Jane came in to say that Aunt Josie's house was in flames—then we all went to the front door—My God! what a scene! It was about four o'clock and the State House was one grand conflagration.

18 Imagine night turning into noonday, only with a blazing, scorching glare that was horrible—a copper colored sky across which swept columns of black rolling smoke glittering with sparks and flying embers, while all around us were falling thickly showers of burning flakes. Everywhere the palpitating blaze walling the streets with solid masses of flames as far as the eye could reach—filling the air with its terrible roar. On every side the crackling and devouring fire, while every instant came the crashing of timbers and the thunder of falling buildings. A quivering molten ocean seemed to fill the air and sky. The Library building opposite us seemed framed by the gushing flames and smoke, while through the windows gleamed the liquid fire.

The College buildings caught. . . . All the physicians and nurses 19
were on the roof trying to save the buildings, and the poor wounded
inmates left to themselves, such as could crawled out while those
who could not move waited to be burned to death. The Common opposite the gate was crowded with homeless women and children, a
few wrapped in blankets and many shivering in the night air. Such a
scene as this with the drunken fiendish soldiery in their dark uniforms, infuriated, cursing, screaming, exulting in their work, came
nearer the material ideal of hell than anything I ever expect to see
again. . . .

The State House of course is burned, and they talk of blowing up 20
the new uncompleted granite one. . . . We dread tonight. O, the sorrow and misery of this unhappy town! From what I can hear their
chief aim, while taunting helpless women, has been to "Humble
their pride—Southern pride." "Where now," they would say, "is all
your pride—see what we have brought you to. This is what you get
for setting yourselves up as better than other folks." . . .

Sunday, February 19. The day has passed quietly as regards the 21
Yankees. . . . I rose, took off my clothes for the first time in three
days, and after bathing and putting on clean clothes felt like another
being. This morning fresh trouble awaited us. We thought the negroes were going to leave us. While we were on the piazza Mary
Ann came to us weeping and saying she feared the Yankees were going to force Henry to go off with them, and of course she would have
to go with her husband. He did not want to go and would not unless
forced. . . . The others, Maria and her children, want to go I think.
They have been dressed in their Sundays best all day. . . .

February 20. . . . Shortly after breakfast—O joyful sight—the two 22
corps encamped behind the Campus back of us marched by with all
their immense wagon trains on their way from Columbia. They tell
us all will be gone by tomorrow evening. . . .

Of course there was no Service in any of the churches yester- 23
day—no Church bells ringing—the Yankees riding up and down the
streets—the provost guard putting up their camp—there was nothing to suggest Sunday. . . .

February 21. A heavy curse has fallen on this town—from a beauti- 24
ful city it is turned into a desert. How desolated and dreary we feel—
how completely cut off from the world. No longer the shrill whistle
of the engine—no daily mail—the morning brings no paper with
news from the outside—there are no lights—no going to and fro. It
is as if a city in the midst of business and activity were suddenly

smitten with some appalling curse. One feels awed if by chance the dreary stillness is broken by a laugh or too loud a voice. . . .

25 *February 22.* I have seen it all—I have seen the "Abomination of Desolation." It is even worse than I thought. The place is literally in ruins. The entire heart of the city is in ashes—only the outer edges remain. On the whole length of Sumter Street not one house beyond the first block after the Campus is standing, except the brick house of Mr. Mordecai. Standing in the centre of town, as far as the eye can reach nothing is to be seen but heaps of rubbish, tall dreary chimneys and shattered brick walls, while "In the hollow windows, dreary horror's sitting." Poor old Columbia—where is all her beauty—so admired by strangers, so loved by her children! . . .

26   Everything has vanished as if by enchantment—stores, merchants, customers—all the eager faces gone—only three or four dismal looking people to be seen picking their way over heaps of rubbish, brick and timbers. The wind moans among the bleak chimneys and whistles through the gaping windows of some hotel or warehouse. The market a ruined shell supported by crumbling arches—its spire fallen in and with it the old town clock whose familiar stroke we miss so much. After trying to distinguish localities and hunting for familiar buildings we turned to Arsenal Hill. Here things looked more natural. The Arsenal was destroyed but comparatively few dwellings. Also the Park and its surroundings looked familiar. As we passed the old State House going back I paused to gaze on the ruins—only the foundation and chimneys—and to recall the brilliant scene enacted there one short month ago. And I compared that scene with its beauty, gayety and festivity, the halls so elaborately decorated, the surging throng, to this. I reached home sad at heart and full of all I had seen. . . .

27 *February 23.* . . . Somehow I feel we cannot be conquered. We have lost everything, but if all this—negroes—property—all could be given back a hundredfold I would not be willing to go back to them. I would rather endure any poverty than live under Yankee rule. . . . I would rather far have France or any other country for a mistress—anything but live as one nation with the *Yankees*—that word in my mind is a synonym for all that is mean, despicable and abhorrent. . . .

Speculations

1. How would you characterize the tone and style of this diary, and what do they reveal about its writer?
2. What stylistic mannerism occasionally betrays the author's youthfulness?

3. Read paragraph 2 carefully. What literary device does the author initially use to make her account of the confusion and panic sweeping the population more dramatic?

4. In what ways do you think this diary would markedly differ if it had been written by a seventeen-year-old today?

5. In paragraph 25 the author puts "Abomination of Desolation" in capitals and quotation marks. Why? Where does this phrase come from, and what does it imply about her?

Spin-offs for writing

1. Narrate the experience of any close call you might have had with fire.

2. In an addition to this diary, write an entry that imaginatively recounts what happened next. Try to imitate the writer's voice and style.

SAMUEL PEPYS

Samuel Pepys (1633–1703) was an English naval official who is ranked among the greatest diarists ever. He was educated at Magdalene College, Cambridge, and began his career as a clerk in the naval office, from which position he rose to become secretary to the admiralty. Written in code, his diary ran from January 1, 1660, to May 31, 1669, chronicling the turbulent period of the English Civil War and the subsequent pleasure-loving Restoration.

The event recorded in this entry, the triumphant return of King Charles II to the throne after exile in France, marks the beginning of the so-called Restoration period of English history. At the time of this writing, Charles had been in exile for eleven years, spending much of that time in want and poverty. He had endured great sufferings, chief among them the beheading of his father, Charles I, by Cromwell in 1649 despite the best efforts of the exiled son to save him. In 1651, Charles II tried to recapture his throne but was defeated by Cromwell in the battle of Worcester. Pepys records the account the King gives of fleeing the battlefield in disguise to France. Writing about this climactic moment in history, Pepys begins the entry aboard a ship off the coast of Holland that is awaiting boarding by the King and his entourage for the return to England.

1. *May 21, 1660.* By letters that came hither in my absence, I understand that the Parliament had ordered all persons to be secured, in order to a trial, that did sit as judges in the late King's death, and all the officers too attending the Court. News brought that the two Dukes are coming on board, which, by and by, they did, in a Dutch boat, the Duke of York in yellow trimmings, the Duke of Gloucester in gray and red. My Lord went in a boat to meet them, the captain, myself, and others, standing at the entering port. So soon as they were entered we shot the guns off round the fleet. After that they went to view the ship all over, and were most exceedingly pleased with it. They seem to be both very fine gentlemen. News is sent us that the King is on shore; so my Lord fired all his guns round twice, and all the fleet after him, which in the end fell into disorder, which seemed very handsome. The gun over against my cabin I fired myself to the King, which was the first time that he had been saluted by his own ships since this change; but holding my head too much over the gun, I had almost spoiled my right eye. Nothing in the world but going of guns almost all this day.

2. *May 23, 1660.* The Doctor and I waked very merry. In the morning came infinity of people on board from the King to go along with him. My Lord, Mr. Crew, and others, go on shore to meet the King as he comes off from shore, where Sir R. Stayner bringing His Majesty into the boat, I hear that His Majesty did with a great deal of

affection kiss my Lord upon his first meeting. The King, with the two Dukes and Queen of Bohemia, Princess Royal, and Prince of Orange, came on board, where I in their coming in kissed the King's, Queen's, and Princess's hands, having done the other before. Infinite shooting off of the guns, and that in a disorder on purpose, which was better than if it had been otherwise. All day nothing but Lords and persons of honor on board, that we were exceeding full. Dined in a great deal of state, the Royal company by themselves in the coach, which was a blessed sight to see. After dinner the King and Duke altered the name of some of the ships, viz., the *Nazeby* into *Charles;* the *Richard, James;* the *Speaker, Mary;* the *Dunbar* (which was not in company with us), the *Henry; Winsly, Happy Return; Wakefield, Richmond; Lambert,* the *Henrietta; Cheriton,* the *Speedwell; Bradford,* the *Success.* This done, the Queen, Princess Royal, and Prince of Orange took leave of the King, and the Duke of York went on board the *London,* and the Duke of Gloucester, the *Swiftsure.* Which done, we weighed anchor, and with a fresh gale and most happy weather we set sail for England. All the afternoon the King walked here and there, up and down (quite contrary to what I thought him to have been), very active and stirring. Upon the quarter-deck he fell into discourse of his escape from Worcester, where it made me ready to weep to hear the stories that he told of his difficulties that he had passed through, as his traveling four days and three nights on foot, every step up to his knees in dirt, with nothing but a green coat and a pair of country breeches on, and a pair of country shoes that made him so sore all over his feet, that he could scarce stir. Yet he was forced to run away from a miller and other company, that took them for rogues. His sitting at table at one place, where the master of the house, that had not seen him in eight years, did know him, but kept it private; when at the same table there was one that had been of his own regiment at Worcester, could not know him, but made him drink the King's health, and said that the King was at least four fingers higher than he. At another place he was by some servants of the house made to drink, that they might know him not to be a Roundhead, which they swore he was. In another place at his inn, the master of the house, as the King was standing, with his hands upon the back of a chair by the fireside, kneeled down and kissed his hand, privately, saying, that he would not ask who he was, but bid God bless him whither he was going. Then the difficulty of getting a boat to get into France, where he was fain to plot with the master thereof to keep his design from the four men and a boy (which was all his ship's company), and so go to Fécamp in France. At Rouen he looked so poorly, that the people went into the rooms before he went away to see whether he had not stolen something or other. The King supped alone in the coach; after that I got a dish, and we four supped in my cabin, as at noon. So to my cabin again, where the company still was, and were talking more of the King's difficulties; as how he was fain to eat a piece of bread and cheese out of a poor boy's pocket; how, at a Catholic house he was fain to lie in the priest's hole a good while in the house for his privacy. Under sail all night, and most glorious weather.

3 *May 24, 1660.* Up, and make myself as fine as I could, with the linning stockings on and wide canons that I bought the other day at Hague. Extraordinary press of noble company, and great mirth all the day. Walking upon the decks, where persons of honor all the afternoon, among others, Thomas Killigrew (a merry droll, but a gentleman of great esteem with the King), who told us many merry stories. After this discourse I was called to write a pass for my Lord Mandeville to take up horses to London, which I wrote in the King's name, and carried it to him to sign, which was the first and only one that ever he signed in the ship *Charles*. To bed, coming in sight of land a little before night.

4 *May 25, 1660.* By the morning we were come close to the land, and every body made ready to get on shore. The King and the two Dukes did eat their breakfast before they went, and there being set some ship's diet before them, only to show them the manner of the ship's diet, they eat of nothing else but peas and pork, and boiled beef. I spoke with the Duke of York about business, who called me Pepys by name, and upon my desire did promise me his future favor. Great expectation of the King's making some knights, but there was none. About noon (though the brigantine that Beale made was there ready to carry him) yet he would go in my Lord's barge with the two Dukes. Our Captain steered, and my Lord went along bare with him. I went, and Mr. Mansell, and one of the King's footmen, with a dog that the King loved, (which [dirtied] the boat, which made us laugh, and methink that a King and all that belong to him are but just as others are), in a boat by ourselves, and so got on shore when the King did, who was received by General Monk with all imaginable love and respect at his entrance upon the land of Dover. Infinite the crowd of people and the horsemen, citizens, and noblemen of all sorts. The Mayor of the town came and gave him his white staff, the badge of his place, which the King did give him again. The Mayor also presented him from the town a very rich Bible, which he took and said it was the thing that he loved above all things in the world. A canopy was provided for him to stand under, which he did, and talked awhile with General Monk and others, and so into a stately coach there set for him, and so away through the town towards Canterbury, without making any stay at Dover. The shouting and joy expressed by all is past imagination. My Lord returned late, and at

his coming did give me order to cause the marke to be gilded, and a Crown and C. R. to be made at the head of the coach table, where the King today with his own hand did mark his height, which accordingly I caused the painter to do, and is not done as is to be seen.

Speculations

1. Why do you think Pepys mentioned the King's renaming of some of the ships in the welcoming fleet? What is so significant about this act?

2. Pepys tells us in paragraph 1 that he almost spoiled his "right eye" by "holding my head too much over the gun." What reasonable inference about Pepys's mood can a reader make from this incident?

3. This diary was, as explained in the headnote, written in a private code that had to be broken before the text could be translated. What reasons do you think Pepys could have had for this effort at concealment?

4. Pepys writes in paragraph 2 that the King was made by some servants to drink "that they might know him not to be a Roundhead, which they swore he was." What is a "Roundhead," and what was the likely identity of these servants?

5. From this brief entry, what can you infer about the personality and temperament of Pepys?

Spin-offs for writing

1. Write a journal about an escape from any perilous situation of your imagining.

2. Write a story in which you narrate any imaginary adventure the disguised King might have had as he fled England for France.

Student Journal–Narration

Lara Vanian

March 10, 1992

Our weekend trip to London was such a mess and so poorly organized that I debated writing about it in my journal at all. Then I decided that, for the sake of posterity, I would write about it in the hopes that looking back on it later, I might actually find it amusing.

It started with a three-hour bus ride from our college in Stratford-upon-Avon to London. Once we reached the city, our teacher, microphone in hand, began pointing out buildings left and right, telling us their names as we drove quickly by. She would often forget buildings only to tell us what they were after we had passed them. The only thing I remember visually from that trip is staring at the backs of the other students' heads as we all strained to catch a glimpse of those cherished buildings. After a while, I became tired and just sat in my seat, unamused, waiting for the journey to end. Little did I know at the time that this was just the beginning of my London experience.

The bus dropped us off by the National Theatre, with all our luggage, to make our own way to the youth hostel where the school had "generously" provided us with discount vouchers. We were alone in a huge and unfamiliar city, and we felt totally lost. After a few long minutes of utter confusion and angst, we found the Underground tube station and asked for the correct platform to reach our destination. Two or three Underground tubes later, we found the right one. We carried our heavy bags through the foreign streets of the lower West End of London. Not without a significant amount of difficulty did we find the "Palace Court" at last.

I wonder if we would have been better off if we had never found it. It seemed like a nightmare transported from the potholes of dementia. Some kind of artificial intoxication might have perhaps softened the blow of that hellish place.

Regardless, we stood in line to check in, as they had not allowed us to reserve rooms in advance. There were no single rooms left. There were no double rooms left. My friend and I were forced to share a room with two complete strangers! We had no other choice, so we paid the fees and tried to locate our room. Pushing our way through the gauntlet of greasy, long-haired men; barefoot, unkempt women; and dirty "white" walls, we ended up in the basement.

Looking around we saw an array of red and black patchy doors with graffiti and explicit signs which included dubious names and clear phone numbers. What struck us as most amazing was the line that had been painted to divide the hallway in two vertical halves. The left side said "My Side" and the right side "Your Side." I thought to myself sarcastically how incredibly "charming" the place was.

We eventually found room number 111. (The woman at the front desk had referred to it as "three ones.") It was a narrow and cold room with two sets of bunk beds that one did not dare touch for fear that they housed rare germs or had strange bugs crawling underneath. There was also an out of place sink and mirror on one wall. A private bathroom would have been a welcomed luxury, but our bathroom was limited to one communal toilet per floor. We were terrified of leaving our belongings in such a deplorable place, so we had them placed under lock and key.

From that point on things became a blur; it became clear that there was no hope of salvaging our weekend. We tried to enjoy our visit as much as possible, but the dark clouds of doom seemed to hang over us no matter how we tried to escape them. Our prayers of going back home were not answered until we boarded the bus two days later to return to Stratford and a bit of sanity. Upon our return, we sought out the proper officials to hear our list of complaints and perhaps save future students from our fate. All we were told was that we could not expect any better for the price we had paid. I could not believe their apathetic response! Right then and there I learned a valuable lesson in trust and confidence. I resented the fact that I could not trust them to complete their obligation to plan a safe and organized tour of London. I thought of the old saying, "If you want something done right, do it yourself," and decided that my next trip to London would be a great success because it would be entirely my own endeavor.

2. DESCRIPTION.

2nd September, 1666. "This fatal night, about ten, began the deplorable fire, near Fleet Street, In London." The Great Fire of London. John Evelyn.

11th November, 1728. "His legs are very thick and very short, and his hoofs exceedingly broad." A Young Buffalo at Sugar-Tree Creek. William Byrd.

November, 1945. "At the end of his life, he was still playing bit parts (utility men, as theater people call them). . . . The death of an old actor. Albert Camus.

---

27 October, 1862. "Of all doleful, dismal, desperate experiences seasickness is certainly the dolefulest, dismalist, and desperate-est!" A 19th-century sea voyage. Charlotte Forten Grimke.

51

CHAPTER 2

Description

Description and narration are as closely related as hand and fist: one is implied in the presence of the other. The writer who describes without narrating is a rarity and is usually dealing with some specialized business such as, for example, the police officer describing the suspect in a crime, or the claims adjuster describing damage to property. Such static descriptions are almost always intended for particularly narrow purposes. In the usual course of events, however, a writer will imbed descriptions in the context of a narrative. Or a narration will encapsulate descriptions, giving movement to passages that would otherwise seem lifelessly static.

The journal descriptions anthologized in this chapter clearly demonstrate the relationship between these two rhetorical modes. John Evelyn describes the catastrophic London fire of the 17th century, but does so in a narrative sequence. William Byrd describes a young buffalo he encountered at Sugar-tree Creek, painting us the picture in the narrative context of a surveying expedition. Albert Camus shows us an old actor at the end of his days, and Charlotte Forten Grimke describes the ghastliness of seasickness, both scenes being imbedded in respective narrations.

What is the difference between the rhetorical modes of narration and description? Primarily it is this: the narrator tells; the describer shows. The narrator is grappling mainly with the management of events in a sequence; this occurs and then that. The describer, on the other hand, is showing us what he or she sees. And this showing is far easier to do when the writer can draw the picture through the eyes of a participant in the action, who functions as a narrator, rather than from a disembodied perspective.

Some few descriptive assignments may ask you to say how a particular object or scene looks. But most will ask you describe some event or thing and will leave it to you to devise the best appropriate strategy. Faced with such a choice, you would be smart to adopt a narrative setting for your description. For example, if you are asked to write a descriptive essay about a thunderstorm, instead of merely sitting down and cataloging what one looks or sounds like, you should put yourself in the middle of trudging through the downpour, describe the pelting of the rain, the earsplitting roar of the thunder, and the serrated bolts of lightning. Not only will the exercise stimulate your imagination, it is also likely to thrill readers by vicariously putting them in your shoes.

There are other well-known techniques for writing a vivid description, all of them on display in this section. The first is unwavering focus. Achieving this single-minded focus means organizing your descriptive passages around a single dominant impression—the part of the scene that strikes you as its most obvious feature. For example, paragraph 3 of the William Byrd description zooms in on the squat bulkiness of the buffalo and carefully amasses details about that and nothing else. Paragraph 4 focuses on the beast's hair and describes its softness and uses as weaving thread. Note that the dominant impression should not be some incidental characteristic of your subject, but the single feature that most accurately sums up its overall look. This is only common sense: John Evelyn's description of the Great London Fire focuses mainly on depicting the massive blaze, not on the halfhearted efforts to put it out.

The second technique, equally well known as the first, is the use of vivid images and colorful words. The best descriptions captivate us with memorable language. But how to make language memorable is a skill that can only be learned through wide reading. The more we expose ourselves to good writing, the more we are likely to unwittingly absorb its lessons. Here is an example of the use of vivid language in a description:

God grant mine eyes may never behold the like, who now saw above 10,000 houses all in one flame! The noise and cracking and thunder of the impetuous flames, the shrieking of women and children, the hurry of people, the fall of the towers, houses, and churches, was like a hideous storm; and the air all about so hot and inflamed that at the last one was not able to approach it, so that they were forced to stand still and let the flames burn on, which they did, for near two miles in length and one in breadth.

Notice that the account is not only infused with the breathlessness of a stunned observer, it also attempts to be exact. So the flames rage "two miles in length and one in breadth" rather than "over a great area"; and the amazed eyes of the reporter "now saw above 10,000 houses all in one flame" rather than merely "a lot of burning houses." Your own descriptions will also benefit from a similar exactness.

As you prepare to write a descriptive essay, you should altogether give up any idea of capturing the essence of your scene in one pass. It is possible to do such a thing, but highly unlikely. Most writers of memorable descriptions freely admit that the effort took repeated rewriting attempts. Journal writers, who write mainly for their own eyes, do not have to be such persistent revisers. But for the objective essayist, constant revision must become a habit.

JOHN EVELYN

English diarist and writer John Evelyn (1620–1706) wrote incidentally on various subjects such as art history, reforestation, and numismatics. His best known work, aside from his diaries, is Life of Mrs. Godolphin. *Next to Pepys, his contemporary, Evelyn is the most renowned of the English diarists. Indeed, both men were acquainted and mention each other in their respective diaries. In his diary, Evelyn was neither as personal nor as confessional as was Pepys, but his observations still give us an invaluable historical glimpse into 17th-century England.*

The subject of this entry, the Great Fire of London, began on September 2nd, 1666, and raged for five days, virtually destroying the entire city. It was a calamitous time in English history. One year earlier the Great Plague had begun, taking some 75,000 lives; barely over a decade before a bloody civil war between Oliver Cromwell and forces loyal to the monarchy had been waged. Evelyn describes not only the fire but the strange passivity and consternation of Londoners in their initial response to the disaster.

1 **2nd September [1666].** This fatal night, about ten, began the deplorable fire, near Fish Street, in London.

2 **3rd.** I had public prayers at home. The fire continuing, after dinner I took coach with my wife and son, and went to the Bankside in Southwark, where we beheld that dismal spectacle, the whole city in dreadful flames near the waterside; all the houses from the Bridge, all Thames Street, and upwards towards Cheapside, down to the Three Cranes were now consumed; and so returned, exceeding astonished what would become of the rest.

3 The fire having continued all this night (if I may call that night which was light as day for ten miles round about, after a dreadful manner), when conspiring with a fierce eastern wind in a very dry season, I went on foot to the same place; and saw the whole south part of the City burning from Cheapside to the Thames, and all along Cornhill (for it likewise kindled back against the wind as well as forward). Tower Street, Fenchurch Street, Gracious Street, and so along to Baynard's Castle, and was now taking hold of St. Paul's Church, to which the scaffolds contributed exceedingly. The conflagration was so universal, and the people so astonished, that, from the beginning, I know not by what despondency or fate, they hardly stirred to quench it; so that there was nothing heard or seen but crying out and lamentation, running about like distracted creatures, without at all attempting to save even their goods; such a strange consternation there was upon them, so as it burned both in breadth and length the churches, public halls, Exchange, hospitals, monuments, and ornaments, leaping after a prodigious manner from house to house, and

street to street, at great distances one from the other. For the heat, with a long set of fair and warm weather, had even ignited the air, and prepared the materials to conceive the fire, which devoured, after an incredible manner, houses, furniture, and everything. Here we saw the Thames covered with goods floating, all the barges and boats laden with what some had time and courage to save, as on the other side carts, &c., carrying out to the fields, which for many miles were strewed with movables of all sorts, and tents erecting to shelter both people and what goods they could get away. Oh, the miserable and calamitous spectacle, such as haply the world had not seen since the foundation of it, nor can be outdone till the universal conflagration thereof! All the sky was of a fiery aspect, like the top of a burning oven, and the light seen above forty miles round about for many nights. God grant mine eyes may never behold the like, who now saw above 10,000 houses all in one flame! The noise and cracking and thunder of the impetuous flames, the shrieking of women and children, the hurry of people, the fall of the towers, houses, and churches, was like a hideous storm; and the air all about so hot and inflamed that at the last one was not able to approach it, so that they were forced to stand still and let the flames burn on, which they did, for near two miles in length and one in breadth. The clouds also of smoke were dismal, and reached, upon computation, near fifty miles in length. Thus, I left it this afternoon burning, a resemblance of Sodom or the last day. It forcibly called to my mind that passage—*non enim hic habemus stabilem civitatem*,[1] the ruins resembling the picture of Troy. London was, but is no more! Thus, I returned.

4th September. The burning still rages, and it is now gotten as far as the Inner Temple. All Fleet Street, the Old Bailey, Ludgate Hill, Warwick Lane, Newgate, Paul's Chain, Watling Street, now flaming, and most of it reduced to ashes; the stones of Paul's flew like grenados, the melting lead running down the streets in a stream, and the very pavements glowing with fiery redness, so as no horse, nor man, was able to tread on them, and the demolition had stopped all the passages so that no help could be applied. The eastern wind still more impetuously driving the flames forward. Nothing but the almighty power of God was able to stop them; for vain was the help of man.

5th September. It crossed towards Whitehall; but oh, the confusion there was then at that court! It pleased his Majesty to command me, among the rest, to look after the quenching of Fetter Lane end, to preserve (if possible) that part of Holborn, whilst the rest of the

[1] "For here we have no continuing city." Hebrew 13:14

gentlemen took their several posts, some at one part, and some at another (for now they began to bestir themselves, and not till now, who hitherto had stood as men intoxicated, with their hands across), and began to consider that nothing was likely to put a stop but the blowing up of so many houses as might make a wider gap than any had yet been made by the ordinary method of pulling them down with engines. This some stout seamen proposed early enough to have saved near the whole city, but this some tenacious and avaricious men, aldermen, &c., would not permit, because their houses must have been of the first. It was, therefore, now commended to be practised; and my concern being particularly for the hospital of St. Bartholomew, near Smithfield, where I had many wounded, and sick men, made me the more diligent to promote it;[2] nor was my care for the Savoy less. It now pleased God, by abating the wind, and by the industry of the people, when almost all was lost infusing a new spirit into them, that the fury of it began sensibly to abate about noon, so as it came no farther than the Temple westward, nor than the entrance of Smithfield, north; but continued all this day and night so impetuous towards Cripplegate and the Tower, as made us all despair. It also brake out again in the Temple; but the courage of the multitude persisting, and many houses being blown up, such gaps and desolations were soon made, as, with the former three days' consumption, the back fire did not so vehemently urge upon the rest as formerly. There was yet no standing near the burning and glowing ruins by near a furlong's space.

6 The coal and wood-wharfs, and magazines of oil, rosin, &c., did infinite mischief, so as the invective which a little before I had dedicated to his Majesty and published, giving warning what probably might be the issue of suffering those shops to be in the City was looked upon as a prophecy.

7 The poor inhabitants were dispersed about St. George's Fields, and Moorfields, as far as Highgate, and several miles in circle, some under tents, some under miserable huts and hovels, many without a rag, or any necessary utensils, bed or board, who from delicateness, riches, and easy accommodations in stately and well furnished houses, were now reduced to extremest misery and poverty.

8 In this calamitous condition, I returned with a sad heart to my house, blessing and adoring the distinguishing mercy of God to me and mine, who, in the midst of all this ruin, was like Lot, in my little Zoar, safe and sound.

---

[2] Evelyn was one of the commissioners for the Care of the Sick and Wounded in the Dutch War.

6th September. Thursday. I represented to his Majesty the case of the French prisoners at war in my custody and besought him that there might be still the same care of watching at all places contiguous to unseized houses. It is not indeed imaginable how extraordinary the vigilance and activity of the King and the Duke was, even labouring in person, and being present to command, order, reward, or encourage workmen, by which he showed his affection to his people, and gained theirs. Having, then, disposed of some under cure at the Savoy, I returned to Whitehall, where I dined at Mr. Offley's, the groom-porter, who was my relation.

7th. I went this morning on foot from Whitehall as far as London Bridge, through the last Fleet Street, Ludgate Hill by St. Paul's, Cheapside, Exchange, Bishopsgate, Aldersgate, and out to Moorfields, thence through Cornhill, &c., with extraordinary difficulty, clambering over heaps of yet smoking rubbish, and frequently mistaking where I was, the ground under my feet so hot that it even burnt the soles of my shoes. In the meantime, his Majesty got to the Tower by water to demolish the houses about the graff,[3] which, being built entirely about it, had they taken fire and attacked the White Tower, where the magazine of powder lay, would undoubtedly not only have beaten down and destroyed all the bridge, but sunk and torn the vessels in the river, and rendered the demolition beyond all expression for several miles about the country.

At my return, I was infinitely concerned to find that goodly church, St. Paul's, now a sad ruin, and that beautiful portico (for structure comparable to any in Europe, as not long before repaired by the late King) now rent in pieces, flakes of large stones split asunder, and nothing remaining entire but the inscription in the architrave, showing by whom it was built, which had not one letter of it defaced! It was astonishing to see what immense stones the heat had in a manner calcined, so that all the ornaments, columns, friezes, capitals, and projectures of massy Portland stone flew off, even to the very roof, where a sheet of lead covering a great space (no less than six acres by measure) was totally melted. The ruins of the vaulted roof falling, broke into St. Faith's, which being filled with the magazines of books belonging to the stationers, and carried thither for safety, they were all consumed, burning for a week following. It is also observable that the lead over the altar at the east end was untouched, and among the divers monuments the body of one bishop remained entire. Thus lay in ashes that most venerable church, one of the most ancient pieces of early piety in the Christian world, besides near one

[3] ditch.

hundred more. The lead, iron-work, bells, plate, &c., melted, the exquisitely wrought Mercers' Chapel, the sumptuous Exchange, the august fabric of Christ Church, all the rest of the Companies' Halls, splendid buildings, arches, entries, all in dust; the fountains dried up and ruined, whilst the very waters remained boiling; the voragos[4] of subterranean cellars, wells, and dungeons, formerly warehouses, still burning in stench and dark clouds of smoke; so that in five or six miles traversing about I did not see one load of timber unconsumed, nor many stones but what were calcined white as snow.

12 The people, who now walked about the ruins, appeared like men in some dismal desert, or rather, in some great city laid waste by a cruel enemy, to which was added the stench that came from some poor creatures' bodies, beds, and other combustible goods. Sir Thomas Gresham's statue, though fallen from its niche in the Royal Exchange, remained entire, when all those of the Kings since the Conquest were broken to pieces. Also the standard in Cornhill, and Queen Elizabeth's effigies, with some arms on Ludgate, continued with but little detriment, whilst the vast iron chains of the City streets, hinges, bars, and gates of prisons, were many of them melted and reduced to cinders by the vehement heat. Nor was I yet able to pass through any of the narrow streets, but kept the widest; the ground and air, smoke and fiery vapour, continued so intense that my hair was almost singed and my feet unsufferably surbated.[5] The bye-lanes and narrow streets were quite filled up with rubbish; nor could one have possibly known where he was, but by the ruins of some church or hall that had some remarkable tower or pinnacle remaining.

13 I then went towards Islington and Highgate, where one might have seen 200,000 people of all ranks and degrees dispersed, and lying along by their heaps of what they could save from the fire, deploring their loss, and, though ready to perish for hunger and destitution, yet not asking one penny for relief, which to me appeared a stranger sight than any I had yet beheld. His Majesty and Council indeed took all imaginable care for their relief, by proclamation for the country to come in and refresh them with provisions.

14 In the midst of all this calamity and confusion there was, I know not how, an alarm begun that the French and Dutch, with whom we were now in hostility, were not only landed but even entering the City. There was, in truth, some days before, great suspicion of those two

---

[4] Abysses.
[5] bruised or made sore by walking.

nations joining, and now that they had been the occasion of firing the town. This report did so terrify that on a sudden there was such an uproar and tumult that they run from their goods, and, taking what weapons they could come at, they could not be stopped from falling on some of those nations whom they casually met, without sense or reason. The clamour and peril grew so excessive that it made the whole Court amazed, and they did with infinite pains and great difficulty reduce and appease the people, sending troops of soldiers and guards to cause them to retire into the fields again, where they were watched all this night. I left them pretty quiet and came home sufficiently weary and broken. Their spirits thus a little calmed, and the affright abated, they now began to repair into the suburbs about the City, where such as had friends or opportunity, got shelter for the present, to which his Majesty's proclamation also invited them.

Still, the plague continuing in our parish, I could not without danger adventure to our church.

10th September. I went again to the ruins, for it was now no longer a city.

13th September. I presented his Majesty with a survey of the ruins, and a plot for a new City, with a discourse on it; whereupon, after dinner, his Majesty sent for me into the Queen's bedchamber, her Majesty and the Duke only being present. They examined each particular, and discoursed on them for near an hour, seeming to be extremely pleased with what I had so early thought on. The Queen was now in her cavalier riding-habit, hat and feather, and horseman's coat, going to take the air.

16th. I went to Greenwich Church, where Mr. Plume preached very well from this text: "Seeing, then, all these things shall be dissolved," &c., taking occasion from the late unparalleled conflagration to mind us how we ought to walk more holy in all manner of conversation.

27th. Dined at Sir William D'Oyly's with that worthy gentleman, Sir John Holland, of Suffolk.

10th October. This day was ordered a general fast through the nation, to humble us on the late dreadful conflagration, added to the plague and war, the most dismal judgments that could be inflicted; but which indeed we highly deserved for our prodigious ingratitude, burning lusts, dissolute court, profane and abominable lives, under such dispensations of God's continued favour in restoring Church, Prince, and People from our late intestine calamities, of which we were altogether unmindful, even to astonishment. This made me resolve to go to our parish assembly, where our doctor preached on Luke xix:41, piously applying it to the occasion. After which was a collection for the distressed losers in the late fire.

Speculations

1. Evelyn names specific districts destroyed in the conflagration. Even though many of these names might be strange to a modern reader, what do you think this specificity adds to the chronicle?
2. What do you think caused the reaction of "despondency" and "strange consternation" that Evelyn observed in the victims of the fire?
3. In his concerns and the steps Evelyn takes to combat the fire, what portrait of him might a modern reader infer?
4. For whom do you think Evelyn was writing this diary? On what do you base this conclusion?
5. What attitude expressed by Evelyn about the cause of the calamity might some modern readers dismiss as unacceptable?

Spin-offs for writing

1. Write an essay describing any accident or natural calamity you have witnessed.
2. Write a description of a forest fire.

WILLIAM BYRD

William Byrd (1674–1744), American Colonial writer, planter, and government official, inherited vast land holdings from his father and laid out the plans on one of his estates for a city that eventually became Richmond, Virginia. Serving in various government capacities in Virginia, he undertook many surveying explorations into the backwoods, which resulted in such books as A Journey to the Land of Eden *and* A Progress to the Mines, *based largely on his diaries. On this particular journey Byrd was surveying the dividing line between Virginia and North Carolina to settle a boundary dispute.*

This excerpt from Byrd's diaries describes an expedition's rare encounter with a young buffalo. Although vast herds of buffalo roamed the prairies at the time, Byrd and his woodsmen obviously had little familiarity with the creatures and regarded the meeting as a stroke of luck.

November 11 [1728]. We had all been so refreshed by our day of rest that we decamped earlier than ordinary, and passed the several fords of Hico River. The woods were thick great part of this day's journey, so that we were forced to scuffle hard to advance seven miles, being equal in fatigue to double that distance of clear and open grounds.

We took up our quarters upon Sugar-tree Creek, in the same camp we had lain in when we came up, and happened to be entertained at supper with a rarity we had never had the fortune to meet with before during the whole expedition.

A little wide of this creek, one of the men had the luck to meet with a young buffalo of two years old. It was a bull which, notwithstanding he was no older, was a big as an ordinary ox. His legs are very thick and very short, and his hoofs exceeding broad. His back rose into a kind of bunch a little above the shoulders, which I believe contributes not a little to that creature's enormous strength. His body is vastly deep from the shoulders to the brisket, sometimes six feet in those that are full grown. The portly figure of this animal is disgraced by a shabby little tail, not above 12 inches long. This he cocks up on end whenever he's in a passion and, instead of lowing or bellowing, grunts with no better grace than a hog.

The hair growing on his head and neck is long and shagged, and so soft that it will spin into thread not unlike mohair, which might be wove into a sort of camlet.[1] Some people have stockings knit of it that would have served an Israelite during his forty years' march through the wilderness.

---

[1] an Eastern fabric, perhaps made of camel's hair.

5 Its horns are short and strong, of which the Indians make large spoons, which they say will split and fall to pieces whenever poison is put into them. Its color is a dirty brown, and its hide so thick that it is scarce penetrable. However, it makes very spongy sole leather by the ordinary method of tanning, though this fault might by good contrivance be mended.

6 As thick as this poor beast's hide was, a bullet made shift to enter it and fetch him down. It was found all alone, though buffaloes seldom are. They usually range about in herds, like other cattle, and, though they differ something in figure, are certainly of the same species. There are two reasons for this opinion: the flesh of both has exactly the same taste, and the mixed breed betwixt both, they say, will generate. All the difference I could perceive between the flesh of buffalo and common beef was that the flesh of the first was much yellower than that of the other, and the lean something tougher.

7 The men were so delighted with this new diet, that the gridiron and frying-pan had no more rest all night than a poor husband subject to curtain lectures. Buffaloes may be easily tamed when they are taken young. The best way to catch them is to carry a milch mare into the woods and, when you find a cow and a calf, to kill the cow and then, having catched the calf, to suckle it upon the mare. After once or twice sucking her, it will follow her home and become as gentle as another calf.

8 If we could get into a breed of them, they might be made very useful not only for the dairy by giving an ocean of milk, but also for drawing vast and cumbersome weights by their prodigious strength. These with the other advantages I mentioned before, would make this sort of cattle more profitable to the owner than any other we are acquainted with, though they would need a world of provender.

Speculations

1. On what implied dominant impression is this description based?
2. What does the appraisal of the buffalo by Byrd implicitly tell us about his attitude towards the woods and its wildlife?
3. What inferences about why the buffalo was nearly hunted to extinction can you draw from Byrd's reactions to the animal?
4. What examples of odd phrasing can you cite to show the antiquity of this diary entry?
5. What does Byrd mean by "curtain lectures" in the opening sentences of paragraph 7?

Spin-offs for writing

1. Describe an animal, whether a personal pet or one seen in a zoo.
2. Find a picture of a buffalo in a book or magazine and write your own description of it.

ALBERT CAMUS

Albert Camus (1913–1960), French writer and philosopher, was born in Algeria and educated at the University of Algiers. Moving to Paris in 1939, he became a member of the French Resistance during the Nazi occupation and editor of an underground publication, Combat. He believed that human life was absurd, yet his novels and plays depicted characters who asserted their dignity and individual will in the face of meaninglessness. His principal works include The Myth of Sisyphus *(1942),* The Stranger *(1946), and* The Rebel *(1954). In 1957 Camus won the Nobel Prize in literature. He was killed in a car accident in 1960.*

Diaries vary in size and intent, and some, especially those kept by writers, are written with a deliberateness that seems oddly at variance with the privacy presumed to be behind the form. Such diaries, usually called notebooks, contain a mix of personal reflections along with roughed out episodes, characters, and plots that later appear in finished work. The following excerpt comes from such a writer's notebook. It relates the poignant story of an old actor at the end of his days.

Nov. 1945

Death of an old actor.

1. One morning in a snowy, muddy Paris. The oldest and most melancholy section in town, the one that houses the Santé, Sainte-Anne, and Cochin.[1] Along the dark, icy streets, the insane, the sick, the poor, and the condemned. As for Cochin: the barracks of poverty and illness, and its walls drip with the filthy humidity that belongs to misfortune.

2. That is where he died. At the end of his life, he was still playing bit parts (utility men, as theater people call them), changing his single threadbare suit yellowing with age for the more or less glittering costumes that have to be provided, willy-nilly, for the minor roles. He had to give up his work. He could no longer drink anything but milk, and besides he had no milk. He was taken to Cochin and he told his friends that he was going to be operated on and then it would be all over. (I recall a line from his part: "When I was a little child," and as a suggestion was made to him about its delivery, "Ah!" he said, "I don't feel it that way.") He wasn't operated on but was sent away, being told he was cured. He even went back to the bit part of a ludicrous little man that he was playing at that time. But he had lost weight. It has always amazed me to what degree the loss a certain amount of weight, a certain manner of having the cheekbones stand

---

[1] On the Boulevard de Port-Royal, near the Métro station of La Glacière, are grouped the Cochin hospital and prisons like La Santé and Sainte-Anne.

out and the gums shrink, is the obvious sign that it's all coming to an end. The one who is losing weight is the only one who never seems to "be aware." Or if he "is aware," it's only intermittently perhaps, and I, of course, have no way of knowing. All I can know is what I see and it so happened that I saw that Liesse was going to die.

He died indeed. He stopped working again. He went back to Cochin. They still didn't operate, but he died without that—one night without a fuss. And in the morning his wife came to see him as usual. No one informed her at the office because no one had been informed. Those in the neighboring beds informed his wife. "You know," they said, "it happened last night."

And this morning there he is, in the little morgue opening on to the rue de la Santé. Two or three of his old associates are there with the widow and the widow's daughter, who is not his daughter. When I arrived, the undertaker (why was he wearing a tricolor sash like a mayor?) told me he could still be seen. I didn't want to; I still had this filthy, clinging morning stuck in my throat. But I went. You could see only his head; what served as a shroud was pulled up to his chin. He had lost more weight; I didn't think anyone in his condition could get still thinner. Yet he had done so, and one could see the thickness of his bones and realize that this strong, nobby head was made to carry a heavy weight of flesh. For lack of flesh, the teeth jutted out, frighteningly . . . But am I going to describe that? A dead body is a dead body, as everyone knows, and the dead must be left to bury the dead. What a pity, though, what a dreadful pity!

The men who were at his head, their hands on the edge of the coffin as if they were presenting him to the visitor, then got under way. Got under way is the word, for those awkward, stiff automata in their coarse clothing suddenly hurled themselves upon the shroud, the cover, and a screwdriver. In a second the top was down and two men were tightening the screws, weighing heavily on them with a brutal motion of the forearm. "Ah!" they seemed to say, "you won't get out now!" Those living men wanted it over with, that could be seen at once. He was carried out. We followed him. The widow and the daughter climbed into the hearse at the same time as the corpse. We piled into a car that followed. Not a flower, nothing but black everywhere.

We were going to the Thiais Cemetery. The widow thought it was far, but the office had forced it on her. We left town by the Porte d'Italie. Never had the sky seemed to me so low over the suburbs of Paris. Fragments of shanties, stakes, a black, spotty vegetation emerged from the piles of snow and mud. Two or three miles of this landscape and we reached the monumental gates of the most hideous cemetery in the world. A guard with a red face came out to stop the procession at the gate and demanded the ticket. "O.K.," he said, once he had it in his hands. For some ten minutes we navigated amid piles of mud and snow. Then we stopped behind another funeral. We were separated from the field of the dead by an embankment of snow. In the snow two crosses were planted askew; one was for Liesse, from what I saw, and the other for a little girl eleven years old. The funeral ahead of us was the little girl's. But the family was just getting back into the hearse. It started off and we were able to advance a few yards. We got out. Tall fellows in blue wearing boots like sewermen dropped the shovels they were holding as they watched the scene. They stepped forward and began to pull the coffin out of the hearse. At that moment, a sort of mailman dressed in blue and red, wearing a bashed-in military cap, suddenly appeared with an invoice with carbon paper between the sheets. Then the sewermen read aloud a number engraved on the coffin: 3237 C. The mailman followed the lines of his invoice with his pencil and he said "O.K." as he checked a number. At that moment they pulled out the coffin. We entered the field. Our feet sank into an oily and elastic mud. The hole was dug among four other holes that surrounded it on all sides. The sewermen slipped the box in rather swiftly. But we were all very far from the hole because the graves kept us from stepping forward and the narrow passage separating them was cluttered with tools and with earth. When the coffin reached the bottom, there was a moment of silence. Everyone looked at one another. There was no priest, no flowers, and not a word of peace or of regret rose from the group. And all felt that the moment should be more solemn, that it should have been emphasized, and no one knew how. Then a sewerman said: "If these ladies and gentlemen want to throw in a little earth." The widow nodded yes. He picked up some earth on a shovel, took a trowel out of his pocket, and picked up some soil on the trowel. The widow stretched out her hand above a mound of earth. She took the trowel and threw the soil in the direction of the hole, rather wildly. The hollow sound of the box could be heard. But the daughter missed her shot. The soil went far beyond the hole. She made a gesture that meant: "Too bad."

7 The bill: "And he was put into the clay soil for an exorbitant price."

8 You know, this is the cemetery of the people put to death.

9 Laval[2] is a little farther on.

---

[2]Pierre Laval (1883–1945), premier of the Vichy government, 1942–44, who was executed for treason.

Speculations

1. What characteristics of this excerpt seem different from the writing one might expect to find in an ordinary diary?

2. What dominant impression of the old actor emerges from the descriptive sketch in paragraph 2?

3. What does a reader learn about Camus from this notebook excerpt?

4. What part does the description of the weather and background scenery play in the overall mood of this piece?

5. How would you characterize the tone of Camus's description of the cemetery?

Spin-offs for writing

1. Write a descriptive essay about any solemn religious rite or ceremony.

2. Describe how you look when you are sick.

CHARLOTTE FORTEN GRIMKE

Charlotte Forten Grimke (1837–1914), African-American teacher, diarist, and abolitionist, was a member of a wealthy Philadelphia family. Her father had her privately educated rather than permit her to attend the segregated schools of Philadelphia. Eventually she was sent to Salem, Massachusetts, whose schools were integrated, and graduated from the Higginson Grammar School, distinguishing herself there as a student and a poet. A passionate proponent of abolition, Charlotte married the Reverend Francis J. Grimke in 1878, who was himself a champion of black rights. She died in 1914, after a lingering illness.

In this excerpt from her journals, Charlotte Forten Grimke describes the seasickness she suffered in 1862 while sailing to Port Royal, South Carolina, which had lately been captured by a Union naval armada. There the Union government had embarked on an ambitious program to educate thousands of freed slaves whose former masters had fled inland, and Charlotte was among the volunteers from the North who offered to help teach them. She remained and taught at St. Helena Island from 1862 to 1864. By the time she returned to Philadelphia, thousands of black children were enrolled in schools, with thousands of former slaves also being taught to read in Sunday sessions before church services.

At Sea.

1 *October 27, Monday.*—Let me see. Where am I? What do I want to write? I am in a state of utter bewilderment. It was on Wed. I rec'd the note. On Thursday I said "good bye" to the friends that are so dear, and the city that is so hateful,[1] and went to N.Y. Spent the night with Mrs. [Peter] W.[illiams]. The next morn did not hurry myself, having heard that the Steamer "United States" w'ld not sail till twelve. Mrs. W.[illiams] and I went to "Lovejoy's" to meet the Hunns'[2] and found there a card from Mr. H.[unn] bidding me hasten to the steamer, as it was advertised to sail at nine. It was then between ten and eleven. After hurrying down and wearying ourselves, found when I got on board that it was not to sail till twelve. But I did not go ashore again. It was too bad, for I had not time to get several things that I wanted much, among them "Les Miserables," which my dear brother H.[enry] had kindly given me the money for. He had not had time to get it in Phila.[delphia].

2 Enjoyed the sail down the harbor perfectly. The shipping is a noble sight. Had no symptoms of sea-sickness until eve. when, being seated

---

[1] Philadelphia

[2] John A. Hunn and his daughter Lizzie, a Quaker family, were going to Port Royal to open a store to benefit the freed slaves.

at the table an inexpressibly singular sensation caused me to make a hasty retreat to the aft-deck, where by keeping perfectly still sitting on a coil of ropes spent a very comfortable eve. and had a pleasant conversation with one of the passengers. Did not get out of sight of land until after dark. I regretted that.

Went below for the night into the close ladies' cabin with many misgivings which proved not unfounded. Was terribly sea-sick that night and all the next morning. Did not reappear on deck till noon of the next day—Saturday. What an experience. Of all the doleful, dismal, desperate experiences sea-sickness is certainly the dolefulest, dismalist, desperate-est!

It was rather a miserable afternoon. Was half sick all the time and scarcely dared to move. There was highly pleasant talk going on around me, to which I could listen in silence—that was all. My companion Lizzie Hunn was sick all the time. Poor girl, she c'ld take no pleasure in anything.

When night came, we both determined that we w'ldn't go below and have a repetition of the agonies of the night before. We heroically resolved to pass the night on deck. A nice little nook was found for us "amidships," and there enveloped in shawls and seated in arm chairs we were made as comfortable as possible, and passed the night without being sick. Two of the passengers—young men from Hilton Head, who were very gentlemanly and attentive, entertained us for some time with some fine singing; then they retired, and we passed the rest of the night in the society of the Ocean alone. How wild and strange it seemed there on deck in the dark night, only the dim outlines of sea and sky to be seen, only the roaring of the waves to be heard. I enjoyed it much. The thought that we were far, far, away from land was a pleasant one to me.

The next day—Sunday—was emphatically a *dismal* day. It rained nearly all the time so that we c'ld not be on deck much of the time. As soon as we established ourselves nicely outside[,] down came the rain and we were driven into the close cabin, which was almost unendurable to me. Tried to read a little in the French Bible which H.[enry Cassey] gave me, but in vain. The day was mostly spent in the interesting occupation of preventing sea-sickness by keeping perfectly quiet and watching the rain drops.

Before night a storm came on. And a terrible storm it was. The steward arranged mattresses and blankets for us in the covered passage way "amidships" and we lay down, but not to rest. It was a veritable grand storm at sea. The vessel rocked and plunged, the planks creaked and groaned; the sea broke upon the boat with thunderous roars, and within[,] one w'ld have thought that all the crockery in the establishment was going to pieces. Such a noise I never heard in my life. Such roaring and plunging, and creaking. Afterward we were told that one of the chains of the vessel broke, and indeed for a time she seemed to be at the mercy of the waves. Some one near us—one of the waiters, I think, was dreadfully frightened, and commenced praying and moaning most piteously, crying "Oh Jesus, dear Jesus," in most lamentable tones, till I began to think we must really be in danger. Then the water came into the ladies' cabin, below. One lady who had a baby with her woke up in the night and c'ld not find the child. It had been rolled away from her by the tossing of the ship, the lamps were out, and after some time, and much terror on the part of the poor woman the baby was found by one of the waiters under the berths. She was very quiet, and did not seem at all alarmed at her involuntary journey. Despite all the alarm and distress and anxiety we c'ld not help being amused at this little episode. During all the storm, however, I felt no fear; and now that the danger has passed, I feel really glad that I have at last experienced a "veritable storm at sea." The most astonishing thing was that I had two or three most refreshing sleeps in the very height of the storm.

8 This morning the sea was still very rough, but I struggled up, and dressed with great difficulty, and with the aid of one of the waiters made my way on deck. The sky was still very much overcast, the great, white capped waves were rising to a great height and breaking against the sides of the vessel. It was a grand sight, and I enjoyed it greatly. It has quite cleared off now, and the day is most lovely. I am feeling well and *luxuriating* in the glorious beauty of sea and sky. But my poor companion is still quite sick, and while I write, sits before me on a coil of ropes, enveloped in shawls, and looking the picture of dolefulness and despair.

9 How grand, how glorious the sea is, to-day! It far more than realizes my highest expectations of it. The sky too is beautiful[,] a deep, delicious blue, with soft, white, fleecy clouds floating over it. We have seen several sails today, in the distance, but still no land, whereat I am rejoiced.

10 There is not much to be said about the passengers on board. There are about a dozen beside ourselves, none of whom seem to me especially interesting, except perhaps our friend from Hilton Head, Mr. B. He is very intelligent, and I sh'ld think even a talented young man. He has read and admires all my favorite authors, and I enjoy talking with him about them. I have rarely found a man with so keen and delicate an appreciation of the beautiful, both in Nature

and Art. There are no soldiers on board but one officer who stalks about the boat looking well pleased with himself and evidently trying to look quite grand, but *sans* success, for he was rather insignificant despite his good figure, fierce moustaches, and epaulettes.

Of the three ladies on board two go South to join their husbands, and the third accompanies hers. The first two are quite talkative, the latter very quiet. I believe that is all that can be said of them. There is a sea captain here whom I like very much. He is a Cape Cod man; has been to sea ever since he was nine years old. Has visited many lands, and I enjoy hearing him talk about them. The other gentlemen do not interest me, so I shall let them pass. Have only been able to go to the table twice. Then there was no difficulty—as I feared there might be. People were kind and polite as possible. Indeed I have had not the least trouble since I have been on board. The waiters are as obliging and attentive as they can be, and bring us our meals out on deck every day.

Afternoon. I have just beheld the most glorious sight I ever saw in my life. With the aid of Mr. B. I staggered to the bow of the ship (which still rolls and pitches terribly) and there saw the sea in all its glory and grandeur. Oh, how beautiful those great waves were as they broke upon the side of the vessel, into foam and spray pure and white as new fallen snow. People talk of the monotony of the sea. I have not found it monotonous for a moment, since I have been well. To me there is "infinite variety," constant enjoyment in it.

I have tried to read, but in vain; there is so much to take off one's attention, besides reading makes my head dizzy. One of the most beautiful sights I have yet seen is the phosphorescence in the water at night—the long line of light in the wake of the steamer, and the stars, and sometimes balls of fire that rise so magically out of the water. It is most strange and beautiful. Had it not been for the storm we should have reached Port Royal to-day. But we shall not get there till to-morrow.

Speculations

1. What can you infer about the author's character and personality from her reaction to the storm?

2. What does the author's appraisals of her fellow passengers aboard ship tell you about her social preferences?

3. In paragraph 11, the author remarks about going to the dining table that "there was no difficulty." What sort of difficulty do you think she anticipated?

4. What dominant impression of the sea underlies the author's descriptions of its raging?

5. Given what we know about the author's social status and background, why do you think she would rejoice at being out of sight of land?

Spin-offs for writing

1. Write a descriptive essay on a thunderstorm.
2. Write an essay describing how you felt during any episode of motion sickness.

Student Journal–Description

Saro Babayan

April 30, 1992

Today was a tragic day for Los Angeles, my city. I want to write down my impressions before they fade from memory.

As the sun was shying away from the face of the earth, with dusk creeping in gradually, the city of Los Angeles was turning into a monstrous ball of fire. Riveted to my television set, I watched in horror as a visit to the local store became as risky as betting your life savings on a horse race. A simple walk along the streets became as hazardous as stepping barefoot on nails. In fact, the once safe streets and sidewalks had suddenly turned into playgrounds for criminals. An immediate curfew, imposed by the local police, shut off the public from any kind of social activity. A deadly disease seemed to have permeated society, forcing families to be quarantined prisoners in their own homes. Chaos and disorderly conduct have disrupted normal and peace-loving people's daily routine. All of these disturbances were taking place because a black man, Rodney King, had been beaten by the police, who—accused and placed on trial—were declared innocent by a jury's verdict.

As soon as the verdict was announced, a lynching mood erupted, and stores and buildings were set on fire by maddened hordes of people, until the Hollywood area turned into a raging inferno, symbolizing the angry mood of the people disgusted by the jury's verdict. They wasted no time in expressing their frustration at what seemed to them a terrible injustice. Blinded by uncontrollable tempers, some resorted to shooting or bludgeoning innocent victims.

Fires were as mesmerizing to the rioters as light is to a moth. Like an octopus devouring it prey, tongues of fire devoured storefronts, cars, and anything else in the way. With clanking horns and whining sirens, firefighter trucks zoomed down the streets in a desperate attempt to salvage the inner city.

Being deprived of some of the basic necessities of life, such as food and medicine, made looting or rioting a justifiable act. Groups of irate people burst into various stores like stampeding buffalo. Clothing, furniture, electronic devices, and food were carried away by greedy adults and even their children. Looters loaded their stolen goods into vans or pickups with expressions of victory pasted all over their faces—as if they had hit the lottery jackpot. Women clung to their items the same way mothers cling to their babies. I watched the streets becoming dump sites after the looters had disposed of the boxes and bags they didn't need. A few looters still lingered long after dark, hoping to accumulate more desirable treasures.

The television screen told me that Los Angeles had turned into a battle zone. Soon the streets were swamped with police cars trying to restore order. The sight of these police officers in their black uniforms, wielding clubs, followed by members of the United States National Guard, holding rifles, added a dimension of awful gloom to the scene.

I do not understand exactly how this terrible tragedy happened, but I want to remember the day's events so that later I can try to understand their origins and causes.

3.

CAUSAL ANALYSIS.

January 1, 1869. "It was then that I left you, my two precious eldest children. I did it and would do it again at any moment, and yet I miss you both and think of you day and night." Why she left her husband and children for Richard Wagner and the price she paid for doing it. Cosima Wagner.

November 24, 1918. "I take some aspirin to help me sleep. But the pain awakens me in the middle of the night, and I think I am going mad." A chronicle of the distressing effect of his homosexual affairs on his marriage. Andre Gide.

August, 1932. "My Lover is in my husband's bed." Duplicity in romance. Anaïs Nin.

11th July, 1942. "Many accuse me of indifference and passivity when I refuse to go into hiding." Why she refused to hide from the Nazis. Etty Hillesum.

CHAPTER 3

Causal Analysis

Causal analysis is the term given to any essay whose practical purpose is to explain the causes or effects of an event. For example, your essay might examine the reasons that a particular marriage broke up or it may focus on the effects of the divorce on the children. In the first example you are looking for antecedents to the breakup, in the second, for consequences likely to ensue from it. This simple diagram illustrates the relationship:

Cause   (past) ——Situation—— Effects   (future)

This diagram simply tells us that cause always precedes an event and effect always follows it. That is why analyzing cause requires us to probe back in time before the event occurred, while analyzing effect requires a prediction of likely consequences to come in the future.

The causal analysis is a rhetorical staple of any discipline whose goal is to explain the material world or behavior. Chemists write essays explaining why compounds interact in certain ways. Social scientists write volumes of causal essays that try to fathom why people commit crimes. Economists try to predict the effects of falling interest rates on the economy, and animal behaviorists labor to explain the navigational instincts of migratory wildfowl. All these essays would be viewed by the rhetorician as causal analyses because they all share a common purpose: to explain cause or to predict effect.

For the diarist, causal analysis is a relatively rare form and hardly ever written with the same calculatedness that we expect to find in the analyses of the essayist. Diarists typically speculate about cause more obliquely than directly, using arguments not framed as specifically as the essayists' and reasoning that is seldom as exact. For example, here is Andre Gide, the famed French writer, reflecting in his diary on the effects of his homosexual nature on his wife and marriage:

> After my conversations with her of three days ago—conversations interrupted by horrible silences and sobbing, yet serious and without one word of reproach by either of us—it seemed to me that never again could I live any kind of life except a life of repentance and contrition. I felt ended, ruined, decomposed. One tear of hers weighed more, I said to myself, than the ocean of my happiness. In brief—why amplify?—I no longer acknowledged my right to build my happiness on the ruin of her despair.

> *But why speak of happiness? It is my life, my very existence that wounds her. And this life I can remove but I cannot change....*
>
> **—Andre Gide**

This sort of fuzzy explanation, while fine for diaries, would be unacceptable in the more public forum of the essay. Here you must be not only specific but also reasonable, which means that you must not make exaggerated claims for causation that you cannot prove. You must avoid simplistic reasoning and dogma and try, instead, to stay with explanations that you can either prove or are generally accepted. For example, even if you believe that people fall in love because of astrological compatibility, you cannot make that the basis of a convincing causal analysis unless you can cite substantial proof. Astrology is not regarded as an empirical science, and many reject its teachings. Better to ground your analysis in some discipline whose findings are attended to with respect. Here, for example, is a paragraph in which a psychiatrist theorizes about falling in love:

> *Falling in love is not an act of will. It is not a conscious choice. No matter how open to or eager for it we may be, the experience may still elude us. Contrarily, the experience may capture us at times when we are definitely not seeking it, when it is inconvenient and undesirable. We are as likely to fall in love with someone with whom we are obviously ill matched as with someone more suitable. Indeed, we may not even like or admire the object of our passion, yet, try as we might, we may not be able to fall in love with a person whom we deeply respect and with whom a deep relationship would be in all ways desirable. This is not to say that the experience of falling in love is immune to discipline. Psychiatrists, for instance, frequently fall in love with their patients, just as their patients fall in love with them, yet out of duty to the patient and their role they are usually able to abort the collapse of their ego boundaries and give up the patient as a romantic object....*
>
> **—M. Scott Peck, "Why We Fall in Love"**

Everything the writer says is commonsensical and reasonable, and anyone who has ever fallen in love is likely to nod with recognition at these truths.

As an essayist, unlike a diarist, you should not write obliquely about cause. Instead, your causal analyses should state exactly what you are trying to explain and should do so in language that makes your purpose unmistakable. Here is an example from an essay entitled "Why a Classic Is a Classic":

> *... Why does the great and universal fame of classical authors continue? The answer is that the fame of classical authors is entirely independent of the majority. Do you suppose that if the fame of*

> Shakespeare depended on the man in the street it would survive a fortnight? The fame of classical authors is originally made, and it is maintained, by the passionate few. Even when a first-class author has enjoyed immense success during his lifetime, the majority have never appreciated him so sincerely as they have appreciated second-rate men. He has always been reinforced by the ardor of the passionate few. And in the case of an author who has emerged into glory after his death the happy sequel has been due solely to the obstinate perseverance of the few. . . .
>
> —**Arnold Bennett, "Why a Classic Is a Classic"**

Word your own causal analysis with a similar directness and your reader will readily get the point.

In writing an essay analyzing cause, never beat around the bush about what you are analyzing or what you believe. State it directly and plainly, using an abundance of words that indicate causation. These range from the ordinary "because" and "since" to the more heavy-footed "the reason why . . . is that" which can almost always be cut. Since they are writing mainly for themselves, diarists may be forgivably roundabout; essayists, on the other hand, have an obligation to be as clear and straightforward as possible.

COSIMA WAGNER

Cosima Wagner (1837–1930), second child of the composer Franz Liszt, abandoned her husband, conductor Hans von Bulow, in 1868 to live with the composer Richard Wagner (1813–1883), who was twenty-four years her senior. For the next fourteen years the two were inseparable. She bore Wagner two daughters and a son, the first two children while she was still living as Hans von Bulow's wife. After Wagner's death, Cosima was instrumental in continuing the Bayreuth Musical Festivals, which the composer had founded.

In 1868, when Cosima went to live with Wagner in Switzerland, she left behind in Munich her two children by Hans von Bulow—Daniela, born 1860, and Blandine, born 1863. As the following excerpt shows, Cosima was tormented by her decision to desert her children for Wagner, to whose genius she devoted the rest of her life. She hoped that her diary would help explain to the children why she had abandoned them.

> ***Friday, January 1.*** On Christmas Day, my 31st birthday, this notebook was to have started, I could not get it in Lucerne. And so the first day of the year will also contain the beginning of my reports to you, my children. You shall know every hour of my life, so that one day you will come to see me as I am; for, if I die young, others will be able to tell you very little about me, and if I live long, I shall probably only wish to remain silent. In this way you will help me do my duty—yes, children, my duty. What I mean by that you will find out later. Your mother intends to tell you everything about her present life, and she believes she can do so.
>
> The year 1868 marks the outward turning-point of my life: in this year it was granted to me to put into action what for the past five years had filled my thoughts. It is an occupation I have not sought after or brought about myself: Fate laid it on me. In order that you may understand, I must confess to you that up to the hour in which I recognized my true inner calling, my life had been a dreary, unbeautiful dream, of which I have no desire to tell you anything, for I do not understand it myself and reject it with the whole of my now purified soul. The outward appearance was and remained calm, but inside all was bleak and dreary, when there came into my life that being who swiftly led me to realize that up to now I had never lived. My love became for me a rebirth, a deliverance, a fading away of all that was trivial and bad in me, and I swore to seal it through death, through pious renunciation or complete devotion. What love had done for me I shall never be able to repay. When the stars decreed that events, about which you will find out elsewhere, should banish into isolation my only friend, the guardian spirit and savior of my soul, the revealer of all that is noble and true, that he should be left

solitary, abandoned, joyless, and unfriended, I cried out to him: I shall come to you and seek my greatest and highest happiness in sharing the burdens of life with you.[1] It was then that I left you, my two precious eldest children. I did it and would do it again at any moment, and yet I miss you both and think of you day and night. For I love you all, each with an equal love; in your hearts I seek the refuge for my earthly memory when my time is past, and I would sacrifice everything to you—everything but the life of this one person. Our separation will be temporary, and you are still so small that you will not feel it as your mother does. This is my hope.

3 Early in the morning the Friend came to greet me and wish me a happy New Year. I am always so overcome by his kindness toward me, in my ever deeper awareness of his greatness, that in his presence I always feel I must dissolve into tears. Afterward I dressed Loldchen and Evchen[2] prettily (white satin frocks and garlands of roses) and we went to give him our good wishes. Then we had breakfast, after which he went to work as usual (making a fair copy of the second act of *Siegfried* and completing his essay on the Jews). I took Evchen and Loldchen into the garden. Before lunch (at one o'clock) my beloved read me what he had written. At table he told me more of the range of his essay, and we discussed his position, that is to say, the position of art as laid down by the Jews, which made me see Mendelssohn for the first time as a tragic figure. After the meal he went for his usual walk, after receiving a telegram from the King and another from you. The latter affected him as it did me; my heart was heavy and full to bursting, because you were not here with me, but a glance at him consoled me and gave me courage—I was looking into a happy future. Then I arranged the Christmas tree, which was lit today for the second time. At about five o'clock Evchen and Loldchen, dressed again as angels, came down and found the Christmas gifts which had been kept back. Richard played for them, they danced, and I thought of you, my absent ones, so far away, and once again I watched the merry scene through a veil of tears, yet here, too, these tears were without bitterness. Then Richard started up a jumping jack, to Loldi's great joy. While the little ones were enjoying their supper, he played me the "Spring Song" from *Die Walküre*. When you one day hear these sounds, my children, you will understand me. I cannot hear them without being transported right away. — We had tea upstairs in my room; I asked my beloved to dictate something to me today (biography) for superstitious reasons (they say that whatever one does on the first

---

[1] In 1868 rumors about the affair between Wagner and Cosima had reached the ears of Wagner's patron, King Ludwig II of Bavaria, who strongly disapproved. Earlier Wagner had alienated the government and people of Munich and had been forced to flee to Switzerland.
[2] Children by Wagner.

day of the year one continues). Although it was an exertion for him, he wanted in his indescribable goodness toward me to do it, and so there emerged two pages about Schopenhauer which for me are beyond all price. At eleven we parted, after once more reviewing the day together and finding it harmonious and good. When he had gone, I sat down at my writing desk to talk to you. The Friend has given me the golden pen with which he wrote *Tristan* and *Siegfried*, and this I consecrate to these communications of mine to you. Thus I signify to you how sacredly I regard this work of a mother's confidences and anxieties; the pen which has traced the sublimest things ever created by a noble spirit shall now be dedicated solely to the depths of a woman's heart. So God bless you, my children, you who are far away, you who are close by, and you lying still unknown within my womb.[3] May your mother's love be a friendly light to you in your path through life! Do not mistake your mother, though you yourselves will never be able to do what she has done, since what Fate has here decreed is something that will not recur. All whom I love are now at rest, and so I, too, will go to my bed. For you and for him my last and friendliest thoughts!

Speculations

1. What do you think Cosima meant by "her duty" in the first paragraph? What does this choice of words say about her motivation for taking this momentous step?

2. From this brief excerpt, how would you characterize Cosima's relationship with, and attitude towards, Wagner?

3. What do you think a modern feminist might say about the relationship between Wagner and Cosima as revealed in these pages?

4. What explanation does Cosima give for her actions, in paragraph 2, and what comfort do you think she might have derived from it?

5. What is your opinion of the argument, made by some musicologists, that Cosima's desertion of her husband and children is at least partly excused by the comfort and help she gave to a musical genius?

Spin-offs for writing

1. Write an essay defending or condemning Cosima's actions.

2. Does extraordinary genius merit exemption from ordinary moral expectations? Write an essay on the pros or cons of this question.

---

[3] Cosima was then pregnant with Wagner's third child and only son, Siegfried.

ANDRE GIDE

Andre Gide (1869–1951) was a French writer noted for his outspoken and unorthodox social opinions, which included a defense of homosexuality and open advocacy of communism, an opinion he later retracted after visiting the Soviet Union. Gide was a versatile writer whose work includes novels, essays, stories, and plays. In several novels he portrayed characters who violated moral norms in a search for their own internal selves. His works include The Immoralist *(1902, tr. 1930),* Strait is the Gate *(1909, tr. 1924), and* The Counterfeiters, *(1926, tr. 1927). Gide was awarded the Nobel Prize in literature in 1947.*

Mirrored in these entries is the conflict that occurred between Gide and his wife, Madeleine, because of the writer's fondness for homosexual lovers. Madeleine, a devout Roman Catholic, could not accept her husband's homosexual tendencies. The two eventually separated over this issue, and when Madeleine died, some suggested it was of a broken heart.

November 24, 1918

1 I take some aspirin to help me sleep. But the pain awakens me in the middle of the night, and I think I am going mad.

2 "It was my most precious possession," she had said to me. "After your departure, when I found myself alone in the big house which you had abandoned, leaving me without anyone to lean on, without knowing what to do or what was to become of me, I thought at first that there was nothing left for me to do but to die. Yes, truly, I believed that my heart had stopped beating and that I was dying. I suffered so much. I burned your letters just to have something to do, to indulge in some kind of activity. But before destroying them, I re-read every one of them, one by one." And then she added, "It was my most precious possession."

3 She would make this sacrifice again, I persuade myself. Independent of all cause for complaint, modesty compelled her toward this act. She could not stand to attract attention of any kind to herself but constantly effaced herself. She never wanted her name to be mentioned anywhere, neither by the lips of friends nor by those of the poor peasants she nursed and who called her "Madame Gille": and, above all, she wanted to suppress her presence in my writing.

4 I respected her modesty to the point that I rarely spoke of her in my note books, and even now, I must stop doing so. Never again shall anyone be what she was to me and what I was to her.

5 I never wrote her real love letters because excessive effusion repulses me, and she could not stand being praised. Consequently, I

usually hid from her the feelings that flooded my heart. Nevertheless, her presence was the strands from which the tissue of my life was woven day by day.

November 25, 1918

Alas! I persuade myself that I have warped her life far worse than she warped mine. Because, to tell the truth, she did not warp mine at all; in fact, it now seems to me that the best part of me came from her. My love for her has dominated my entire life, without subtracting anything, but only adding conflict.

It would be totally erroneous for anyone to believe that I modelled the character of Alissa after Madeleine in my novel *The Narrow Door*. There was never anything forced or excessive in her virtue. It seems simply that everything in her asked only to blossom softly and tenderly. . . . It is that which renders me inconsolable. Occasionally I persuade myself that she never feared anyone except me.

After my conversations with her of three days ago—conversations interrupted by horrible silences and sobbing, yet serious and without one word of accusation or reproach by either of us—it seemed to me that never again could I live any kind of life except a life of repentance and contrition. I felt ended, ruined, decomposed. One tear of hers weighed more, I said to myself, than the ocean of my happiness. In brief—why amplify?—I no longer acknowledged my right to build my happiness on the ruins of her despair.

But why speak of happiness? It is my life, my very existence that wounds her. And this life I can remove but I cannot change. And it is not only the sun but the air itself of which I should now be deprived.

Since all my life seemed meant for fails. . .

December 11, 1918

I have been back from Paris for four days—four atrocious days.

My back aches and I can no longer bear the burden of yesterday's joys. How can I ever rekindle the confidence that helped me live? I have no desire to do anything whatsoever, and all of the light beams in my sky have been extinguished.

December 19, 1918

I keep myself busy reviewing my memoirs and turning the rough draft into a complete text in case I wish to entrust it to Verbecke. I am not very satisfied with what I reread. The sentences are flabby; the whole work is too self-conscious, too supervised, too literary.

14 I sit at the piano and play *The Well-tempered Clavier.* Once again I feel this too calm, suffocating life, from which I cannot escape without a new laceration. Weakness and extreme aging. That which could cause my heart once again to beat with rapture would be for her suffering and horror. Anything that would affirm me would only wound her. Only in destroying myself can I assure her happiness.

December 22, 1918

15 Certain days, and especially certain nights, I feel crushed by the regret caused by those letters she destroyed. It was through them that I had hoped to survive.

January 20, 1919

16 The entire act [of her burning the letters] implied a sort of contract in which the other party was not consulted—a contract which I imposed on her only because my nature imposed on me the same peremptory conditions.

17 From now on my work shall be nothing more than a symphony missing the most tender harmonies, an uncrowned edifice.

Cuverville, October 8, 1918

18 (Date of my wedding anniversary). I do not know which is more dreadful—to no longer be loved or to watch the one you still love, and who still loves you, cease believing in your love for her. I did not succeed in loving her less, and I remain near her, my heart bleeding, but mute. Ah! Will I never speak to her again? . . . What is the use of insisting to the world that I love her above all others? She would not believe me. Alas! now it is in my power only to bruise her more.

January 6, 1919

19 I am leaving Cuverville tomorrow. The physical and moral condition in which I find myself here is most depressing, and my work has suffered immensely. I no longer taste here the joy of making her happy; that is, I no longer have that illusion. And the thought of this failure haunts my nights. I have even come to believe that my love was a burden to her, and sometimes I accuse this love of being like a weakness, like a folly—and I try to persuade myself to no longer

suffer from it. . . . But I cannot take my share of the divorce of our thoughts. I love only her in this world and I can love no other but her. I cannot live without her love. I accept having the entire world turn against me, but not her. And I must hide all of this from her. I must play with her, and like her, a comedy of happiness.

Paris, May 15, 1921

Madeleine announces her arrival for Tuesday. I expected her Thursday; then Friday I went to the station to meet her. The idea that she will travel on a holiday and in a train packed with other people keeps me in a state of continued anguish. My love for her is just as much part of my life as it ever was, and I can no more tear her out of my heart than I can tear out the desires of my flesh.

Monday, May 29, 1921

She leaves me at four o'clock. I drive her to the Saint Lazare train station.

For a few brief instants I was able to rediscover her face—her smile and expression—despite the fatigue that was so visible. It is that face I loved more than anything else in the world.

December 12, 1921

What shall I do? Whom shall I become? Where shall I go? I cannot stop loving her. On certain days her face—her angelic smile—fills my heart with ecstasy, love, and hopelessness. The hopelessness is a result of not being able to tell her. Not one day, not one moment was I able to speak to her. Both of us remained imprisoned in our silence. Yet, sometimes I told myself that not to speak was the best way since all that I could tell her would simply be a prelude to further agonies for her.

I cannot imagine life without her. Without her I would never have amounted to anything at all. Each of my thoughts was born to function for her. For whom else would I have felt the urgent need to explain myself? And was it not the "despite so much love" that gave my thoughts so much force?

January 3, 1922

Madeleine wrote me this: "What bothers me considerably is the bad attacks that have begun to be levelled against you. Of course it is the power of your thought and its authority that have unleashed them.

Ah! If you were invulnerable, I would not tremble. But you are vulnerable and you know it, and I know it."

26 Vulnerable I am not, except through her. Since her letter, I don't care anymore, and I fear nothing. After all, what can I lose that I still want to hold on to?

[On April 17, 1938, Gide's wife died—as a result of neglecting her health and having been tortured by her relationship with Gide. The following entry was written after her death.]

27 Last evening I thought of her. I was speaking with her as I had done so often, almost more easily in my imagination than if she had been present in reality. Then suddenly I said to myself, "But she is dead. . . ."

28 In the past I had often spent long passages of time away from her; yet, from childhood on I developed the habit of reporting to her the events of my days and to associate her in my mind with all of my joys as well as my sorrows. I was reporting to her in this way last evening when I suddenly remembered that she was dead.

29 As soon as I realized the true nature of the situation, all my thoughts became tarnished and dull—the thoughts about my times away from her and the very recollection of them, for I really relived them in memory only for her. I came to understand that having lost her I had also lost my reason for being and my purpose for living.

Translated by Jo Ray McCuen

Speculations

1. What picture of Madeleine and the relationship between her and Gide emerge from this diary?
2. What can you infer from this diary about Gide's attitude towards his homosexual inclinations?
3. What evidence can you glean from the diary to indicate that perhaps Gide was writing not only for himself, but also for posterity?
4. In paragraph 14 Gide writes, "Only in destroying myself can I assure her happiness." What do you think he meant by that?
5. What symbolic meaning can you attach to Madeleine's burning of the love letters she received from Gide? What meaning did Gide seem to give this act?

Causal Analysis

Spin-offs for writing

1. Write an essay analyzing the causes or effects of sexual jealousy. You may cite the example of a relationship, real or hypothetical, to make your point.

2. Is jealousy decreased or increased when the other person is involved in a same-sex relationship? Write an essay exploring this question.

ANAÏS NIN

Anaïs Nin (1903–1977) was a Paris born American writer who came to the United States at age nine with her Spanish composer father, Joaquin Nin. Her novels mainly depict the dilemmas of women and include Winter of Artifice *(1939),* A Spy in the House of Love *(1954), and other works. She is best known today, however, for her voluminous diaries comprising 35,000 handwritten pages, now owned by the Special Collections Department of the University of California at Los Angeles.*

The excerpt below tells part of the story of the passionate love affair that raged between the writer Henry Miller (1891–1990), his wife June, and Anaïs Nin, who confessed a strong attraction to both. A compulsive diarist, Nin kept a diary for sixty-one years, often reshaping the material for use in a novel, but never, as she once noted, putting the pages of her fiction in her diaries. This excerpt comes from a manuscript edited to emphasize the relationship that existed between Nin and the Millers, carried on behind the back of her husband, Hugh Guiler. It was Nin's wish, the executor of her estate commented, to "have the full story told."

August, 1932

1 As Hugo and I walked tonight from the top of the hill I saw Paris lying in a heat haze. Paris. Henry. I did not think of him as a man, but as life.

2 Perfidiously, I said to Hugo, "It is so fearfully hot. Couldn't we ask Fred and Henry and Paulette for a visit overnight?"

3 This, because I received this morning the first pages of his new book, stupendous pages. He is doing his best writing now, fevered yet cohesive. Every word now hits the mark. The man is whole, strong, as he never was. I want to breathe his presence for a few hours, feed him, cool him, fill him with that heavy breath of earth and trees which whip his blood. God, this is like living every moment in an orgasm, with only pauses between plunges.

4 I want Henry to know this: that I can subordinate the jealous grasping of woman to a passionate devotion to the writer. I feel a proud servitude. There is splendor in his writing, a splendor which transfigures everything he touches.

5 Last night Henry and Hugo talked for each other, admired each other. Hugo's generosity blossomed. When we were in our bedroom, I compensated him. At breakfast, in the garden, he read Henry's latest pages. His enthusiasm flared. I took advantage of it to suggest we open our home to him, the great writer. Holding my hand, weighing my words of reassurance—"Henry interests me as a writer, that's

all"—he assented to all I wanted. I go to the gate to see him off. He is happy just to be loved, and I am astonished by my own lies, my acting.

I did not come out unscathed from the inferno of Henry's overnight visit. The development of those two days was intricate. Just as I was beginning to act like June, "capable of worship, devotion, but also of the greatest callousness to obtain what she wants," as Henry had said, he fell into a sentimental mood.

It was after Hugo had gone off to work. Henry said, "He is so sensitive, one ought not to hurt a man like that." This roused a storm in me. I left the table and went to my room. He came to watch me weeping, and he was glad to see me weep, showing the absence of callousness. But I became tense, poisonous.

When Hugo returned in the evening, Henry began again to listen to him attentively, to speak his language, to talk gravely, ponderously. The three of us were sitting in the garden.

Our talk was at first desultory, until Henry began to ask questions on psychology. (Sometime during the day, probably out of jealousy of June, I had said something which had aroused Henry's jealousy of Allendy.[1]) Everything I had read the previous year, all my talks with Allendy, my own broodings on the subject, all this gushed out of me with amazing energy and clarity.

Suddenly Henry stopped me and said, "I don't trust either Allendy's ideas or your thinking, Anaïs. Why, I only saw him once. He is a brutish, sensual man, lethargic, with a fund of fanaticism in the back of his eyes. And you—why, you put things so clearly and beautifully to me—so crystal clear—it looks simple and true. You are so terribly nimble, so clever. I distrust your cleverness. You make a wonderful pattern, everything is in its place, it looks convincingly clear, too clear. And meanwhile, where are you? Not on the clear surface of your ideas, but you have already sunk deeper, into darker regions, so that one only thinks one has been given all your thoughts, one only imagines you have emptied yourself in that clarity. But there are layers and layers—you're bottomless, unfathomable. Your clearness is deceptive. You're the thinker who arouses most confusion in me, most doubt, most disturbance."

This is the outline of his attack. It was set forth with extraordinary irritation and vehemence. Hugo added quietly, "One feels that she

---

[1] Nin's therapist.

gives you a neat pattern and then slips out of it herself and laughs at you."

12 "Exactly," said Henry.

13 I laughed. I realized that the sum total of his criticism was flattering, and I was joyful at having irritated and puzzled him, but then I felt raked by bitterness at the idea that he should suddenly fight me. Yes, war was inevitable. He and Hugo continued talking while I was trying to toughen myself. It was too unexpected for me. Henry's admiration of Hugo too, was puzzling, after all he had said.

14 I remember thinking, now the two slow-minded ones, the ponderous German and the unflashy Scotchman, have found solidarity against my nimbleness. Well, I will be more nimble and more treacherous. Henry identifies himself with Hugo, the husband, as I identify with June. June and I would have flagellated the two men with pleasure.

15 What a night! How one can go to sleep poisoned, heavy with tears, with rage still smoking. Go ahead, Henry, pity Hugo, because I am going to deceive him a hundred times. I would deceive the greatest and finest man on earth. The ideal of faithfulness is a joke. Remember what I taught you tonight: psychology tries to reestablish the basis of life not on ideals but on sincerity with one's self. Hit, hit all you want to. I'll hit back.

16 I went to sleep full of hatred and love for Henry. Hugo awakened me later with caresses and was trying to make love to me. Half asleep, I pushed him away, without feeling. I found excuses for it afterwards.

17 In the morning I awoke heavy, brittle. Henry sat in the garden. He had stayed on to talk. He was worried about the previous night. I just listened. He told me that he acted in his usual way. He said and did things he did not mean. "Did not mean?" I repeat. Yes, he had been carried away by his intention to dissimulate his love for me. He did not admire Hugo as much as he said, not nearly. The truth was he had been swept off his feet by my tirade. He wanted to embrace me. He had never seen me go to the bottom of a subject like that. Most of my thinking was like shorthand to him. He had fought against a feeling of admiration, jealousy of Allendy, also a perverse hatred of the person who can tell him something new. I had opened worlds to him.

18 It occurred to me that he might be acting, one comedy following another, that now, for some reason, he was playing with me. I told him so. He said quietly, "So help me God, Anaïs, I never lie to you. I cannot help it if you will not believe me."

His explanation sounded weak. What need to dissimulate? I was taking care of Hugo's blindness. Was it not, rather, that he enjoyed difficulties, that our last week of interpenetration, harmony, confidence, now brought on his usual perverse craving for discord? "No, Anaïs, I don't want war. But I lost my confidence. You said that Allendy . . ." Oh, Allendy. So I had wounded him, started him off. Jealousy inspired him. I said, "I will not deprive you of the pleasure you find in jealousy by answering your questions."

Then he said something which moved me. It began: "What a man wants [what a man wants!] is to believe that a woman can love him so much that no other man can interest her. I know that's impossible. I know that every joy carries its own tragedy." Then we could again have openness? If I were truthful? "Listen," I said awkwardly, "what a man wants is what I have given you to date, with an absolutism you could never imagine."

"That is wonderful," he said, very tenderly, dazed. Our first duel had come to an end.

There was a great deal of insanity in all this, more in his explanations than in his initial actions. Was this really a scene of jealousy or the first expression of his instability in human relationships, his unaccountableness? For once I stand before a nature more complicated than my own. It may be that we have become more interesting to each other at the expense of trust. He is glad to have seen me, like an instrument, giving out all its range of sounds. Humanly, I have lost something. Faith, perhaps. In place of that blind openness to him, I summon my cleverness.

Later, when he weeps while telling me his father is starving, I sit paralyzed and my pity does not flow. I would give anything to know if he has sent his father some of the money I have given him, starving himself to do so. All I need to know is: Can he lie to me? I have been able to both love him and lie to him. I see myself wrapped in lies, which do not seem to penetrate my soul, as if they are not really a part of me. They are like costumes. When I loved Henry, as I did those four days, I loved him with a naked body that had shed its costumes and forgotten its lies. Perhaps it is not so with Henry. But love, in all this, trembles like a spear in a sand dune. To lie, of course, is to engender insanity. The minute I step into the cavern of my lies I drop into darkness.

I have had no time to write down the lies. I want to begin. I suppose I have not wanted to look at them. If unity is impossible to the writer who is a "sea of spiritual protoplasm, capable of flowing in all directions, of engulfing every object in its path, of trickling into every crevice, of filling every mold," as Aldous Huxley said in *Point Counter Point*, at least truth is possible, or sincerity about one's insincerities. It is true, as Allendy said, that what my mind engenders fictionally I enrich with true feeling, and I am taken in, in good faith, by my own inventions. He called me "*le plus sympathique*" of the insincere ones. Yes, I am the noblest of the hypocrites. My motives, psychoanalysis reveals, possess the smallest degree of malevolence. It is not to hurt anyone that I let my lover sleep in my husband's bed. It is because I have no sense of sacredness. If Henry himself were more courageous, I would have given Hugo a sleeping potion during Henry's visit so I could have gone and slept with him. He was too timid, however, to steal a kiss. Only when Hugo had left did he throw me on the ivy leaves, in the back of the garden. . . .

25 The estrangement between Hugo's body and mine will drive me mad. His constant caresses are intolerable to me. Up to now I could steel myself, find a tender pleasure in his closeness. But today I might be living with a stranger. I hate it when he sits near me, running his hands up my legs and around my breasts. This morning when he touched me, I jumped away angrily. He was terribly taken aback. I can't bear his desire. I want to run away. My body is dead to his. What is my life going to be now? How can I go on pretending? My excuses are so futile, so feeble—bad health, bad moods. They are transparent lies. I will hurt him. How I crave my liberty!

26 During our siesta Hugo tried to possess me again. I closed my eyes and let go, but without pleasure. If it is true that this year I have reached new peaks of joy, it is also true that I have never reached such black depths. Tonight I am afraid of myself. I could leave Hugo this minute and become a derelict. I would sell myself, take drugs, die with voluptuous pleasure.

27 I said to Hugo, who was boasting of being a little drunk, "Well, tell me something about yourself that I do not know, tell me something new. You have nothing to confess? And you couldn't invent something?"

28 He did not get my meaning. Nor did he get my meaning when I jumped away from his caresses. Sweet faith. To be laughed at, made use of. Why aren't you cleverer, less believing? Why don't you hit back, why have you no aberrations, no passions, no comedies to play, no cruelty?

From Anaïs Nin, *Henry and June*, pp. 226–233

Speculations

1. Why is Nin, after successfully deceiving her husband, also enraged at his credulousness?

2. How do you think Henry Miller might have reacted if Nin hadn't stormed away in anger after her husband left for work as described in paragraph 7? Why was he "glad to see" her weep?

3. Nin says she let her lover sleep in her husband's bed because she has "no sense of sacredness." What is your opinion of that statement?

4. How does Hugo emerge from these pages? What do you imagine might have been his profession?

5. What explanation of Nin's behavior might be plausibly constructed from the feminist perspective?

Spin-offs for writing

1. Using any perspective you prefer—psychological, philosophical, feminist, or commonsensical—write a causal explanation of Anaïs Nin's behavior towards her husband.

2. Write an analysis of effect specifying the consequences you foresee resulting from a husband's or wife's discovery of the other's unfaithfulness.

ETTY HILLESUM

Etty Hillesum (1914–1943) was a Dutch Jew who perished in the Nazi concentration camp at Auschwitz. The daughter of a scholarly father and Russian mother, Etty (her given name was Esther) studied law in Amsterdam and taught Russian. After the Nazi occupation of the Netherlands, she worked briefly for the Jewish Council of Amsterdam before voluntarily becoming a prisoner in the Westerbork transit camp for Jews. Allowed free movement in and out of the camp, she had many opportunities to escape but resolved, instead, to stay behind and share in the fate of her people. She was shipped to Auschwitz on September 7, 1943, where she died two months later.

Etty kept a diary from March 9, 1941 to October 11, 1942, which she prophetically entrusted to the care of friends before entering the prison camp. In it she openly addressed her fears and doubts to God, vowing that if God could not help her, she would have to "help God." The excerpt opens with Etty's apprehensions about what she would encounter in the Westerbork prison camp, for which she knew she was eventually destined, and closes with a poetic and remarkable prayer brimming with faith and hope. Shortly after this entry, she did get the job with the Jewish Council but later gave it up to enter the camp from which she and her two brothers never returned.

1 **11 July 1942, Saturday morning, 11 o'clock.** We must only speak about the ultimate and most serious things in life when the words well up inside us as simply and as naturally as water from a spring.

2 And if God does not help me to go on, then I shall have to help God. The surface of the earth is gradually turning into one great prison camp and soon there will be nobody left outside. The Jews here are telling each other lovely stories: they say that the Germans are burying us alive or exterminating us with gas. But what is the point of repeating such things even if they should be true?

3 It hasn't stopped pouring with rain since last night. I have already cleared out one of the drawers in my desk. I rediscovered the one photograph I have of S.[1] which I mislaid nearly a year ago. I have always been absolutely convinced that it would turn up again. And there it suddenly was, at the bottom of that untidy drawer. That's typical of me: I just know with some things, big or small, that they will turn out all right in the end. I never worry about tomorrow. For instance I know I am going to have to leave here very soon and I haven't the faintest idea where I'll end up or how I shall earn my living, but I know that something will turn up. If one burdens the future

---

[1] Julius Spier, founder of 'psychochirology'—the study of palm prints—and Etty's lover.

with one's worries, it cannot grow organically. I am filled with confidence, not that I shall succeed in worldly things but that even when things go badly for me I shall still find life good and worth living.

I catch myself making all sorts of minor but telling adjustments in anticipation of life in a labour camp. Last night when I was walking along the quay beside him in a pair of comfortable sandals, I suddenly thought, 'I shall take these sandals along as well, I can wear them instead of the heavier shoes from time to time.' What goes on in my head at moments like that? Such light-hearted, almost playful good humour. Yesterday was a hard, a very hard day, when I suffered agonies. Yet once more I was able to brave it all, everything that came storming at me, and now I can bear a little more than I was able to bear yesterday. And that probably explains my cheerfulness and inner peace: that I am able, time after time, to cope all by myself, that my heart does not shrivel up with the bitterness of it all, and that even the moments of deepest sadness and black despair finally make me stronger. I don't fool myself about the real state of affairs and I've even dropped the pretence that I'm out to help others. I shall merely try to help God as best I can and if I succeed in doing that, then I shall be of use to others as well. But I mustn't have heroic illusions about that either.

But how shall I really feel and act, I keep wondering, with a call-up card for Germany in my bag and orders to leave in a week's time? Supposing the card came tomorrow, how would I act then? I wouldn't tell a soul at first but retire to the quietest spot in the house, withdraw into myself and gather what strength I could from every cranny of my body and soul. I would have my hair cut short and throw my lipstick away. I would try to finish reading the Rilke letters before the week was out. And I'd have a pair of trousers and a jacket made out of that heavy winter coat material I've got left over. I would try to see my parents, of course, and do my best to reassure them, and every spare minute I would want to write to him, to the man I shall always long for—I now know that for certain. Yes, when I think about having to leave him and never being able to know what is happening to him, I feel as if I were dying already.

In a few day's time I shall go to the dentist and have lots and lots of holes in my teeth filled. For that really would be awful: suffering from toothache out there. I shall try to get hold of a rucksack and pack only what is absolutely essential, though everything must be of good quality. I shall take a Bible along and that slim volume *Letters to a Young Poet*, and surely I'll be able to find some corner for the *Book of Hours*. I won't take along any photographs of those I love; I'll just take all the faces and familiar gestures I have collected and hang them up along the walls of my inner space so that they will always be with me.

7 And even now I keep telling my heart that we two will have to carry on even if I am separated from those without whom I now think I cannot live. Each moment I free myself more from dependence on eternal props and draw closer inwardly to those from whom I cannot be separated however far apart we happen to be. And yet, when I walk with him hand in hand along the quay, which looked so autumnal and stormy last night, and then warm myself in his little room on his open and loving gestures, I am flooded with human, oh so human, hopes and desires: why can't we stay together after all? Nothing else would really matter if only we could be together. I don't ever want to leave him. Yet sometimes I say to myself: it is probably easier to pray for someone far away than to witness him suffering by your side.

8 In this tempestuous, havoc-ridden world of ours, all real communication comes from the heart. Outwardly we are being torn apart and the paths to each other lie buried under so much debris that we often fail to find the person we seek. We can only continue to live together in our hearts, and hope that one day we may walk hand in hand again.

9 I cannot tell, of course, how I shall react when I really do have to leave him. His voice over the telephone this morning still rings in my ear; tonight we shall have a meal together; tomorrow morning we shall work together and then lunch at Liesl and Werner's, and in the afternoon we shall play music together. He is still here. And perhaps in my heart of hearts I do not really accept that all of us are about to be separated. A human being, after all, is only human.

10 Many accuse me of indifference and passivity when I refuse to go into hiding; they say that I have given up. They say everyone who can must try to stay out of their clutches, it's our bounden duty to try. But that argument is specious. For while everyone tries to save himself, vast numbers are nevertheless disappearing. And the funny thing is I don't feel I'm in their clutches anyway, whether I stay or am sent away. I find all that talk so cliché-ridden and naive and can't go along with it any more. I don't feel in anybody's clutches; I feel safe in God's arms, to put it rhetorically, and no matter whether I am sitting at this beloved old desk now, or in a bare room in the Jewish district or perhaps in a labour camp under SS guards in a month's time—I shall always feel safe in God's arms. They may well succeed in breaking me physically, but no more than that. I may face cruelty and deprivation the likes of which I cannot imagine in even

my wildest fantasies. Yet all this is as nothing to the immeasurable expanse of my faith in God and my inner receptiveness.

I shall always be able to stand on my own two feet even when they are planted on the hardest soil of the harshest reality. And my acceptance is not indifference or helplessness. I feel deep moral indignation at a regime that treats human beings in such a way. But events have become too overwhelming and too demonic to be stemmed with personal resentment and bitterness. These responses strike me as being utterly childish and unequal to the fateful course of events.

People often get worked up when I say it doesn't really matter whether I go or somebody else does, the main thing is that so many thousands *have* to go. It is not as if I want to fall into the arms of destruction with a resigned smile—far from it. I am only bowing to the inevitable and even as I do so I am sustained by the certain knowledge that ultimately they cannot rob us of anything that matters. But I don't think I would feel happy if I were exempted from what so many others have to suffer. They keep telling me that someone like me has a duty to go into hiding, because I have so many things to do in life, so much to give. But I know that whatever I may have to give to others, I can give it no matter where I am, here in the circle of my friends or over there, in a concentration camp. And it is sheer arrogance to think oneself too good to share the fate of the masses.

And if God Himself should feel that I still have a great deal to do, well then, I shall do it after I have suffered what all the others have to suffer. And whether or not I am a valuable human being will only become clear from my behaviour in more arduous circumstances. And if I should not survive, how I die will show me who I really am. Of course that doesn't mean I will turn down a medical exemption if they give me one on account of my inflamed kidneys and bladder. And I have been recommended for some sort of soft job with the Jewish Council. They had permission to hire 180 people last week, and the desperate are thronging there in droves, as shipwrecked people might cling for dear life to a piece of driftwood. But that is as far as I am prepared to go and, beyond that, I am not willing to pull any strings. In any case, the Jewish Council seems to have become a hotbed of intrigue, and resentment against this strange agency is growing by the hour. And sooner or later it will be their turn to go, anyway.

But, of course, by then the English may have landed. At least that's what those people say who have not yet abandoned all political hope. I believe that we must rid ourselves of all expectations of help from the outside world, that we must stop guessing about the duration of the war and so on. And now I am going to set the table.

15 *Sunday morning prayer*. 'Dear God, these are anxious times. Tonight for the first time I lay in the dark with burning eyes as scene after scene of human suffering passed before me. I shall promise You one thing, God, just one very small thing: I shall never burden my today with cares about my tomorrow, although that takes some practice. Each day is sufficient unto itself. I shall try to help You, God, to stop my strength ebbing away, though I cannot vouch for it in advance. But one thing is becoming increasingly clear to me: that You cannot help us, that we must help You to help ourselves. And that is all we can manage these days and also all that really matters: that we safeguard that little piece of You, God, in ourselves. And perhaps in others as well. Alas, there doesn't seem to be much You Yourself can do about our circumstances, about our lives. Neither do I hold You responsible. You cannot help us but we must help You and defend Your dwelling place inside us to the last. There are, it is true, some who, even at this late stage, are putting their vacuum cleaners and silver forks and spoons in safe keeping instead of guarding You, dear God. And there are those who want to put their bodies in safe keeping but who are nothing more now than a shelter for a thousand fears and bitter feelings. And they say, "I shan't let them get me into their clutches." But they forget that no one is in their clutches who is in Your arms. I am beginning to feel a little more peaceful, God, thanks to this conversation with You. I shall have many more conversations with You. You are sure to go through lean times with me now and then, when my faith weakens a little, but believe me, I shall always labour for You and remain faithful to You and I shall never drive You from my presence.

16 'I have strength enough, God, for suffering on a grand scale, but there are more than a thousand everyday cares that leap up on me without warning like so many fleas. So I scratch away desperately and tell myself, "This day has been taken care of now, the protective walls of an hospitable home still surround me like a well-worn, familiar piece of clothing, there is food enough for today and the bed with the white sheets and the warm blankets stands waiting for me tonight, so don't let me waste even one atom of my strength on petty material cares. Let me use and spend every minute and turn this into a fruitful day, one stone more in the foundations on which to build our so uncertain future." The jasmine behind my house has been completely ruined by the rains and storms of the last few days, its white blossoms are floating about in muddy black pools on the low garage roof. But somewhere inside me the jasmine continues to

blossom undisturbed, just as profusely and delicately as ever it did. And it spreads its scent round the House in which You dwell, oh God. You can see, I look after You, I bring You not only my tears and my forebodings on this stormy, grey Sunday morning, I even bring you scented jasmine. And I shall bring You all the flowers I shall meet on my way, and truly there are many of those. I shall try to make You at home always. Even if I should be locked up in a narrow cell and a cloud should drift past my small barred window, then I shall bring you that cloud, oh God, while there is still the strength in me to do so. I cannot promise You anything for tomorrow, but my intentions are good, You can see.'

And now I shall venture out upon this day. I shall meet a great many 17 people today and evil rumours and threats will again assault me like so many enemy soldiers besieging an inviolable fortress.

Speculations

1. What is your attitude towards Etty's steadfast refusal to try and save herself from the horrors of Nazi captivity?

2. In what ways can human beings help God, as Etty vows that she is determined to do?

3. In paragraph 6, Etty writes that in preparation for the concentration camp she intends to go to the dentist and have her teeth filled. What does this intention tell us about her frame of mind as she contemplates imprisonment?

4. How do you think a fundamentalist Christian might take this statement by Etty: "I shall merely try to help God as best as I can and if I succeed in doing that, then I shall be of use to others as well"?

5. How would you describe the conception of God in which Etty believes?

Spin-offs for writing

1. Write an essay analyzing Etty's approach to morality as a pragmatic ethic for life today.

2. What is the duty of one who is confronted with oppression and evil? Write an essay on this question.

Student Journal—Causal Analysis

Rebecca Curtis

March 19, 1992

Tomorrow, March 20th, the first day of spring, is my birthday. I will turn forty. They say forty is fatal, or life begins at forty. I am experiencing a conflict of emotions at this milestone. It seems that youth is fleeting. My passion is tempered by reason.

Spring is in the air. I did yard work all morning. I love the feel of the cold earth, dirt under my fingernails. Our backyard is in a lush canyon. It is filled with surprises. A woodpecker in a nearby tree is busy at work tapping. J. T. calls him Woody. A pair of blue scrub jays have taken up residency in the trees. They approach the patio carefully, flying down from the canyon, one tree at a time, until they come very close to the spot where J. T. has dropped his crackers. They snatch the cracker and fly off with the prize. Birds fill this canyon.

The past summer was so hot that a lot of foliage and plants died off. We spend days clearing out and cutting back the summer scorch. Then the winter frost came, killing the cactus and the bougainvillea. But there is a renewal in the air today as I plant new seeds in the ground. Spring is the promise of a new beginning. I am planting Lady Banks roses and replanting a tree. I am helping to regenerate and recycle life. Maybe in some small way it is my contribution to the environment, this, our oasis, in the middle of Los Angeles.

Here in my oasis there is only the beauty of the earth. There is only the silent sound of the wind. Softness rests on every leaf. There is only the delicacy of sunlight. I reflect on reaching the age of forty.

I hear only the music of the birds, the buzz of the bees, and the beating of my heart.

There is only eternity, which makes me wonder, Was Plato right? Can these images I see be only illusions? Does the real ideal world exist somewhere far beyond my imagination?

Were Aristotle, Newton, and Einstein correct about science, biology, species renewal, quantum physics, anti-matter and negative infinity? Can the answers to the universe be found? Are they within our grasp?

These trees leave their seed on the ground for another tree to take their place. My husband and I have left our son. But what of our thoughts? Do our brains cease to function with the beatless heart, or is there essentialism? Can we defy explanation, reason?

I want to believe because, like all humans, I do not want to die without purpose. Is man superior or just a fluke of nature with a large brain? Is man's enormous ego capable of throwing off the balance of nature and destroying the environmental beauty that has existed for billions of years?

This contemplation seems to be being brought on by my fortieth birthday. I shed a tear for my missed childhood experiences, opportunities. The future is closing in on us all. Whatever forty is, it is now. Now is better than yesterday. Who knows about tomorrow? Now is the sun in my face, the wind at my back. Now is the joy of my son. Now is the love of my husband—his idealism, his fears, our common threads. And our common dreaded age, forty.

4.
PROCESS.

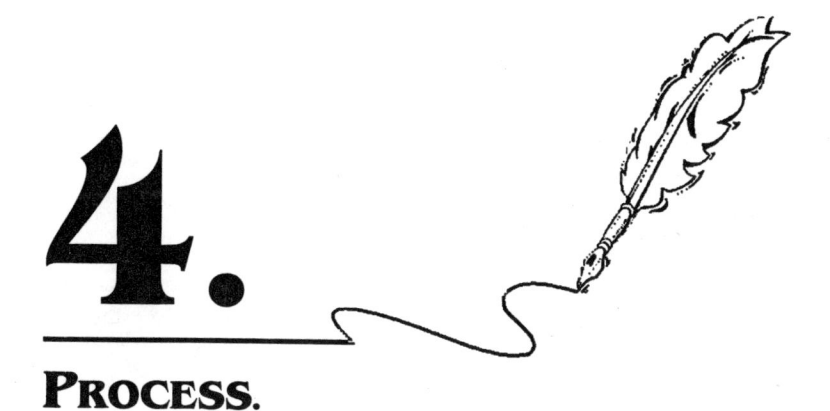

April 9, 1853. "Started from home at about 11 o'clock and traveled 8 miles and camped in an old house; night cold and frosty." The process of travelling across the plains in a covered wagon. Amelia Steward Knight.

July, 1943. "I believe that the Führer will carry the thing through to a successful end." The Battle of Stalingrad as seen by an anonymous German soldier. Anonymous.

July 12, 1955. "Here I am, in the Passevant Hospital, for a three-day checkup." The process of a physical. Noël Coward.

February 16, 1964. "I was nervous, fearing the baby would have pain." The process involved in a Jewish *Briss* or circumcision ceremony. Frances Karlen Santamaria.

CHAPTER 4

Process

Process refers to any writing that aims to explain anything in a step-by-step fashion, giving directions or instructions about how to do a task or perform an action. This use, however, is rare in a medium of solitary musing such as the diary. Instead, most process entries in diaries will specify in step-by-step fashion how something *was* done or some action or ceremony *was* performed.

It is in this second sense that all the diary excerpts in this section are classifiable as process pieces. All recount events in systematic step-by-step fashion, although they do not give directions or instructions. For example, in the first piece, Amelia Stewart Knight tells us how she crossed the prairies in a wagon train in 1853. An anonymous German soldier, slain in the World War II battle for the Russian city of Stalingrad, unwittingly depicts the process by which a warrior's dreams of glory turn to despair. Noël Coward, the renowned composer and playwright, treats us to a humorous account of a physical he underwent in 1955, while Frances Karlen Santamaria depicts for us the process of the Jewish *briss* performed on her firstborn son, Joshua. None of these excerpts is a process pattern in the traditional sense of transmitting instructions or directions. However, they qualify as representatives of the type by portraying, in step-by-step fashion, how an event unfolded or how an action was accomplished.

The writer of straightforward process assignments meant to impart how-to instructions must not only be more systematic than these diarists but also more detailed. This kind of process writing is simple to do if you observe some commonsense rules.

The first rule of writing a good process piece is to begin with a clear statement of your intent. If you are explaining how a dictionary is made, for example, specifically say so, making note of any exceptions to your explanations, as the following example does:

> *Let us see how dictionaries are made and how the editors arrive at definitions. What follows applies, incidentally, only to those dictionary offices where first-hand, original research goes on—not those in which editors simply copy existing dictionaries....*
>
> **—S. I. Hayakawa, "How Dictionaries Are Made"**

The exception is important because otherwise we might think that all dictionaries are prepared in this way, when in fact the process covers only those dictionaries whose original definitions are prepared by a team of editors.

The second rule is never to assume anything about your audience. Begin always at the beginning, define every term, and systematically link every step in the chain of actions that must be taken to accomplish the job. Many process essays frustrate their readers by failing to follow this advice. Terms are not defined; steps are taken for granted and not adequately covered; readers are assumed to know more than they actually do. This is the mistake the writers of manuals and how-to instructions consistently make, as anyone who has ever sat up late on Christmas Eve trying to assemble a "simple" toy can attest. For example, consider these instructions for warding off a cold:

> *The first thing to try is moisturizing spray. Spray the inside of your nose thoroughly every hour or two. Keep warm and get a good night's sleep. This program alone will stop some colds in their tracks.*

These instructions are mystifying unless you have first defined what you mean by a "moisturizing spray," as this writer earlier did:

> *Use home-made moisturizing nose spray. You can banish dry crusts and help you nose's defense by using this moisturizing spray:*
>
> > *1 teaspoon glycerin, obtained from any drugstore without a prescription*
> >
> > *1 1/2 tablespoons 70% alcohol (rubbing alcohol strength)*
> >
> > *1 teaspoon table salt*
> >
> > *1 pint tap or distilled water*
>
> *If your tap water has a heavy odor of chlorine, let it stand overnight in an open vessel. Mix the ingredients and stir until salt is thoroughly dissolved. Pour into clean bottle and stopper firmly.*
>
> *Get a plastic pocket atomizer for about 35 cents at the drugstore, fill it with this solution, and use it several times a day as needed.*
>
> **—John E. Eichenlaub, "How To Fight Cold-proneness"**

It is now plain what the writer meant when he recommended that we use a moisturizing spray to ward off colds.

The third rule of process writing is to always use language that is plain and direct. Most process essays are not trying to capture shades of meaning or subtleties: they are simply trying to instruct in a specific task. And exactness of language is the best technique for furthering this aim. Call items by their exact names; give exact instructions; be exact about what comes first and what next. Practice only this one commonsense rule and your process essays are likely to be clearer than most how-to manuals.

AMELIA STEWART KNIGHT

In 1853 Amelia Stewart Knight began a five-month-long wagon train journey that took her from Monroe County, Iowa, to the Oregon Territory. Pregnant at the time, she traveled in the company of her husband and seven children. She gave birth along the rugged trail, an event that must have been an unimaginable ordeal but is barely mentioned in her diary. Eventually the family reached its destination and settled into a small windowless log cabin, much to the relief of the diarist.

1. *Saturday, April 9, 1853.* STARTED FROM HOME about 11 o'clock and traveled 8 miles and camped in an old house; night cold and frosty.

2. *Sunday, April 10th.* Cool and pleasant, road hard and dusty. Evening—Came 8 ½ miles and camped close to the Fulkersons house.

3. *Monday, April 11th.* Morn. Cloudy and sign of rain, about 10 o'clock it began to rain. At noon it rains so hard we turn out and camp in a school house after traveling 11½ miles; rains all the afternoon and all night, very unpleasant. Jefferson and Lucy have the mumps. Poor cattle bawled all night.

4. *Tuesday, April 12th.* Warm and sultry. Still cloudy, road very muddy, traveled 10 miles and camp on Soap creek bottom. Creek bank full; have to wait till it falls.

5. *Wednesday, April 13th.* Fair weather, have to overhaul all wagons and dry things. Evening—still in camp.

6. *Thursday, April 14th.* Quite cold. Little ewes crying with cold feet. Sixteen wagons all getting ready to cross the creek. Hurrah and bustle to get breakfast over. Feed the cattle. Hurrah boys, all ready, we will be the first to cross the creek this morning. Gee up Tip and Tyler, and away we go the sun just rising. Evening—We have traveled 24 miles today and are about to camp in a large prairie without wood. Cold and chilly; east wind. The men have pitched the tent and are hunting something to make a fire to get supper. I have the sick headache and must leave the boys to get it themselves the best they can.

7. *Friday, April 15th.* Cold and cloudy, wind still east. Bad luck last night. Three of our horses got away. Suppose they have gone back. One of the boys has gone after them, and we are going on slowly. Evening—Henry has come back with the horses all right again. It is beginning to rain; the boys have pitched the tent and I must get supper.

Saturday, April 16th. Camped last night three miles east of Chariton Point in the prairie. Made our beds down in the tent in the wet and mud. Bed clothes nearly spoiled. Cold and cloudy this morning, and every body out of humour. Seneca is half sick. Plutarch has broke his saddle girth. Husband is scolding and hurrying all hands (and the cook) and Almira says she wished she was home, and I say ditto. "Home, Sweet Home."...

Sunday, April 17th. [This party did not rest on the Sabbath. It continued to travel over rolling prairies.]

Monday, April 18th. Cold; breaking fast the first thing; very disagreeable weather; wind east cold and rainy, no fire. We are on a very large prairie, no timber to be seen as far as the eye can reach. Evening—Have crossed several bad streams today, and more than once have been stuck in the mud....

Came 22 miles today. My head aches, but the fire is kindled and I must make some tea, that will help if not cure it.

Tuesday, April 19th...

Wednesday, April 20th. Cloudy. We are creeping along slowly, one wagon after another, the *same* old gait; and the same thing over, out of one mud hole into another all day. Crossed a branch where the water run into the wagons. No corn to be had within 75 miles. Came 18 miles and camp.

Thursday, April 21st. Rained all night; is still raining. I have just counted 17 wagons traveling ahead of us in the mud and water. No feed for our poor stock to be got at any price. Have to feed them flour and meal. Traveled 22 miles today.

Friday, April 22nd. Still bad weather. no sun; traveling on, mile after mile in the mud, mud....

Saturday, April 23rd. Still in camp, it rained hard all night, and blew a hurricane almost. All the tents were blown down, and some wagons capsized. Evening—It has been raining hard all day; everything is wet and muddy. One of the oxen is missing; the boys have been hunting him all day. (Dreary times, wet and muddy, and crowded in the tent, cold and wet and uncomfortable in the wagon. No place for the poor children.) I have been busy cooking roasting coffee, etc. today, and have come into the wagon to write this and make our bed.

Sunday, April 24th...

Monday, April 25th...

19 *Tuesday, April 26th.* Cold and clear; found corn last night at 2 dollars a bushel. Paid 12 dollars for about half a feed for our stock. I can count twenty wagons winding up the hill ahead of us. Traveled 20 miles and camp.

20 *Wednesday, April 27th.* A nice spring morning; warm and pleasant; the road is covered with wagons and cattle. (Paid two dollars 40 cts. for crossing a bridge.) Traveled 25 miles. . . .

21 *Thursday, April 28th . . .*

22 *Friday, April 29th.* Cool and pleasant; saw the first Indians today. Lucy and Almira afraid and run into the wagon to hide. Done some washing and sewing.

23 *Saturday, April 30th.* Fine weather; spent this day in washing, baking, and overhauling the wagons. Several more wagons have camped around us.

24 *Sunday, May 1st.* Still fine weather; wash and scrub all the children.

25 *Monday, May 2nd.* Pleasant evening; have been cooking, and packing things away for an early start in the morning. Threw away several jars, some wooden buckets, and all our pickles. Too unhandy to carry. Indians came to our camp every day, begging money and something to eat. Children are getting used to them.

26 *Tuesday, May 3rd . . . .* here Plutarch is taken sick.

27 *Wednesday, May 4th . . .*

28 *Thursday, May 5th . . .*

29 *Friday, May 6th . . . .* Here we passed a train of wagons on their way back, the head man had been drowned a few days before, in a river called Elkhorn, while getting some cattle across and his wife was lying in the wagon quite sick, and children were mourning for the father gone. With sadness and pity I passed those who perhaps a few days before had been well and happy as ourselves. Came 20 miles today.

30 *Saturday, May 7th.* Cold morning, thermometer down to 48 in the wagon. No wood, only enough to boil some coffee. Good grass for the stock. We have crossed a small creek, with a narrow Indian bridge across it. Paid the Indians 75 cents toll. My hands are numb with cold. . . .

31 *Sunday, May 8th.* Still in camp. Waiting to cross [the Elkhorn River]. There are three hundred or more wagons in sight and as far as the eye

can reach, the bottom is covered, on each side of the river, with cattle and horses. There is no ferry here and the men will have to make one out of the tightest wagon-bed (every company should have a waterproof wagon-bed for this purpose.) Everything must now be hauled out of the wagons head over heels (and he who knows where to find anything will be a smart fellow.) then the wagons must be all taken to pieces, and then by means of a strong rope stretched across the river with a tight wagon-bed attached to the middle of it, the rope must be long enough to pull from one side to the other, with men on each side of the river to pull it. In this way we have to cross everything a little at a time. Women and children last, and then swim the cattle and horses. There were three horses and some cattle drowned while crossing this place yesterday. It is quite lively and merry here this morning and the weather is fine. We are camped on a large bottom, with the broad, deep river on one side of us and a high bluff on the other.

Monday, May 9th. Morning cold, within 4 degrees of freezing; we are all on the right side of the river this morning. . . . 32

Tuesday, May 10th . . . 33

Wednesday, May 11th. Evening. It has been very dusty yesterday and today. (The men all have their false eyes on to keep the dust out.) . . . as far as eye can reach the road is covered with teams. Plutarch is well and able to drive. Came 23 miles. 34

Thursday, May 12. Thursday Noon—Beautiful weather, but very dusty. We are camped on the bank of Loup Fork, awaiting our turn to cross. There are two ferry boats running, and a number of wagons ahead of us, all waiting to cross. Have to pay three dollars a wagon for three wagons and swim the stock. Traveled 12 miles today. We hear there are 700 teams on the road ahead of us. Wash and cook this afternoon. 35

Friday, May 13th. It is thundering and bids fair for rain. Crossed the river early this morning before breakfast. (Got breakfast over after a fashion. Sand all around ankle deep; wind blowing; no matter, hurry it over. Them that eat the most breakfast eat the most sand. . . .) 36

Saturday, May 14th . . . . Winds so high that we dare not make a fire, impossible to pitch the tent, the wagons could hardly stand the wind. All that find room crowded into the wagons; those that can't, have to stay out in the storm. Some of the boys have lost their hats. 37

Sunday, May 15th . . . 38

Monday, May 16th. Evening—We have had all kinds of weather today. This morning was dry, dusty and sandy. This afternoon it 39 rained, hailed, and the wind was very high. Have been traveling all the afternoon in mud and water up to our hubs. Broke chains and stuck in the mud several times. The men and boys are all wet and muddy. Hard times but they say misery loves company. We are not alone on these bare plains, it is covered with cattle and wagons. . . .

40 *Tuesday, May 17th.* We had a dreadful storm of rain and hail last night and very sharp lighting. It killed two oxen and one man. We have just encamped on a large flat prairie, when the storm commenced in all its fury and two minutes after the cattle were taken from the wagons every brute was gone out of sight, cows, calves, horses, all gone before the storm like so many wild beasts. I never saw such a storm. The wind was so high I thought it would tear the wagons to pieces. Nothing but the stoutest covers could stand it. The rain beat into the wagons so that everything was wet, in less than 2 hours the water was a foot deep all over our camp grounds. As we could have no tents pitched, all had to crowd into the wagons and sleep in wet beds with their wet clothes on, without supper. The wind blew hard all night and this morning presents a dreary prospect surrounded by water, and our saddles have been soaking in it all night and are almost spoiled! . . .

41 *Wednesday, May 18th—Monday, May 23rd . . .*

42 *Tuesday, May 24th . . .* I had the sick headache all night, some better this morning; must do a day's work.

43 *Wednesday, May 25th—Monday, May 30th . . .*

44 *Tuesday, May 31st.* Evening—Traveled 25 miles today. When we started this morning there were two large droves of cattle and about 50 wagons ahead of us, and we either had to stay poking behind them in the dust or hurry up and drive past them. It was no fool of a job to be mixed up with several hundred head of cattle, and only one road to travel in, and the drovers threatening to drive their cattle over you if you attempted to pass them. They even took out their pistols. Husband came up just as one man held his pistol at Wilson Carl and saw what the fuss was and said, "Boys, follow me," and he drove our team out of the road entirely, and the cattle seemed to understand it all, for they went into the trot most of the way. The rest of the boys followed with their teams and the rest of the stock. I had rather a rough ride to be sure, but was glad to get away from such a lawless set, which we did by noon. The head teamster done his best by whipping and hollowing to his cattle. He found it no use and got up into his wagon to take it easy. We left some swearing men behind us. We drove a good ways ahead and stopped to rest the cattle and eat some dinner. While we were eating we saw them coming. All hands

jumped for their teams saying they had earned the road too dearly to let them pass us again, and in a few moments we were all on the go again. Had been very warm today. Thermometer at 98 in the wagon at one o'clock. Towards evening there came up a light thunderstorm which cooled the air down to 60. We are now within 100 miles of Fort Laramie.

Wednesday, June 1st. It has been raining all day long and we have been traveling in it so as to be able to keep ahead of the large droves. The men and boys are all soaking wet and look sad and comfortless. (The little ones and myself are shut up in the wagons from the rain. Still it will find its way in and many things are wet; and take us all together we are a poor looking set, and all this for Oregon. I am thinking while I write, "Oh, Oregon, you must be a wonderful country." Came 18 miles today.)

Thursday, June 2nd—Sunday, June 5th . . .

Monday, June 6th. Still in camp, husband and myself being sick (caused, we suppose by drinking the river water, as it looks more like dirty suds than anything else), we concluded to stay in camp and each take a vomit, which we did and are much better. The boys and myself have been washing some today. The prickly pear grows in great abundance along this Platte River road.

Tuesday, June 7th. Rained some last night; quite warm today. Just passed Fort Laramie, situated on the opposite side of the river. This afternoon we passed a large village of Sioux Indians. Numbers of them came around our wagons. Some of the women had moccasins and beads, which they wanted to trade for bread. I gave the women and children all the cakes I had baked. Husband traded a big Indian a lot of hard crackers for a pair of moccasins and after we had started on he came up with us again making a great fuss, and wanted them back (they had eaten part of the crackers). He did not seem to be satisfied, or else he wished to cause us some trouble, or perhaps get into a fight. However, we handed the moccasins to him in a hurry and drove away from them as soon as possible. . . .

Wednesday, June 8th . . .

Thursday, June 9th . . .

Friday, June 10th. It has been very warm today. Thermometer up to 99 at noon. . . . one of our hands, left. . . .

Saturday, June 11th . . . we crossed this afternoon over the roughest and most desolate piece of ground that was ever made (called by some the Devil's Crater) (Not a drop of water, nor a spear of grass to be seen, nothing but barren hills, bare and broken rock, sand and dust)....

53 *Sunday, June 12th.* ... I have just washed the dust out of my eyes so that I can see to get supper.

54 *Monday, June 13th* ...

55 *Tuesday, June 14th.* ... Had a great deal of trouble to keep the stock from drinking the poison or alkali water. It is almost sure to kill man or beast who drink it.

56 *Wednesday, June 15th.* ... passed Independence Rock this afternoon, and crossed Sweetwater River on a bridge. Paid 3 dollars a wagon and swam the stock across. The river is very high and swift. ...

57 *Friday, June 17th* .... Have been washing and cooking today. The mosquitoes are very bad here....

58 *Saturday, June 18th* ...

59 *Sunday, June 19th.* On our way again, Traveling in the sand and dust. Sand ankle deep—hard traveling. ...

60 *Monday, June 20th* ...

61 *Tuesday, June 21st.* We have traveled over a very rough, rocky, road today; over mountains close to banks of snow. Had plenty of snow water to drink. Husband brought me a large bucket of snow and one of our hands brought me a beautiful bunch of flowers which he said was growing close to the snow, which was about 6 feet deep....

62 *Wednesday, June 22nd—Saturday, June 25th* ...

63 *Sunday, June 26th* .... Evening—All hands come into camp tired and out of heart. Husband and myself sick. No feed for the stock. One ox lame. Camp on the bank of Big Sandy again.

64 *Monday, June 27th.* Cold, cloudy and very windy—more like November than June. I am not well enough to get out of the wagon this morning. The men have just got their breakfast over and drove up the stock. (It is all hurry and bustle to get things in order. It's children milk the cows, all hands help yoke these cattle the d—l's in them. Plutarch answers "I can't. I must hold the tent up, it is blowing away." Hurray boys. Who tied these horses? "Seneca, don't stand there with your hands in your pocket. Get your saddles and be ready.") ...

Tuesday, June 28th. Still in camp waiting to cross. Nothing for the stock to eat. As far as the eye can reach it is nothing but a sandy desert, and the stench is awful. . . . (all along this road we see white men living with Indians; many of them have trading posts; they are mostly French and have squaw wives.) . . .

Wednesday, June 29th. Cold and cloudy. The wagons are all crowded up to the ferry waiting with impatience to cross. There are 30 or more to cross before us. Have to cross one at a time. Have to pay 8 dollars for a wagon; 1 dollar for a horse or a cow. We swim all our stock. . . .

Thursday, June 30th—Sunday, July 3rd . . .

Monday, July 4th. It has been very warm today. Thermometer up to 110. . . . I never saw mosquitoes as bad as they are here. Chat has been sick all day with fever, partly caused by mosquitoe bites. . . .

Tuesday, July 5th . . . . Chatfield is sick yet; had fever all night. . . .

Wednesday, July 6th—Wednesday, July 13th . . .

Thursday, July 14th. It is dust from morning until night, with now and then a sprinkling of gnats and mosquitoes, and as far as the eye can reach it is nothing but a sandy desert, covered with wild sage brush, dried up with heat; however, it makes good firewood. Evening—I have not felt well today and the road has been very tedious to me. I have ridden in the wagon and taken care of Chatfield till I got tired, then I got out and walked in the sand and through stinking sage brush till I gave out; and I feel thankful that we are about to camp after traveling 22 miles, on the bank of Raft River, about dark; river high.

Friday, July 15th. Last night I helped get supper and went to bed too sick to eat any myself. Had fever all night and all day. It is sundown and the fever has left me. I am able to creep around and look at things and brighten up a little; the sun has been very hot today. . . .

Saturday, July 16th . . .

Sunday, July 17th. We are traveling through the Digger Indians' country, but have not seen any yet. (We crossed Swamp Creek this morning, and Goose Creek this afternoon. Goose Creek is almost straight down, and then straight up again. Several things pitched out of the wagons into the Creek. Travel over some very rocky ground. Here Chat fell out of the wagon, but did not get hurt much.)

75 **Monday, July 18th.** Traveled 22 miles. Crossed one small creek and have camped on one called Rock Creek. It is here the Indians are so troublesome. This creek is covered with small timber and thick underbrush, a great hiding place; and while in this part of the country the men have to guard the stock all night. One man traveling ahead of us had all his horses stolen and never found them as we know of. (I was very much frightened while at this camp. I lay awake all night. I expected every minute we would be killed. However, we all found our scalps on in the morning.) There are people killed at this place every year.

76 **Tuesday, July 19th—Thursday, July 21st . . .**

77 **Friday, July 22nd.** Crossed the river before daybreak and found the smell of carrion so bad that we left as soon as possible. The dead cattle were lying in every direction. Still there were a good many getting their breakfast among all the stench. I walked off among the rocks, while the men were getting the cattle ready; then we drove a mile or so, and halted to get breakfast. (Here Chat had a very narrow escape from being run over. Just as we were all getting ready to start, Chatfield the rascal, came around the forward wheel to get into the wagon and at that moment the cattle started and he fell under the wagon. Somehow he kept from under the wheels and escaped with only a good or I should say, a bad scare. I never was so much frightened in my life.) I was in the wagon at the time, putting things in order, and supposed Francis was taking care of him. . . .

78 **Saturday, July 23rd.** We took a fresh start this morning with everything in order, for a good day's drive. Travel about 5 miles and here we are, up a stump again, with a worse place than we ever had before us to be crossed, called Bridge Creek. I presume it takes its name from a natural bridge which crosses it. This bridge is only wide enough to admit one person at a time. A frightful place, with the water roaring and tumbling ten or fifteen feet below it. This bridge is composed of rocks, and all around us, it is nothing but a solid mass of rocks, with the water ripping and tearing over them. Here we have to unload all the wagons and pack everything by hand, and then we are only on an island. There is a worse place to cross yet, a branch of the same. Have to stay on the island all night, and wait our turn to cross. (There are a good many camped on the island.) and there are camps on each side of it. There is no chance to pitch a tent, and this island is a solid rock, so we must sleep the best way we can, with the water roaring on each side of us. The empty wagons, cattle, and horses have to be taken further up the river and crossed by means of chains and ropes. The way we cross this branch is to climb down about 6 feet on rocks, and then a wagon bed bottom will just reach

across, from rocks to rocks. It must then be fastened at each end with ropes or chains so that you can cross on it, and then we climb up the rocks on the other side, and in this way everything has to be taken across. Some take their wagons to pieces and take them over in that way.

Sunday, July 24th . . .

Monday, July 25th. Bad luck this morning to start with. A calf took sick and died before breakfast. Soon after starting one of our best cows was taken sick and died in a short time. Presumed they were both poisoned with water or weeds. Left our poor cow for the wolves and started on. . . .

Tuesday, July 26th . . .

Wednesday, July 27th. Another fine cow died this afternoon. Came 15 miles today, and have camped at the boiling springs, a great curiosity. They bubble up out of the earth boiling hot. I have only to pour water on to my tea and it is made. There is no cold water in this part. (Husband and myself wandered far down this branch, as far as we dare, to find it cool enough to bathe in. It was still very hot, and I believe I never spent such an uneasy sleepless night in my life. I felt as if I was in the bad place. I still believe it was not very far off.) I was glad when morning came and we left.

Thursday, July 28th . . . Chat is quite sick with scarlet fever.

Friday, July 29th—Sunday, July 31st . . .

Monday, August 1st. . . . This evening another of our best milk cows died. Cattle are dying off very fast all along this road. We are hardly ever out of sight of dead cattle, on this side of Snake River. This cow was well and fat an hour before she died. Cut the second cheese today.

Tuesday, August 2nd . . .

[There is no entry for August 3]

Thursday, August 4th . . . Have also a good many Indians and bought fish of them. They all seem peaceful and friendly.

Friday, August 5th . . . (Snake River Ferry) . . . Our turn to cross will come sometime tomorrow. There is one small ferry boat running here, owned by the Hudson's Bay Company. Have to pay three dollars a wagon. Our worst trouble at these large rivers is swimming the stock over. Often after swimming half way over the poor things will turn and come out again. At this place, however, there are Indians who swim the river from morning till night. There is many a drove of cattle that could not be got over without their help. By paying them a small sum, they will take a horse by the bridle or halter and swim over with him. The rest of the horses all follow and by driving and hurrahing to the cattle they will almost always follow the horses, sometimes they fail and turn back. This Fort Boise is nothing more than three new buildings, its inhabitants, the Hudsons Bay Company officials, a few Frenchmen, some half-naked Indians, half breeds, etc.

89 *Saturday, August 6th* . . .

90 *Sunday, August 7th* . . . . The roads have been very dusty, no water, nothing but dust and dead cattle all day, the air filled with the odor from the dead cattle.

91 *Monday, August 8th.* We have to make a drive of 22 miles, without water today. Have our cans filled to drink. Here we left unknowingly our Lucy behind, not a soul had missed her until we had gone some miles, when we stopped a while to rest the cattle; just then another train drove up behind us with Lucy. She was terribly frightened and so were some more of us when we found out what a narrow escape she had run. She said she was sitting under the bank of the river, when we started, busy watching some wagons cross, and did not know we were ready. And I supposed she was in Mr. Carl's wagon, as he always took care of Francis and Lucy, and I took care of Myra and Chat, when starting he asked for Lucy, and Francis said "She is in Mother's wagon," as she often went there to have her hair combed. It was a lesson to all of us.[1] Evening—It is near dark and we are still toiling on till we find a camping place. The little ones have curled down and gone to sleep without supper. Wind high, and it is cold enough for a great coat and mittens.

92 *Tuesday, August 9th.* Came into camp last night at nine o'clock after traveling 19½ miles with enough water in our cans to make tea for supper; men all tired and hungry. I groped around in the dark and got supper over, after a fashion. . . .

93 *Wednesday, August 10th* . . .

94 *Thursday, August 11th* . . . . Frost this morning. Three of our hands got discontented and left this morning, to pack through. I am pleased,

---

[1] The loss of a child in all the confusion and disorder of travel was a fear that haunted many mothers, and indeed similar accounts to this one appear in a number of women's diaries.

as we shall get along just as well without them and I shall have three less to wait on. . . .

Friday, August 12th . . . . Came 12 miles today. Crossed Burnt River twice. Lost some of our oxen. We were traveling along slowly, when he dropped dead in the yoke. We unyoked and turned out the odd ox, and drove around the dead one, and so it is all along the road, we are continually driving around the dead cattle, and shame on the man who has no pity for the poor dumb brutes that have to travel and toil month after month on this desolate road. (I could hardly help shedding tears, when we drove round this poor ox who had helped us along thus far, and has given us his very last step.) We have camped on a branch of Burnt River.

***Saturday, August 13th—Tuesday, August 16th* . . .**

Wednesday, August 17th. Crossed the Grand Ronde Valley, which is 8 miles across and have camped close to the foot of the mountains. Good water and feed plenty. There 50 or more wagons camped around us. (Lucy and Myra have their feet and legs poisoned, which gives me a good deal of trouble. Bought some fresh salmon of the Indians this evening, which is quite a treat to us.) It is the first we have seen.

***Thursday, August 18* . . .**

Friday, August 19th. Quite cold this morning, water frozen over in the buckets. Traveled 13 miles over very bad roads without water. After looking in vain for water, we were about to give up as it was near night, when husband came across a company of friendly Cayuse Indians about to camp, who showed him where to find water. The men and boys have driven the cattle down to water and I am waiting for water to get supper. This forenoon we bought a few potatoes from an Indian, which will be a treat for our supper.

***Saturday, August 20th—Tuesday, August 30th* . . .**

***Wednesday, August 31st* . . .** It blew so hard last night as to blow our buckets and pans from under the wagons, and this morning we found them (and other things which were not secured) scattered all over the valley. One or two pans came up missing. Everything is packed up ready for a start. The men folks are out hunting the cattle. The children and myself are out shivering around in the wagons, nothing for fires in these parts, and the weather is very disagreeable.

***Thursday, September 1st* . . .** we have encamped not far from the Columbia River. Made a nice dinner of fried salmon. Quite a number of Indians were camped around us, for the purpose of selling salmon to the emigrants.

103 *Friday, September 2nd.* Came 5 miles this morning, and are now crossing Fall (or Deschutes[2] it is called here) River on a ferry boat pay 3 dollars a wagon and swim the stock. This river is very swift and full of rapids. . . .

104 *Saturday, September 3rd.* Cool and pleasant. Had a fine shower last night which laid the dust and makes traveling much better. Here husband (being run out of money) sold his sorrel mare (Fan) for a hundred and twenty-five dollars.

105 *Sunday, September 4th* . . .

106 *Monday, September 5th.* Passed a sleepless night last night as a good many of the Indians camped around us were drunk and noisy and kept up a continual racket, which made all hands uneasy and kept our poor dog on the watch all night. I say poor dog, because he is nearly worn out with traveling through the day and should rest at night; but he hates an Indian and will not let one come near the wagons if he can help it; and doubtless they would have done some mischief but for him. Ascended a long steep hill this morning, which was very hard on the cattle, and also on myself, as I thought I never should get to the top, although I rested two or three times. . . .

[Within twelve days' time, Amelia Knight would give birth to her eighth child. As the last entries are read, one must imagine her in the final days of her pregnancy, stumbling over rocks and fallen trees, carrying her youngest child.]

107 *Tuesday, September 6th.* Still in camp, washing and overhauling the wagons to make as light as possible to cross the mountains. Evening—After throwing away a good many things and burning up most of the deck boards of our wagons so as to lighten them, got my washing and cooking done and started on again. Crossed two branches, traveled 3 miles and have camped near the gate or foot of the Cascade Mountains (here I was sick all night, caused by my washing and working too hard).

108 *Wednesday, September 7th* . . .

109 *Thursday, September 8th.* Traveled 14 miles over the worst road that was ever made, up and down, very steep, rough and rocky hills, through mud holes, twisting and winding around stumps, logs and

[2]The Deschutes River is a tributary of the Columbia River.

fallen trees. Now we are on the end of a log, now over a big root of a tree; now bounce down in a mud hole, then bang goes the other side of the wagon, and woe be to whatever is inside. There is very little chance to turn out of this road, on account of timber and fallen trees, for these mountains are a dense forest of pines, fir, white cedar or redwood (the handsomest timber in the world must be here in these Cascade Mountains). Many of the trees are 300 feet high and so dense to almost exclude the light of heaven, and for my own part I dare not look to the top of them for fear of breaking my neck. We have camped on a little stream called Sandy. No feed for the stock except flour and by driving them a mile or so, they can get a little swamp grass or pick brush.

Friday, September 9th. Came eight and a half miles. Crossed Sandy 4 times; came over corduroy roads, through swamps, over rocks and hummocks, and the worst road that could be imagined or thought of, and have encamped about one o'clock in a little opening near the road. The men have driven the cattle a mile off from the road to try and find grass and rest them till morning. (We hear the road is still worse ahead.) There is a great deal of laurel growing here, which will poison the stock if they eat it. There is no end to the wagons, buggies, yokes, chains, etc. that are lying all along this road. Some splendid good wagons just left standing, perhaps with the owners names on them and many the poor horses, mules, oxen, cows, etc. that are lying dead in these mountains. Afternoon—Slight shower.

Saturday, September 10th. It would be useless for me with my pencil to describe the awful road we have just passed over. Let fancy picture a train of wagons and cattle passing through a crooked chimney and we have Big Laurel Hill. After descending several bad hills, one called Lityle Laurel Hill, which I thought is as bad as could be, but in reality it was nothing to this last one called Big Laurel. It is something more than half mile long very rocky all the way, quite steep, winding, sideling, deep down, slippery and muddy, made so by a spring running the entire length of the road, and this road is cut down so deep that at times the cattle and wagons are almost out of sight, with no room for the drivers except on the bank, a very difficult place to drive, also dangerous, and to make the matter worse, there was a slow poking train ahead of us, which kept stopping every few minutes, and another behind us which kept swearing and hurrying our folks on and there they all were, with the poor cattle all on the strain, holding back the heavy wagons on the slippery road. The men and boys all had their hands full and I was obliged to take care of myself and little ones as best I could, there being no path or road except the one where the teams traveled. We kept as near the road as we could, winding around the fallen timber and brush, climbing over logs creeping under fallen timber, sometimes lifting and carrying Chat. To keep from smelling the carrion, I, as others, holding my nose. . . . I was sick all night and not able to get out of the wagon in the morning.

112 *Sunday, September 11th . . .*

113 *Monday, September 12th . . .*

114 *Tuesday, September 13th . . .* Ascended three steep, muddy hills this morning. Drove over some muddy, miry ground and through mud holes and have just halted at the first farm to noon and rest awhile and buy feed for the stock. Paid 1.50 per hundred for hay. Price of fresh beef 16 and 18 cts. per pound, butter ditto 1 dollar, eggs, 1 dollar a dozen, onion 4 and 5 dollars per bushel, all too dear for poor folks, so we have treated ourselves to some small turnips at the rate of 25 cents per dozen. Got rested and are now ready to travel again. . . . there we are in Oregon making our camp in an ugly bottom, with no home, except our wagons and tent. It is drizzling and the weather looks dark and gloomy. . . .

115 *Wednesday, Sept. 14th.* Still in camp. Raining and quite disagreeable.

116 *Thursday, Sept. 15th.* Still in camp and still raining. (I was sick all night.)

117 *Friday, Sept. 17th.* In camp yet. Still raining. Noon—It has cleared off and we are all ready for a start again, for some place we don't know where. . . .

118 A few days later my eighth child was born. After this we picked up and ferried across the Columbia River, utilizing skiff, canoes and flatboat to get across, taking three days to complete. Here husband traded two yoke of oxen for a half section of land with one-half acre planted to potatoes and a small log cabin and lean-to with no windows. This is the journey's end.

(finis)

Speculations

1. How would you characterize the relationship between the pioneers and the Indians as portrayed in this diary?

2. Later on, the Indians became hostile and began attacking the wagon trains. (See Narration, "A Pioneer Woman's Diary.") What incidents in

this early chronicle foreshadow an impending change in the attitude of the Plains Indians towards the pioneers?

3. How would you characterize the degree of intimacy and self-revelation in this diary? What do the author's omissions indirectly say about her and her times?

4. Bearing in mind the harsh conditions under which this diary was written, what evident purpose do you infer the writer had for keeping it?

5. From the concerns and observations of this diary, what can you infer about the mind of its writer?

Spin-offs for writing

1. Write a process essay enumerating the steps you have to take when you embark on an extended trip.

2. Write an essay about Amelia Stewart Knight, reconstructing her personality and disposition from this diary excerpt.

ANONYMOUS

The diary from which this excerpt comes was found among German soldiers slain during the World War II battle of Stalingrad that ended with the surrender of the German Sixth Army on February 2, 1943. Its author has never been identified.

In step-by-step fashion, this diary depicts the disillusionment with war suffered by a German infantryman. It opens on the euphoria of conquests and closes on a grim note of desperation.

1 Today, after we'd had a bath, the company commander told us that if our future operations are as successful, we'll soon reach the Volga, take Stalingrad and then the war will inevitably soon be over. Perhaps we'll be home by Christmas.

2 *July 29.* . . . The company commander says the Russian troops are completely broken, and cannot hold out any longer. To reach the Volga and take Stalingrad is not so difficult for us. The Führer knows where the Russians' weak point is. Victory is not far away. . . .

3 *August 2.* . . . What great spaces the Soviets occupy, what rich fields there are to be had here after the war's over! Only let's get it over with quickly. I believe that the Führer will carry the thing through to a successful end.

4 *August 10.* . . . The Führer's orders were read out to us. He expects victory of us. We are all convinced that they can't stop us.

5 *August 12.* We are advancing towards Stalingrad along the railway lines. Yesterday Russian "katyushi" and then tanks halted our regiment. "The Russians are throwing in their last forces," Captain Werner explained to me. Large-scale help is coming up for us, and the Russians will be beaten.

6 This morning outstanding soldiers were presented with decorations. . . . Will I really go back to Elsa without a decoration? I believe that for Stalingrad the Führer will decorate even me. . . .

7 *August 23.* Splendid news—north of Stalingrad our troops have reached the Volga and captured part of the city. The Russians have two alternatives, either to flee across the Volga or give themselves up. Our company's interpreter has interrogated a captured Russian officer. He was wounded, but asserted that the Russians would fight for Stalingrad to the last round. Something incomprehensible is, in fact, going on. In the north our troops capture a part of Stalingrad and reach the Volga, but in the south the doomed divisions are continuing to resist bitterly. Fanaticism. . . .

August 27. A continuous cannonade on all sides. We are slowly advancing. Less than twenty miles to go to Stalingrad. In the daytime we can see the smoke of fires, at night-time the bright glow. They say that the city is on fire; on the Führer's orders our Luftwaffe has sent it up in flames. That's what the Russians need, to stop them from resisting . . .

September 4. We are being sent northward along the front towards Stalingrad. We marched all night and by dawn had reached Voroponovo Station. We can already see the smoking town. It's a happy thought that the end of the war is getting nearer. That's what everyone is saying. If only the days and nights would pass more quickly . . .

September 5. Our regiment has been ordered to attack Sadovaya station—that's nearly in Stalingrad. Are the Russians really thinking of holding out in the city itself? We had no peace all night from the Russian artillery and aeroplanes. Lots of wounded are being brought by. God protect me . . .

September 8. Two days of non-stop fighting. The Russians are defending themselves with insane stubbornness. Our regiment has lost many men from the "katyushi," which belch out terrible fire. I have been sent to work at battalion H.Q. It must be mother's prayers that have taken me away from the company's trenches . . .

September 11. Our battalion is fighting in the suburbs in Stalingrad. We can already see the Volga; firing is going on all the time. Wherever you look is fire and flames. . . . Russian cannon and machine-guns are firing out of the burning city. Fanatics . . .

September 13. An unlucky number. This morning "katyushi" attacks caused the company heavy losses: twenty-seven dead and fifty wounded. The Russians are fighting desperately like wild beasts, don't give themselves up, but come up close and then throw grenades. Lieutenant Kraus was killed yesterday, and there is no company commander.

September 16. Our battalion, plus tanks, is attacking the [grain storage] elevator, from which smoke is pouring—the grain in it is burning, the Russians seem to have set light to it themselves. Barbarism. The battalion is suffering heavy losses. There are not more than sixty men left in each company. The elevator is occupied not by men but by devils that no flames or bullets can destroy.

September 18. Fighting is going on inside the elevator. The Russians inside are condemned men; the battalion commander says: "The commissars have ordered those men to die in the elevator."

16 If all the buildings of Stalingrad are defended like this then none of our soldiers will get back to Germany. I had a letter from Elsa today. She's expecting me home when victory's won.

17 *September 20.* The battle for the elevator is still going on. The Russians are firing on all sides. We stay in our cellar; you can't go out into the street. Sergeant-Major Nuschke was killed today running across a street. Poor fellow, he's got three children.

18 *September 22.* Russian resistance in the elevator has been broken. Our troops are advancing towards the Volga. . . .

19 . . . Our old soldiers have never experienced such bitter fighting before.

20 *September 26.* Our regiment is involved in constant heavy fighting. After the elevator was taken the Russians continued to defend themselves just as stubbornly. You don't see them at all, they have established themselves in houses and cellars and are firing on all sides, including from our rear—barbarians, they use gangster methods.

21 In the blocks captured two days ago Russian soldiers appeared from somewhere or other and fighting has flared up with fresh vigour. Our men are being killed not only in the firing line, but in the rear, in buildings we have already occupied.

22 The Russians have stopped surrendering at all. If we take any prisoners it's because they are hopelessly wounded, and can't move by themselves. Stalingrad is hell. Those who are merely wounded are lucky; they will doubtless be at home and celebrate victory with their families. . . .

23 *September 28.* Our regiment, and the whole division, are today celebrating victory. Together with our tank crews we have taken the southern part of the city and reached the Volga. We paid dearly for our victory. In three weeks we have occupied about five and a half square miles. The commander has congratulated us on our victory. . . .

24 *October 3.* After marching through the night we have established ourselves in a shrub-covered gully. We are apparently going to attack the factories, the chimneys of which we can see clearly. Behind them is the Volga. We have entered a new area. It was night but we saw many crosses without helmets on top. Have we really lost so many men? Damn this Stalingrad!

October 4. Our regiment is attacking the Barrikady settlement. A lot of Russian tommy-gunners have appeared. Where are they bringing them from?

October 5. Our battalion has gone into the attack four times, and got stopped each time. Russian snipers hit anyone who shows himself carelessly from behind shelter.

October 10. The Russians are so close to us that our planes cannot bomb them. We are preparing for a decisive attack. The Führer has ordered the whole of Stalingrad to be taken as rapidly as possible.

October 14. It has been fantastic since morning: our aeroplanes and artillery have been hammering the Russian positions for hours on end; everything in sight is being blotted from the face of the earth....

October 22. Our regiment has failed to break into the factory. We have lost many men; every time you move you have to jump over bodies. You can scarcely breathe in the daytime: there is nowhere and no one to remove the bodies, so they are left there to rot. Who would have thought three months ago that instead of the joy of victory we would have to endure such sacrifice and torture, the end of which is nowhere in sight?...

The soldiers are calling Stalingrad the mass grave of the Wehrmacht [German army]. There are very few men left in the companies. We have been told we are soon going to be withdrawn to be brought back up to strength.

October 27. Our troops have captured the whole of the Barrikady factory, but we cannot break through to the Volga. The Russians are not men, but some kind of cast-iron creatures; they never get tired and are not afraid of fire. We are absolutely exhausted; our regiment now has barely the strength of a company. The Russian artillery at the other side of the Volga won't let you lift your head....

October 28. Every soldier sees himself as a condemned man. The only hope is to be wounded and taken back to the rear....

November 3. In the last few days our battalion has several times tried to attack the Russian positions, ... to no avail. On this sector also the Russians won't let you lift your head. There have been a number of cases of self-inflicted wounds and malingering among the men. Every day I write two or three reports about them.

34 *November 10.* A letter from Elsa today. Everyone expects us home for Christmas. In Germany everyone believes we already hold Stalingrad. How wrong they are. If they could only see what Stalingrad has done to our army.

35 *November 18.* Our attack with tanks yesterday had no success. After our attack the field was littered with dead.

36 *November 21.* The Russians have gone over to the offensive along the whole front. Fierce fighting is going on. So, there it is—the Volga, victory and soon home to our families! We shall obviously be seeing them next in the other world.

37 *November 29.* We are encircled. It was announced this morning that the Führer has said: "The army can trust me to do everything necessary to ensure supplies and rapidly break the encirclement."

38 *December 3.* We are on hunger rations and waiting for the rescue that the Führer promised.

39 I send letters home, but there is no reply.

40 *December 7.* Rations have been cut to such an extent that the soldiers are suffering terribly from hunger; they are issuing one loaf of stale bread for five men.

41 *December 11.* Three questions are obsessing every soldier and officer: When will the Russians stop firing and let us sleep in peace, if only for one night? How and with what are we going to fill our empty stomachs, which, apart from 3½–7 ozs of bread, receive virtually nothing at all? And when will Hitler take any decisive steps to free our armies from encirclement?

42 *December 14.* Everybody is racked with hunger. Frozen potatoes are the best meal, but to get them out of the ice-covered ground under fire from Russian bullets is not so easy.

43 *December 18.* The officer today told the soldiers to be prepared for action. General Manstein is approaching Stalingrad from the south with strong forces. This news brought hope to the soldiers' hearts. God, let it be!

44 *December 21.* We are waiting for the order, but for some reason or other it has been a long time coming. Can it be that it is not true about Manstein? This is worse than any torture.

45 *December 23.* Still no orders. It was all a bluff with Manstein. Or has he been defeated at the approaches to Stalingrad?

December 25. The Russian radio has announced the defeat of Manstein. Ahead of us is either death or captivity. 46

December 26. The horses have already been eaten. I would eat a cat; 47 they say its meat is also tasty. The soldiers look like corpses or lunatics, looking for something to put in their mouths. They no longer take cover from Russian shells; they haven't the strength to walk, run away and hide. A curse on this war! ...

Speculations
1. Aside from what he says, what evidence can you glean from the diary to indicate that its author was hard pressed and beleaguered?
2. What can you infer from the diary about the condition of the German troops at the outset?
3. What might a reader of history find particularly ironic about the writer's attitude towards the Russian defenders?
4. What subtle sign can you find in the diary that signals a change in the writer's attitude towards Adolf Hitler?
5. The author writes on December 23, 1942: "I send letters home, but there is no reply." Why do you think he received no replies to his letters?

Spin-offs for writing
1. Write an essay specifying in step-by-step fashion some change in feelings or attitude you have had over a period of time towards a person, event, or holiday.
2. Write an essay on the process of falling in, or out of, love.

NOEL COWARD

Noël Coward (1899–1973) British playwright, actor, composer, and novelist, became a child star at the age of ten and endured through six decades of theatrical history. He is renowned as the author of such theatrical hits as Fallen Angels *(1925),* Hay Fever *(1925),* Private Lives *(1930), and* Blithe Spirit *(1941). He was also the composer of 281 songs and the screenwriter of such films as* In Which We Serve *(1942) and* Brief Encounter *(1946). His autobiographical works include* Present Indicative *(1937) and* Future Indefinite *(1954). Coward, who was knighted in 1970, died three years later while at home in his "beloved Jamaica."*

In 1955 Coward checked into a Chicago hospital to undergo a three-day physical examination. He recorded the event in a diary entry that combined humorous observations about Americans with a step-by-step recounting of the process involved.

Chicago

Tuesday 12 July

1 Here I am, in the Passevant Hospital, for a three-day check-up. I arrived last night under the assumed name of Nicholas Cole. Coley[1] unpacked for me and then he and Alfred[2] departed for Genesee Depot, leaving me weary but cheerful enough in a small green room with a functional bed. The curtains refuse to draw completely, the waste plug in the lavatory basin doesn't work, and outside in the warm humid Chicago air the Shriners are holding their Annual Convention. This consists of many thousand old men and young men dressed in fancy clothes marching about to a series of excruciating brass bands. A pleasant doctor (Walters) came to see me and extracted my life's history, after which he examined me with the utmost thoroughness even to tickling my balls and, after giving me a sleeping-pill, left.

2 This morning I woke at seven owing to the light striking my eyes like a sword through the non-drawing curtains. A series of different ladies appeared from time to time, some on errands, some apparently vaguely as though they had nowhere else to go. One of these latter said 'How ya comin?' I replied that in my present mood I saw little hope of such a contingency arising, whereupon she looked at me blankly, said 'Okay,' and went away.

3 Another lady arrived and, having stuck a large syringe into one of my arm veins, extracted a lot of my blood and also went away. She was followed by a big, moist William Bendix[3] character who, with

---

[1] Coley—Cole Lesley, who was Coward's secretary and factotum.
[2] Alfred—Alfred Lunt (1892–1977), stage and film star.
[3] William Bendix was a rough-looking film actor frequently cast as an amiable simpleton.

almost maternal sympathy, rammed an enema up my bottom and that was that. Presently some cereal was brought to me, and a cup of coffee. While I was enjoying this, a very ramshackle man arrived with a ladder to fix the curtains while the Shriners struck up 'God Bless America.' Presently Dr. Bigg himself arrived looking very like Michel St. Denis,[4] and we had a purposeful little chat. Following on his visit, two men came in to fix the wash-basin, which they failed to do, then a few other ladies bounced in and out for no apparent reason. At about 10.30 I was taken down in the elevator by a personable young Jew called Tony. Here I was led into a small lavatory and told to take off my dressing-gown and pyjamas and put on a strange garment which tied at the side and made me look like a rather skittish Roman matron. In this I was led into a large, depressing room and laid on a slab. Over me and all round me were vast machines. Two men appeared and proceeded to administer a barium enema, a very unpleasant procedure indeed. One of them inserted a tube into my arse while the Shriners, slightly muffled by distance, struck up 'The Darktown Strutters Ball.' Then, in the pitch dark, accompanied by whirrings and whizzings, I was blown up with barium until I thought I should burst. Meanwhile the whizzings and whirrings were photographing what was going on. One of the men massaged my stomach and genitals rather hard, which was painful. At long last it was over and I was allowed to retire to the loo and sit on it until most of my inside had dropped out. Dr. Walters appeared and gave me a cigarette. After half an hour or so I was taken to another room and my chest was x-rayed.

Then I was led back to my room and allowed to relax for a few minutes until yet another very brisk lady came in with an electric apparatus. She proceeded to sandpaper different parts of my skin until it glowed like an ember and clamped electric things on to me and switched on the current. It was quite painless and apparently took a movie of my heart. When she had gone a grey woman arrived with a menu. I chose and marked devilled-egg salad, cheese, rye bread, French dressing and iced tea. An hour or so later a tray was brought me on which was a cup of vegetable soup, a pear in a bed of lettuce with mayonnaise, a hunk of hamburger covered in ketchup accompanied by two moist boiled potatoes, a corn on the cob which I didn't attempt on account of my teeth, and a pistachio ice-cream which tasted like brilliantine. I ate very little of all this ambrosia, but enjoyed the coffee which came instead of the iced tea. So far that is all that has happened to me today, and thank God the Shriners have at last moved off in ragged formation to lacerate the nerves of the rest of Chicago.

[4] Michel St. Denis, distinguished French theatre director in Paris and London.

Wednesday 13 July

5 This has not been a good day. Whatever I write of it will be prejudiced by nervous exhaustion, physical exhaustion and quivering exasperation. First of all, let me state unequivocally that I do not think American women make good nurses. With one or two exceptions those I have encountered in this hospital are smart, bossy and overwhelmingly pleased with themselves. They represent the dominant sex all right in this country and they bloody well know it. The male orderlies are kind, gentle and cowed. Last night, after a meal of fruit only and a pleasant conversation with Dr. Bigg, who is obviously a wise man and a first-rate doctor, I retired to sleep at 11.30 with a sleeping pill. I have been moved into a much nicer room which overlooks the lake (it also overlooks a parking lot in process of construction, a fact that was withheld from me until this morning when the hydraulic drills began at 7.30). At 3.30 a.m. I was torn from a deep sleep by a light being flashed in my eyes and a brisk nurse saying, 'I'm only checking up; go to sleep again.'

6 From that moment I was done for and never closed an eye until 5.30, when I gave up trying and read Tolstoy's *War and Peace* which has saved my reason. From 5.30 until 9.30 I waited without breakfast because I was to have barium for further x-rays. During this time the drills went on outside, while inside different nurses bounced in and out for no apparent reason. After I had returned from the second x-ray jaunt at 2.30 I was allowed breakfast. I ordered poached eggs, bacon and coffee, but when the tray finally arrived the eggs were lying sullenly in the water they'd been poached in, which was not very appetizing. By mid-afternoon I began to feel really beastly and the slight infection in my urinary tract started to give me trouble. Dr. Bigg appeared and, to my intense relief, all my organs are healthy: liver, prostate and heart particularly so. He was wise and comforting and of course the main cause for jubilation is that I am neither festooned with ulcers nor riddled with cancer. Finally, after he had given me a belladonna and opium suppository to ease my discomfort, he went.

Wisconsin

Friday 15 July

7 Yesterday was fairly restful except for the hydraulic drills which happily stopped at 4.30 p.m., having been going since 7.30 a.m. At about five o'clock I had a long talk to Dr. Bigg. He lectured me firmly about my future health, with emphasis on my 'nervous' stomach. He said nothing organic was wrong with me, except a slight

curving of the spine which can be remedied or at least prevented from curving more by watching my posture and walking and sitting with more care, but that I must remember that I am fifty-five and not twenty-five, and live sensibly and moderately and *not* give myself so much to other people and their problems. He also said that I should create more and perform less and, for the rest of my life, drink as little alcohol as socially possible. He also told me not to be fussy about my diet, but to eat little and well. He specified that roughage was bad for my colon, which apparently is over-sensitive, like so many of my friends. He said that all the old wives' tales about cooked green vegetables being good for me was nonsense and that meat and fish, eggs, potatoes, bread and sugar were much better! He advised the latter in moderation on account of my figure. In fact he advised moderation in everything. We then got into a long discussion of morals and sex taboos and homosexuality, which convinced me that he is one of the wisest and most thoroughly sensible men I have ever met. I shall go to him once a year.

I arrived at Milwaukee at 3.15 and was met by Lynnie and Cole. We had a peaceful evening, played my Las Vegas record, which is excellent, and I went to bed early and finished *War and Peace*. Yes, yes, yes, it is a great book but it is far too long and although all the characters are brilliantly drawn they are, most of them, bloody bores, particularly the hero and heroine, Pierre and Natasha, whom I personally find absolutely idiotic. Prince Andrei is, to me, the only sympathetic creature in the whole book and even he gets a bit fuzzy and mystic before he kicks the bucket. 8

Well, I have finished it and I am very, very proud.

Speculations

1. In what specific ways would the procedure differ if Coward were being given a physical today?

2. How would you characterize the tone of the exchange between Coward and the nurse as reported in paragraph 2?

3. Coward writes in paragraph 5 that American women "represent the dominant sex in this country and they bloody well know it." What is your opinion of this view?

4. In what ways does Coward's account of his hospitalization bear the imprint of his many years of theatrical experience?

5. Read the advice given Coward by his doctor in paragraph 7. How does this differ radically from what a modern doctor might recommend?

Spin-offs for writing

1. Write an essay on the process involved in any visit to the doctor or any stay in a hospital.
2. Write a process essay on your most horrible medical experience.

FRANCES KARLEN SANTAMARIA

Frances Karlen Santamaria, born and raised in Cleveland, attended Antioch College. She began keeping a diary at fifteen, as she says, "to relieve the burden" of her adolescence. Parts of it were eventually published as Joshua Firstborn, *commemorating the wonders and labors of first-time motherhood. She gave birth to her son, Joshua, in Greece.*

The **briss** *is a Jewish circumcision ritual that family and close friends of the parents are invited to witness. Performed by a* **moyl**, *an accredited circumciser, it is an occasion of religious observances and celebration. This diary entry takes us through the process involved.*

February 16, 1964

Plans for the *Briss*, the Jewish circumcision ceremony, began immediately, as Joshua was still uncircumcised. (The Greeks do not circumcise.)

It took place the next Thursday afternoon in my in-laws' living room where we had been married five years before. The relatives started to come. My father and brother had flown in from Cleveland although my father was weak from pneumonia (later I found out it was terminal cancer).

I was nervous, fearing the baby would have pain. We were not prepared for the sight of the *moyl* who arrived at three o'clock. At the circumcisions of nephews and cousins there had always been a ubiquitous little old man in a black coat and hat with a wrinkled, efficient wife to whom he spoke in Yiddish as he performed the little operation in the privacy of the bedroom. ("They say he sucks the blood," someone would inevitably whisper.) The mother, always wearing a brand-new blue nylon bathrobe kept out of sight of the proceedings until the ceremony was over and the party had begun.

Our *moyl*, a Mr. Shoulson, turned out to be a radiant young man with a fresh skin that seemed unearthly smooth and white, and a handsome goatee. (He was a weekend folk-singer we found out later and a frustrated would-be medical student.) His suit was fashionable and his head with the white *yarmalka* was strong and beautiful. He worked with surgical equipment at a card table in the dining room making preparations while the baby lay happily upstairs kicking in the crib with Thel, his godmother, bending over him. He was dressed up for the occasion (*sacrifice*, I kept thinking) in a blue shirt and striped blue-and-white pants, and white booties with pom-poms she had brought that day. He was the size and weight of a six-month baby and he laughed delightedly and unsuspectingly in his deep, husky voice.

5 Nervous, I had a drink. When our *moyl*, the folksinger, was ready, the godfather proudly carried Joshua downstairs. He looked around at the crowd of great-uncles and aunts and grandparents with sweetness and open-eyed curiosity. Shoulson smiled and talked to him, commenting he'd never performed the operation on any but an eight-day-old child.

6 The baby was passed from the arms of his godfather to his father while prayers were said in Hebrew and English. Then he was placed on the crossed arms of both his grandfathers while the *moyl* prayed. Finally, he was put on the little board on the table. His arms were tied up over his head in a receiving blanket. His sturdy legs were put into wide leather bands on the board. Arno seemed excited but felt, I think, calmer than I.

7 The crowd gathered around the table. We took off his striped shorts and diaper. I felt giddy and terribly worried. Mother came into the room and left quickly, refusing to watch. When the icy anesthetic was sprayed on him, Josh began to cry. He tried to wave his arms but they were pinned and he screamed with fright and surprise. There was nothing for me to do but go to him. "Give him his bottle," said the *moyl*. "It will take his mind off it."

8 "But he won't drink a bottle." I filled one quickly though and tried to put it to his lips and, as he had for the past month, Joshua refused anything but the breast. I leaned over him, our faces inches apart and spoke to him. He stared up at me from the board and screamed and sobbed. I could feel the *moyl* working, cutting the foreskin, stared at my baby, spoke steadily, held him, our eyes locked—his frightened and angry as though I were betraying him. And so we were, for what seemed an endless time.

9 I did not even know my father had stepped forward to hold his legs, and when the foreskin came away and the tiny organ was revealed, red and raw, my father, holding the small legs, buckled and asked my brother for a whiskey. I did not hear. I spoke to Arno who stood by, and felt the crowd, heard laughter and whispers and realized dimly that the ordeal was probably not so terrible as it seemed, and yet my son cried and held me reproachfully with his eyes for the first time, and time did not move for me.

10 Finally it was done. The dressing was put on and I stepped back as the *moyl* released his arms and legs, and picked him up, arranging the diaper, the blue and white pants. The crying ceased. Shoulson held him in his arms and made a joke or two. Then he continued with the ceremony. He prayed in Hebrew in half-chant, half-song. Then

in English. His robe was white and the front embroidered in heavy silver thread. Brown-bearded, white-capped, shining in silver and silk, he held my baby and prayed.

"And prolong the life of this infant—Amen." 11

I heard the rich syllables of the Hebrew name for the first time: 12
Yehoshua ben Chuna. Joshua, son of Arno. We said Amen. Wine was poured. "Why is everyone crying?" I asked.

Arno and his brother embraced and I took Joshua upstairs to nurse 13
him. Later the *moyl* told us that there had been a complication—the baby had been born, he said, "with a great redundancy of foreskin." I flushed with a kind of blank pride as though told one had acquitted oneself with a flourish, made an especially fine arabesque.

He cried on and off for the rest of the evening. Arno fixed his aspirin, 14
and, since he was crying, to my distress, at the sight of me (he associated my face with his afternoon ordeal), his father put him to sleep, carrying him back and forth in the darkened room, and then tried to convince me I had not betrayed my son.

As I waited outside the room I realized how much we have changed 15
in the past three months; how much I have learned about loving. I had expected that, like a little girl mocking love to her doll, my love would at once envelop my baby; instead I had to learn it, grow into it. Love doesn't come from the child's cooing and smiling, his cuteness or beauty. We are rewarded by these things at odd moments. Love comes gradually with our worry, relief, and care—with what we have invested of ourselves. We must learn the loving of a first child step by step, as we learn to sustain love in marriage. The loving of a first baby is like an acquired gift, or skill. The second child, I imagine, comes into that love ready-made.

These days, surrounded by his family, Arno seems different with the 16
baby, as though other people, acknowledging the relationship between him and his child (that great, binding link, again) help him, too, to feel it, make it real. The extended family works to make a family of us; the symbolically linked hands and crossed arms of godfather, father, grandfather at the *briss*, the sense of generations of males, gives my husband a place to stand with his son.

And so, through one little crisis, one painful shot and a sore vaccina- 17
tion, many nights of crying and hurried consultation, and now the tiny wounded cock, we begin to be parents, and Joshua is truly, profoundly, ours.

Speculations

1. How would you describe the specific steps involved in the Jewish ritual of the *briss*?

2. With what Christian ceremony does the *briss* seem to be symbolically linked? In what way?

3. What contrasts can you see in the reported attitudes of the mother and father towards the *briss*?

4. The author mentions in passing that her father flew in from Cleveland, though she later discovered that he was stricken with terminal cancer. Why do you think she chose to tell us that?

5. From the author's description of the ceremony, whom do you think she intended as the audience of this piece?

Spin-offs for writing

1. Write a process essay on any religious ritual or ceremony.

2. Write an essay depicting the process involved in any ceremony, religious or otherwise, in which you have participated.

Student Journal–Process

Jon Cotton

January 1, 1993

Just back from a week of skiing at Alta with Mom, Dad, Grandma, Sean, and Michael. Despite the whistling wind and whipping snow, we had a great time trying to conquer the various runs by blindly jumping over moguls and keeping our boots together as we landed and then crunched out our turns without really being able to define the terrain of the hill.

Later on, back at our condo, Grandma talked about her mother, Great Grandma Beach, who is now ninety-one and waiting for death—unable to walk, talk, or understand what is happening around her. I think about this and how life can slowly deteriorate at the end of the line. Grandma Beach had always been an extremely nice southern lady, who let Sean, Michael, and me stage imaginary fights with her ebony elephants from Africa and who had stowed away a whole set of colorful wooden blocks with which we could build imaginary fortresses, castles, and villages. I loved sprawling on her Persian carpet to stack my fantasy world, interrupted only by snacking on the cookies she had baked for us. But Grandma Beach is failing rapidly. She is no longer what she was in those days. And it seems to me that I can mark the stages of her decline.

As I recall, the first time I noticed something wrong with Grandma Beach was years ago at one of our annual family picnics. I always liked these picnics. This was one of the only times, throughout the year, that I got to see my relatives. She was just as nice and caring as ever, but suddenly her memory seemed rattled. She asked me, "Jon, what grade are you in?" I told her, "I'm in the seventh grade." Fine and well, but one minute later she asked me the same question, and again I answered, "I'm in the seventh grade." Then she asked me that same question over and over again—as if she had never listened to my answer. At one point I saw her point to Mom and ask Aunt Colette, "Who is that pretty girl over there?" The experts call this phase of senility "short-term memory loss." How embarrassing to repeat yourself so tiringly. How sad not to remember your grandson's wife whom you have known and recognized for years.

The next time I saw Grandma Beach was two years later. I couldn't believe how she had deteriorated. She basically looked the same, always smiling. She was still that same kind and caring woman, but she was incapable of making a grammatical sentence. She would begin a sentence in one direction, but then trail off into another, unrelated to the first. She hugged and kissed me affectionately, but her comments made no sense. Also, she seemed to think all of us had come from Switzerland, where she had lived all during World War II. Dad tells me that this phase is just part of *senile dementia*, the mind's inability to process language in a logically connected way. It seems that the neurons in a senile brain don't fire off correctly. This time the family went to lunch at Marie Callender's popular pie place. Grandma Beach sat in her chair—perfectly happy to be part of the group physically, but unable to take part in the conversation.

Now more than two years have passed, and I can't see how Grandma's condition can get much worse. The last time I saw her, she was lying in bed—no longer able to get up and walk—babbling and having no clue who I was. She seemed to act normal, but her words were jumbled into nonsense phrases or meaningless sounds. All I could do was smile at her. But I was struck by the fact that even in this hopelessly deteriorated state—an old woman lying in bed and waiting for death—she was still very kind and caring. Her gray eyes stared vacantly as if she were half in another world unknown to me.

Today, at the beginning of a new year, I wonder what it will be like when I am old. I guess the end of a long life is no bed of roses. I wonder if you strain to remember and if you feel terrible about losing it all. I think it would be frustrating to be senile, repeating the same questions and not remembering anything. You would be such a burden on everyone else.

Two thoughts come to mind as I sit here writing in my diary: First, if I get that senile, I want a paid nurse to take care of me so I won't be a burden to my family. Second, I plan to be kind, patient, and caring with senile people. They can't help their condition, and most of us, if we live long enough, will end up that way.

Still, I wonder if science will someday find a cure for extreme senility.

5.

DIVISION AND CLASSIFICATION.

August 26, 1805. "The Shoshonees are a small tribe of the nation called Snake Indians. . . ." Classification of the Shoshone Indians. Meriwether Lewis.

January, 1839. "And here it may be well to inform you that the slaves on this plantation are divided into fieldhands and mechanics or artisans." Kinds of slaves on an antebellum southern plantation. Fanny Kemble.

July 22, 1903. "Next came Hardy—Tess of the D'Urbervilles, which is of a very different type." The kinds of books she enjoyed reading in the country. Virginia Woolf.

March 12, 1865. "In the afternoon Chaplain Lovering came up and held forth. . ." Types of Civil War chaplains. Private John W. Haley, 17th Maine Regiment.

CHAPTER 5

Division and Classification

Division and classification is the rhetorical pattern most commonly used in any discipline that requires systematic thinking. The aim of division is to break down a larger subject into its smaller units; on the other hand, the aim of classification is to identify and discuss a smaller unit as part of a larger whole. For example, the first excerpt in this section, by Meriwether Lewis, is a classification. Lewis informs us that the Shoshones belong to a particular Indian nation; against this context, he then writes at length about Shoshone culture. The next excerpt, by Fanny Kemble, is a division. She divides the slaves found on a Southern plantation into primary types and discusses the particular functions of each.

Division and classification is a useful way of thinking because of the control we get from grouping items, objects, and ideas into known types. For example, a physician must be able to identify the type of germ that causes a given disease, for then he or she knows what particular kinds of antibiotics or treatments are likely to work. An airline pilot knows that a certain type of aircraft has a specific range as well as a limited capacity, and this information enables him or her to plan a safe trip. On a less urgent level, a critic who knows that the work of an artist belongs to a particular movement is better able to judge its merits. Being able to sort items into types, classes, and kinds liberates us from the tyranny of the particular. Without this capacity in our thinking, we would find the world a bewildering wonderland whose daily newness would be incomprehensible.

But division and classification is also a mode of thinking that is so intellectual as to be almost entirely absent from diaries. Diarists are mainly reflective, solitary writers, many of whom begin and end their diaries with no conscious intention of ever seeing them published. When they do classify, it is done informally and briefly. Virginia Woolf, for example, tells us about the types of books she likes to read while staying in the country, but she does so offhandedly. Likewise, John Haley, who fought on the Union side during the Civil War, writes about the kinds of chaplains who ministered to his regiment, but he does so only in passing.

For the essayist, there are certain ideals that, if followed, promise a sound division and classification essay. The first is to select a single principle for the classification. This means choosing a significant rather than a trivial feature to divide the whole into its parts. For example, if you wanted to divide fiction, you could choose physical length as your principle, yielding four general types: the short-short story, the short story, the novelette, and the novel. Length is a significant enough feature to yield a meaningful division that tells us something about fiction. A meaningless division of fiction, and an illogical essay, would result from using as your dividing principle some frivolous measure such as kind of cover. That fiction is published in hardback and paperback is no doubt true, but it is also a dead-end observation that says nothing about the genre.

The second ideal in writing a sound essay is to make your classification complete. For example, if you wrote an essay about the sailing rigs of pleasure craft and asserted that there are three types—the cutter, the sloop, and the ketch—you would be guilty of leaving out at least three others—the catboat, the schooner, and the yawl. Your essay, even if well written and carefully presented, would still lack the logic of completeness.

The third ideal is for the division and classification essay to yield separate and complete types. This is basically a simple notion and means, for example, that your essay should not divide automobiles into sedans, coupes, and four-wheel drives, since it is possible for a sedan and a coupe also to be a four-wheel drive. Each category should be exclusive and complete and not overlap with another. Although this mistake is basically a flaw of thinking, making it will still result in an illogical essay.

Finally, the fourth ideal is to be balanced in your discussion of the types or categories into which you have divided the whole. The writer who is guilty of the oversight of imbalance will spend pages discussing one type and a paragraph on the other. It is the commonest error in division and classification essays. Fairness and logic require that if you divide, say, poetic meter into five types, then you not write pages on the iambic pentameter and only one line on the spondee. Sometimes, however, one part of your division will have relatively more importance than another and will deserve more attention. However, you should always make it clear why that is so from the outset.

Division and classification is an exercise in thinking intellectually about a subject. As a writing assignment, it ranks among the most academic since a writer must know a subject intimately before attempting to divide or classify it. Inspiration helps in all kinds of writing, but for writing this particular kind of essay, nothing is better than careful research.

MERIWETHER LEWIS

Meriwether Lewis (1774–1809), American explorer, was one of the leaders of the famous Lewis and Clark Expedition undertaken between 1803 and 1806 to survey land comprising the Louisiana Purchase and beyond. One purpose of the trip was to find an overland route to the Pacific; another, to solidify American claims to the Oregon Territory. The expedition was highly successful and cost the life of only one man in the party. Lewis, who was later made governor of the Louisiana Territory in 1807, died under mysterious circumstances two years later.

Lewis kept a journal of the expedition, in which he made notes about the terrain the explorers covered and the Indians they encountered. In this excerpt he undertakes what, for diarists, is a rare act of classification: he first identifies the Shoshone Indians as belonging to the Snake Indian Nation before proceeding to discuss their ways and habits.

1 The Shoshonees are a small tribe of the nation called Snake Indians, a vague denomination, which embraces at once the inhabitants of the southern parts of the Rocky mountains and of the plains on each side. The Shoshonees with whom we now are, amount to about one hundred warriors, and three times that number of women and children. Within their own recollection they formerly lived in the plains, but they have been driven into the mountains by the Pawkees, or the roving Indians of the Sascatchawain, and are now obliged to visit occasionally, and by stealth, the country of their ancestors. Their lives are indeed migratory. From the middle of May to the beginning of September, they reside on the waters of the Columbia, where they consider themselves perfectly secure from the Pawkees who have never yet found their way to that retreat. During this time they subsist chiefly on salmon, and as that fish disappears on the approach of autumn, they are obliged to seek subsistence elsewhere. They then cross the ridge to the waters of the Missouri, down which they proceed slowly and cautiously, till they are joined near the three forks by other bands, either of their own nation or of the Flatheads, with whom they associate against the common enemy. Being now strong in numbers, they venture to hunt buffaloe in the plains eastward of the mountains, near which they spend the winter, till the return of the salmon invites them to the Columbia. But such is their terror of the Pawkees, that as long as they can obtain the scantiest subsistence, they do not leave the interior of the mountains; and as soon as they collect a large stock of dried meat, they again retreat, and thus alternately obtaining their food at the hazard of their lives, and hiding themselves to consume it. In this loose and wandering existence they suffer the extremes of want; for two thirds of the year they are forced to live in the mountains, passing whole weeks without meat, and

with nothing to eat but a few fish and roots. Nor can any thing be imagined more wretched than their condition at the present time, when the salmon is fast retiring, when roots are becoming scarce, and they have not yet acquired strength to hazard an encounter with their enemies. So insensible are they however to these calamities, that the Shoshonees are not only cheerful but even gay; and their character, which is more interesting than that of any Indians we have seen, has in it much of the dignity of misfortune. In their intercourse with strangers they are frank and communicative, in their dealings perfectly fair, nor have we had during our stay with them, any reason to suspect that the display of all our new and valuable wealth has tempted them into a single act of dishonesty. While they have generally shared with us the little they possess, they have always abstained from begging any thing from us. With their liveliness of temper, they are fond of gaudy dresses, and of all sorts of amusements, particularly to games of hazard; and like most Indians fond of boasting of their own warlike exploits, whether real or fictitious. In their conduct towards ourselves, they were kind and obliging, and though on one occasion they seemed willing to neglect us, yet we scarcely knew how to blame the treatment by which we suffered, when we recollected how few civilized chiefs would have hazarded the comforts or the subsistence of their people for the sake of a few strangers. This manliness of character may cause or it may be formed by the nature of their government, which is perfectly free from any restraint. Each individual is his own master, and the only control to which his conduct is subjected, is the advice of a chief supported by his influence over the opinions of the rest of the tribe. The chief himself is in fact no more than the most confidential person among the warriors, a rank neither distinguished by any external honor, nor invested by any ceremony, but gradually acquired from the good wishes of his companions and by superior merit. Such an officer has therefore strictly no power; he may recommend or advise or influence, but his commands have no effect on those who incline to disobey, and who may at any time withdraw from their voluntary allegiance. His shadowy authority which cannot survive the confidence which supports it, often decays with the personal vigour of the chief, or is transferred to some more fortunate or favourite hero.

In their domestic economy, the man is equally sovereign. The man is the sole proprietor of his wives and daughters, and can barter them away, or dispose of them in any manner he may think proper. The children are seldom corrected; the boys, particularly, soon become their own masters; they are never whipped, for they say that it breaks their spirit, and that after being flogged they never recover their independence of mind, even when they grow to manhood. A plurality of wives is very common; but these are not generally sisters, as among the Minnetarees and Mandans, but are purchased of different fathers. The infant daughters are often betrothed by the father to men who are grown, either for themselves or for their sons, for whom they are desirous of providing wives. The compensation to the father is usually made in horses or mules; and the girl remains with her parents till the age of puberty, which is thirteen or fourteen, when she is surrendered to her husband. At the same time the father often makes a present to the husband equal to what he had formerly received as the price of his daughter, though this return is optional with her parent. Sacajawea[1] had been contracted in this way before she was taken prisoner, and when we brought her back, her betrothed was still living. Although he was double the age of Sacajawea, and had two other wives, he claimed her, but on finding that she had a child by her new husband, Chaboneau, he relinquished his pretensions and said he did not want her.

3 The chastity of the women does not appear to be held in much estimation. The husband will for a trifling present lend his wife for a night to a stranger, and the loan may be protracted by increasing the value of the present. Yet strange as it may seem, notwithstanding this facility, any connexion of this kind not authorized by the husband, is considered highly offensive and quite as disgraceful to his character as the same licentiousness in civilized societies. The Shoshonees are not so importunate in volunteering the services of their wives as we found the Sioux were; and indeed we observed among them some women who appeared to be held in more respect than those of any nation we had seen. But the mass of the females are condemned, as among all savage nations, to the lowest and most laborious drudgery. When the tribe is stationary, they collect the roots, and cook; they build the huts, dress the skins and make clothing; collect the wood, and assist in taking care of the horses on the route; they load the horses and have the charge of all the baggage. The only business of the man is to fight; he therefore takes on himself the care of his horse, the companion of his warfare; but he will descend to no other labour than to hunt and to fish. He would consider himself degraded by being compelled to walk any distance; and were he so poor as to possess only two horses, he would ride the best of them, and leave the other for his wives and children and their baggage; and if he has too many wives or too much baggage for the horse, the wives have no alternative but to follow him on foot; they are not however often reduced to those extremities, for their stock of

---

[1] Sacajawea (1784–1884?)—An Indian guide and member of the Shoshone Indians who was the only woman on the Lewis and Clark Expedition.

horses is very ample. Notwithstanding their losses this spring they still have at least seven hundred, among which are about forty colts, and half that number of mules. There are no horses here which can be considered as wild; we have seen two only on this side of the Muscleshell river which were without owners, and even those although shy, showed every mark of having been once in the possession of man. The original stock was procured from the Spaniards, but they now raise their own. The horses are generally very fine, of a good size, vigorous and patient of fatigue as well as hunger. Each warrior has one or two tied to a stake near his hut both day and night, so as to be always prepared for action. The mules are obtained in the course of trade from the Spaniards, with whose brands several of them are marked, or stolen from them by the frontier Indians. They are the finest animals of that kind we have ever seen, and at this distance from the Spanish colonies are very highly valued. The worse are considered as worth the price of two horses, and a good mule cannot be obtained for less than three and sometimes four horses.

We also saw a bridle bit, stirrups and several other articles which, like the mules, came from the Spanish colonies. The Shoshonees say that they can reach those settlements in ten days' march by the route of the Yellowstone river; but we readily perceive that the Spaniards are by no means favourites. They complain that the Spaniards refuse to let them have fire arms under pretence that these dangerous weapons will only induce them to kill each other. In the meantime, say the Shoshonees, we are left to the mercy of the Minnetarees, who having arms, plunder them of their horses, and put them to death without mercy. "But this should not be," said Cameahwait fiercely, "if we had guns, instead of hiding ourselves in the mountains and living like the bears on roots and berries, we would then go down and live in the buffaloe country in spite of our enemies, whom we never fear when we meet on equal terms."

As war is the chief occupation, bravery is the first virtue among the Shoshonees. None can hope to be distinguished without having given proofs of it, nor can there be any preferment, or influence among the nation, without some warlike achievement. Those important events which give reputation to a warrior, and which entitle him to a new name, are killing a white bear, stealing individually the horses of the enemy, leading out a party who happen to be successful either in plundering horses or destroying the enemy, and lastly scalping a warrior. These acts seem of nearly equal dignity, but the last, that of taking an enemy's scalp, is an honour quite independent of the act of vanquishing him. To kill your adversary is of no importance unless the scalp is brought from the field of battle, and were a warrior to slay any number of his enemies in action, and others were to obtain the scalps or first touch the dead, they would have all the honours, since they have borne off the trophy.

6 The Shoshonees are of a diminutive stature, with thick flat feet and ankles, crooked legs, and are, generally speaking, worse formed than any nation of Indians we have seen. Their complexion resembles that of the Sioux, and is darker than that of the Minnetarees, Mandans, or Shawnees. The hair in both sexes is suffered to fall loosely over the face and down the shoulders: some men, however, divide it by means of thongs of dressed leather or otter skin into two equal queues, which hang over the ears and are drawn in front of the body; but at the present moment, when the nation is afflicted by the loss of so many relations killed in war, most of them have the hair cut quite short in the neck, and Cameahwait has the hair cut short all over his head, this being the customary mourning for a deceased kindred.

7 They have many more children than might have been expected, considering their precarious means of support and their wandering life. This inconvenience is however balanced by the wonderful facility with which their females undergo the operations of child-birth. In the most advanced state of pregnancy they continue their usual occupations, which are scarcely interrupted longer than the mere time of bringing the child into the world.

8 The old men are few in number, and do not appear to be treated with much tenderness or respect.

9 The tobacco used by the Shoshonees is not cultivated among them, but obtained from the Indians of the Rocky mountains, and from some of the bands of their own nation who live south of them: it is the same plant which is in use among the Minnetarees, Mandans, and Ricaras.

10 Their chief intercourse with other nations seems to consist in their association with other Snake Indians, and with the Flatheads when they go eastward to hunt buffaloe, and in the occasional visits made by the Flatheads to the waters of the Columbia for the purpose of fishing. Their intercourse with the Spaniards is much more rare, and it furnishes them with a few articles, such as mules, and some bridles, and other ornaments for horses, which, as well as some of their kitchen utensils, are also furnished by the bands of Snake Indians from the Yellowstone. The pearl ornaments which they esteem so highly come from other bands, whom they represent as their friends and relations, living to the southwest beyond the barren plains on the other side of the mountains: these relations they say inhabit a good country, abounding with elk, deer, bear, and antelope, where horses and mules

are much more abundant than they are here, or to use their own expression, as numerous as the grass of the plains.

The names of the Indians varies in the course of their life: originally 11 given in childhood, from the mere necessity of distinguishing objects, or from some accidental resemblance to external objects, the young warrior is impatient to change it by some achievement of his own. Any important event, the stealing of horses, the scalping an enemy, or killing a brown bear, entitles him at once to a new name which he then selects for himself, and it is confirmed by the nation. Sometimes the two names subsist together: thus, the chief Cameahwait, which means, "one who never walks," has the war name of Tooettecone, or "black gun," which he acquired when he first signalized himself. As each new action gives a warrior a right to change his name, many of them have had several in the course of their lives. To give to a friend his own name is an act of high courtesy, and a pledge like that of pulling off the moccasin of sincerity and hospitality. The chief in this way gave his name to captain Clarke when he first arrived, and he was afterwards known among the Shoshonees by the name of Cameahwait.

The diseases incident to this state of life may be supposed to be few, 12 and chiefly the result of accidents. We were particularly anxious to ascertain whether they had any knowledge of the venereal disorder. After inquiring by means of the interpreter and his wife, we learnt that they sometimes suffered from it, and that they most usually die with it; nor could we discover what was their remedy. It is possible that this disease may have reached them in their circuitous communications with the whites through the intermediate Indians; but the situation of the Shoshonees is so insulated, that it is not probable that it could have reached them in that way, and the existence of such a disorder among the Rocky mountains seems rather a proof of its being aboriginal.

Speculations

1. What characteristics of substance and style differentiate this excerpt from a personal diary?

2. The author says that Shoshones valued their mules much more highly than their horses, although he does not say why. What logical reasons can you infer from the narrative to explain this preference?

3. The author finds it "strange" that a Shoshone man will readily lend his wife to another man for "a trifling present" but that liaisons unauthorized by the husband are considered "highly offensive." What explanation can you give for this inconsistency?

4. If you read between the lines in paragraph 4, what do you surmise to be the real reason that the Spaniards refused to let the Shoshones have guns?

5. In what ways was the division of labor between the sexes among the Shoshones similar to or different from the division of labor that existed among the early white settlers or pioneers? How do you explain this similarity or difference?

Spin-offs for writing

1. Write an essay that classifies and discusses any group to which you belong.

2. Write an essay dividing your home town or your campus into the ethnic or cultural types that predominate.

FANNY KEMBLE

Fanny Kemble (1809–1893), English actress of much acclaim in her day, married Pierce Butler of Georgia in 1834 and lived with him for a while on his slave plantation. Disgusted by slavery, she soon divorced her husband and moved back to England, where she wrote anti-slavery essays. Her Journal of a Residence on a Georgia Plantation in 1838–1839 *has become a much quoted source about the practices of slavery.*

During her stay on her husband's plantation in Georgia, Kemble recorded information about the divisions of function, labor, and class among the slaves. She noted with a sardonic eye the roles assigned to the different classes of slaves and described their exercise of them. Her division is not as systematic as we would expect to find in an essay, but she has a keen eye for detail and a good sense of how to structure her observations.

January, 1839

Our servants—those who have been selected to wait upon us in the house—consist of a man, who is quite a tolerable cook (I believe this is a natural gift with them, as with Frenchmen); a dairy-woman, who churns for us; a laundry-woman; her daughter, our housemaid, the aforesaid Mary; and two young lads of from fifteen to twenty, who wait upon us in the capacity of footmen.

And here it may be well to inform you that the slaves on this plantation are divided into field-hands and mechanics or artisans. The former, the great majority, are the more stupid and brutish of the tribe; the others, who are regularly taught their trades, are not only exceedingly expert at them, but exhibit a greater general activity of intellect, which must necessarily result from even a partial degree of cultivation. There are here a gang (for that is the honourable term) of coopers, of blacksmiths, of brick-layers, of carpenters, all well acquainted with their peculiar trades.

The latter constructed the wash-hand stands, clothes-presses, sofas, tables, etc., with which our house is furnished, and they are very neat pieces of workmanship—neither veneered or polished indeed, nor of very costly materials, but of the white pine wood planed as smooth as marble—a species of furniture not very luxurious perhaps, but all the better adapted therefore to the house itself, which is certainly rather more devoid of the conveniences and adornments of modern existence than any thing I ever took up my abode in before....

Of our three apartments, one is our sitting, eating, and living room, and is sixteen feet by fifteen. The walls are plastered indeed, but neither painted nor papered; it is divided from our bedroom (a similarly elegant and comfortable chamber) by a dingy wooden partition covered all over with hooks, pegs, and nails, to which hats, caps, keys, etc., etc., are suspended in graceful irregularity. The doors open by wooden latches, raised by means of small bits of pack-thread—I imagine, the same primitive order of fastening celebrated in the touching chronicle of Red Riding Hood; how they shut I will not attempt to describe, as the shutting of a door is a process of extremely rare occurrence throughout the whole Southern country.

5 The third room, a chamber with sloping ceiling, immediately over our sitting-room and under the roof, is appropriated to the nurse and my two babies. Of the closets, one is the overseer's bedroom, the other his office or place of business; and the third, adjoining our bedroom, and opening immediately out of doors, is Mr Butler's dressing-room and cabinet d'affaires, where he gives audiences to the negroes, redresses grievances, distributes red woollen caps (a singular gratification to a slave), shaves himself, and performs the other offices of his toilet.

6 Such being our abode, I think you will allow there is little danger of my being dazzled by the luxurious splendours of a Southern slave residence.

7 At the upper end of the row of houses, and nearest to our overseer's residence, is the hut of the head driver. Let me explain, by the way, his office. The negroes, as I before told you, are divided into troops or gangs, as they are called; at the head of each gang is a driver, who stands over them, whip in hand, while they perform their daily task, who renders an account of each individual slave and his work every evening to the overseer, and receives from him directions for their next day's tasks.

8 Each driver is allowed to inflict a dozen lashes upon any refractory slave in the field, and at the time of the offence; they may not, however, extend the chastisement, and if it is found ineffectual, their remedy lies in reporting the unmanageable individual either to the head driver or the overseer, the former of whom has power to inflict three dozen lashes at his own discretion, and the latter as many as he himself sees fit, within the number of fifty; which limit, however, I must tell you, is an arbitrary one on this plantation, appointed by the founder of the estate, Major Butler, Mr Butler's grandfather, many of whose regulations, indeed I believe most of them, are still observed in the government of the plantation.

9 To return to our head driver, or, as he is familiarly called, head man, Frank—he is second in authority only to the overseer, and exercises rule alike over the drivers and the gangs in the absence of the

sovereign white man from the estate, which happens whenever the overseer visits the other two plantations at Woodville and St Simon's.

He is sole master and governor of the island, appoints the work, pronounces punishments, gives permission to the men to leave the island (without it they never may do so), and exercises all functions of undisputed mastery over his fellow-slaves, for you will observe that all this while he is just as much a slave as any of the rest. Trustworthy, upright, intelligent, he may be flogged tomorrow if the overseer or Mr Butler so please it, and sold the next day, like a carthorse, at the will of the latter.

Besides his various other responsibilities, he has the key of all the stores, and gives out the people's rations weekly; nor is it only the people's provisions that are put under his charge—meat, which is only given out to them occasionally, and provisions for the use of the family, are also intrusted to his care.

Thus you see, among these inferior creatures, their own masters yet look to find, surviving all their best efforts to destroy them, good sense, honesty, self-denial, and all the qualities, mental and moral, that make one man worthy to be trusted by another. . . .

Speculations

1. How would you characterize Kemble's observation that cooking "is a natural gift" with Negro slaves as it is with Frenchmen?
2. What does the overall tone of this entry imply about the attitude of the author towards what she observes? Find specific examples to support your answer.
3. Of what is Kemble indirectly complaining when she says in paragraph 4 that "the shutting of a door is a process of extremely rare occurrence throughout the whole Southern country"?
4. What implicit principle does the author use in her division of the slaves?
5. To what does Kemble attribute the differences she observes between the common field-hands and the more expert artisans? What does this attribution imply about Southern slave society?

Spin-offs for writing

1. Write an essay dividing the workers of any business or industry with which you are familiar. Use whatever principle you think most reasonable to make your division.
2. Write an essay dividing your teachers by their methods of teaching.

VIRGINIA WOOLF

Virginia Woolf (1882–1941), English novelist and essayist, is considered one of the most significant novelists of this century. Educated at home, she married Leonard Woolf in 1912, and their house soon became the meeting place for a circle of intellectual friends who later became known as the Bloomsbury Group. Woolf is regarded not only as a master novelist but also as a brilliant essayist. Her novels include The Voyage Out *(1915),* Night and Day *(1919), and* Mrs. Dalloway *(1925). Her essays were published in such collections as* The Common Reader *(1925) and* The Death of the Moth and Other Essays *(1942). Following a series of mental breakdowns, Woolf drowned herself in 1941.*

Diarists are, as previously noted, not natural classifiers. Division and classification is far too intellectual a rhetorical pattern for most diarists, who are more intent on sketching the fleeting pulse of the day in their pages than on classifying the objects they see around them. This particular entry by Woolf is a rough classification, not systematic or formal, of the kinds of books she read during summers spent in the country. It was written when the author was only 21.

July 1, 1903

1 I foresee that one day I shall write a book of maxims—like a Frenchwoman. I often think of things that sound to me remarkably like what in English we call 'Thoughts'. But mine have this drawback—they are very obvious—a little false—& after all where will one sentence lead you? All the thoughts, maxims &c. &c. &c. which we see so laboriously printed & translated from one language to another as though no one literature could be selfish enough to keep these treasures for itself—all, I say, have only one moment of legitimate life. I can imagine that they sound well at a dinner table—go off with an enlivening pop, as of dexterous little crackers. But they won't blow up anything or do much in the way of illumination. I am sorry that I began to write this page—I forget now where it was to lead me, or why I chose this circuitous path.

2 Well, I say, we are getting ready for Salisbury[1]—Heaven knows what that has to do with maxims! The pleasantest part of going anywhere almost is the thought of it beforehand. I am laying in books. That is what I mean by getting ready. I collect books on all conceivable subjects & sew together paper books like this I write in—thick enough to hold all the maxims in the world. I delight to plan what I shall read this summer—I believe I begin putting aside books in my mind, to read in the summer, about October, Shakespeare for

---

[1] The author's family rented Netherhampton House, about 3 miles west of Salisbury, for their seven weeks' summer holiday.

instance & the Bible—Then the time really comes, & I actually take a bit of paper & write Homer, Dante, Burkes Speeches[2] &c. &c. upon it. I feel already as though I had read some way in these books & profited greatly. I get the volumes together—lay them out on my table, & I think exultingly that all that thickness of paper will be passed through my mind. I wish I felt sure it would leave any impression there, but that is a doubt I put far from me, before I begin. It is quite true that I read more during these 8 weeks in the country than in six London months perhaps. Learning seems natural to the country. I think I could go on browsing & munching steadily through all kinds of books as long as I lived at Salisbury say. The London atmosphere is too hot—too fretful. I read—then I lay down the book & say—what right have I, a woman to read all these things that men have done? They would laugh if they saw me. But I am going to forget all that in the country. This summer holiday has always—almost—been a very happy time—I imagine that it is the nearest kind of thing to happiness that any of us get—not being a very cheerful race.

We settle into a very free out of door life. We are very full of talk & family jokes. 3

Family life, of a very independent kind, such as suits us four[3] self willed young animals only really flourishes in the country. But this is not what I meant to write. 4

I read a great deal, I say: all the big books I have read I have read in the country. Besides this I write—with greater ease, at times, than ever in London. But the books are the things that I enjoy—on the whole—most. I feel sometimes for hours together as though the physical stuff of my brain were expanding, larger & larger, throbbing quicker & quicker with new blood—& there is no more delicious sensation than this. I read some history: it is suddenly all alive, branching forwards & backwards & connected with every kind of thing that seemed entirely remote before. I seem to feel Napoleon's influence on our quiet evening in the garden for instance—I think I see for a moment how our minds are all threaded together—how any live mind today is of the very same stuff as Plato's & Euripides. It is only a continuation & development of the same thing. It is this common mind that binds the whole world together; & all the world is mind. Then I read a poem say—& the same thing is repeated. I feel as though I had grasped the central meaning of the world, & all these 5

---

[2]Edmund Burke (1729–97), Irish-born statesman and political writer.
[3]Vanessa, Thoby, Adrian, and the author. Vanessa was her older sister, Thoby and Adrian her older and younger brothers.

poets & historians & philosophers were only following out paths branching from that centre in which I stand. And then—some speck of dust gets into my machine I suppose, & the whole thing goes wrong again. I open my Greek book next morning, & feel worlds away from it all—worse than that—the writing is entirely indifferent to me. Then I go out into the country—plodding along as fast as I can go—not much thinking of what I see, or of anything, but the movement in the free air soothes & makes me sensitive at once. As long as one can feel anything—life may lead one where it likes. In London undoubtedly there are too many people—all different—all claiming something or losing something—& they must all be reconciled to the scheme of the universe before you can let yourself think what that scheme is. Of course, people too, if one read them rightly, might illuminate as much as if not more than books. It is probably best therefore in the long run to live in the midst of men & women—to get the light strong in your eyes as it were—not reflected through cool green leaves as it is in books.

6 But I think of my great box of books all littered about in the wide country room I am to have—with entire joy now—Nine months surely is enough to spend with ones kind!

August, 1903

7 It must be confessed that that boast of reading in the country has not been altogether fulfilled. I was not really happy in my choice of books—& I have brought some which no compulsion will drive me to open while we are here. I have read though, one or two that pleased me—Roderick Hudson[4] to begin with—That is a book which reminds me of an infinitely fine pencil drawing; it lacks colour, it lacks outline, but it is full of exquisite drawing, as an artist would say—& the slightest stroke, you see, has its meaning. You dont get any of that spontaneous & unreflecting pleasure out of it that you do out of the great books, [ ] but you get a marvellous amount of reasoned enjoyment. It is the enjoyment of the intellectual palate tickled by something fine & rare—you need be a little of an epicure to see how very fine & rare it is. [ ] But this isn't an altogether satisfactory style of art.

8 Next came Hardy—Tess of the D'Urbervilles,[5] which is of a very different type. He has taken a grim subject and stuck to it till the bitter end. It is [ ] written with the purpose of showing how a girl may be as pure as snow, & do things that women may not do—how in spite of her purity, the judgment of a brutal world descends upon her,

---

[4] Henry James, *Roderick Hudson*, 1876.
[5] Thomas Hardy, *Tess of the D'Urbervilles*, 1891.

ruins her life, & sends her to the gallows. All this is set forth with an almost savage insistence; the writer is so sternly determined that we shall see the brutality of certain social conventions that he tends to spoil his novel as a novel. Tess & Clare & D'Urberville have to represent types, & rather lose their individual features. But it is an impressive bit of work—& many things in it are purely admirable— Joan Durbeyfield for instance—the Dairy maids at the Farm, & Hardy is one of the few writers who can bring the fresh air into their books. His country is solid. [ ]

I read here too, Boswells Hebrides[6]—which has fired me to read all I can find of Johnson. What is the receipt I wonder for making such a book as this? Boswell apparently sat up at night—fuddled with wine as likely as not—& wrote down word for word the sayings that had dropped from Johnson's lips during the day. Many people could do this & have done it—but without success. The result is invariably a succession of bald & disconnected sentiments which might have been dropped by an eagle or a mummy. Boswell somehow manages to cut out a whole chunk of the earth & air & stick it all alive under a glass case for us to come & see.

Speculations

1. How would you characterize Woolf's tone and mood at the beginning of this entry?
2. If this were a more systematic classification, how do you think it should begin and proceed?
3. With Woolf's eagerness for books as a contrast, to what can you attribute the so-called "decline of reading" that theorists allege is so widespread today?
4. What evidence can you find to suggest that perhaps Woolf intended her diaries to be private rather than eventually published?
5. What can you infer about the education of Virginia Woolf from her choice of books?

Spin-offs for writing

1. Write an essay that divides and classifies your own reading over a term or summer.
2. Write an essay, organized any way you wish, on the presumed decline of reading in our day.

[6]James Boswell, *Boswell's Journal of a Tour to the Hebrides with Samuel Johnson, 1773.*

JOHN HALEY

John Haley (1840–1921), Civil War veteran, served in the 17th Maine Volunteer Regiment from August 7, 1862 until June 10, 1865, the day the Regiment was mustered out of the Union army. He saw action in most of the major battles of the Civil War, recording his daily impressions in a journal that he hand published shortly before his death in 1921. The journal was rediscovered and commercially published in 1985.

Typically, Haley the diarist does not engage in the sort of methodical classifying found in the works of essayists. Here he sums up the types of chaplains his regiment had been burdened with over the course of the war, but his observations are only informally structured in a classifying pattern.

March 12th, 1865

1 Sunday. A full inspection this morning. In the afternoon Chaplain Lovering came up and held forth, this being the first time he has done so since Thanksgiving up in Fort Rice. Lovering has been at the hospital, caring for those who are sick and wounded in body and not troubling about their souls. Still, Lovering is the best we have been favored with.

2 Our first chaplain, Hersey, was a disgrace to the regiment, and more so to his profession. He had no sooner arrived in camp than he joined himself unto the "sons of Belial" and could soon guzzle more whiskey than the fattest of them. As he couldn't get enough to drink in legitimate ways, he resorted to illegitimate ones, even to stealing. He also stole a horse when we marched through Maryland in the fall of 1862. On the whole, he acted so much like Satan that his career with us soon ended.

3 Our next chaplain, Hayden, was taken from the ranks and, as he thought, elevated above *us*. He was a cheap buffoon and a very prince of gas-bags. His alleged preaching and attempts to expound the scriptures excited both pity and disgust. While he expounded the Word, the officers used to sit around and make game of him by telling cheap stories and uttering base plagiarisms of venerable jokes. If there can be a more pitiable or humiliating sight than that of one who occupies so high a calling prostituting the same in such a way, I don't know about it. The officers, seeing what a fool Hayden was and how susceptible to flattery, pasted it onto him so thick that it fell off in flakes, and he began to think himself greater even than Beecher.

4 The next victim was the present incompetent, Lovering, a person holding the Unitarian faith, which is altogether too high-toned for

the army as it is too noncommittal. (We have seen the extremes, for Hayden was a Baptist of the hard-shell persuasion.) I have never heard anything against the character of Lovering, and think him the best of the lot so far. This is damning the man with faint praise, but it is the best I can do. He is unpopular because he keeps aloof from both officers and men, so his preaching is mere emptiness.

Speculations

1. What does this brief excerpt tell you about Haley, the man?
2. Haley laboriously copied out his rough diary into three hand-printed books because he wanted to do "something for posterity." Based on this excerpt, how do you think this self-conscious act of transcription and publishing might have affected his diary?
3. What is the Unitarian faith? Why do you think Haley regarded it as "too high-toned for the army"?
4. What do you think Haley means when he characterizes Hayden as a "Baptist of the hard-shell persuasion"?
5. Which of the religious creeds mentioned by Haley do you think would more likely appeal to American troops today? Why?

Spin-offs for writing

1. Write an essay dividing or classifying the clerics of any religion with which you are familiar.
2. Write an essay on the consolations and comforts of religion.

Student Journal–Division and Classification

Karineh J. Arzumanian

August 10, 1992

It is the last week of my stay in Washington, D.C. As I look back on my summer interning for the Department of Justice, I realize that I have had the opportunity to meet a variety of people. With one hundred thirty University of California interns living under the same roof, I was bound to come across people with all sorts of ambitions.

Interns are, by nature, a different breed of people. They are hungry for work that nobody else will do in a prestigious establishment. Some do it for glory; others do it for fun. Some do it for both. All one hundred thirty of us travelled three thousand miles across the country, paying for every penny of our expenses to do work VOLUNTARILY. There was no monetary satisfaction for the kind of grunt work we did. However, I believe that, more or less, everybody enjoyed being an intern.

I have to be very careful to generalize hastily, but I think that the bulk of us could be distinguished into three specific categories according to why we came here and what we tried to get out of our internships. The first class of interns are the kind that came here with a specific career goal—to earn invaluable experience at a price. I consider myself part of this group. Interns like myself have realized the necessity of committing to such an experience if we want to get into the graduate school of our choice. If I want to go to the "right" law school, then I have to present something more captivating to that school than the average student background. By seeking a position with the Department of Justice I was grasping an opportunity outside the range of normal, average school experience. This is what most interns who have a specific goal in mind are seeking. After spending thousands of dollars in travel, rent, living expenses, and the loss of two-months' pay we have made an investment for the future that will hopefully pay off soon.

Then there are those interns who are on the opposite end of the spectrum. They have come here for a good time at the expense of their parents while they are far away from home, and the rent and utilities are paid for by Mom and Dad who send spending money every week. And the city is stocked with bars and nightclubs where they can spend it all. In return, they have promised to volunteer their time at an organization that is more than willing to have a warm body to do their grunt work for free. These interns are fully aware of the nature of their internships, and they fully understand the maxim that since they are not getting paid, they don't have to try as hard. This is a pretty good trade-off for a two-month's vacation on Mom and Dad in the nation's "happy hour" capitol. At five o'clock every bar in town is bursting with young men in suits and young women in heels shoving dollars at the bartenders. I have to admit, the nightlife is great in this town, seven days a week. So I can see how some opportunists could take advantage of it. I admit, I have just as much fun at these bars.

Then there are those interns who have a real thirst for political circles. This being an election year the city is swamped with eager interns on Capitol Hill dying to get a foot in the door. They work for the "right" people, they socialize with the "right" people, they even spend most of their leisure time with the "right" people, all in the hopes of making the kind of connection that will eventually lead to a career in politics. I was disappointed to find out that some interns who used to be good friends before coming here, stopped going out with our group because they had to go out with the "right" people instead. I guess ambition leads people down different paths in life. We each choose our own paths.

This internship has not only been a work experience, but it has also been a life experience. I have come to learn many peculiarities about the people around me as well as about myself. We are a small cross-section of America's college population come together for a single purpose.

6. DEFINITION.

January 13, 1901. "I have attained an egotism that is rare indeed." Definition of herself. Mary MacLane.

April 8, 1942. "It seems to me absurd to talk about "happy" and "unhappy" marriages. Real marriages are both at the same time." Her definition of marriage. Anne Morrow Lindbergh.

July, 1960 "No one ever told me that grief felt so like fear." Defining the terrible grief he felt upon the death of his beloved wife. C. S. Lewis.

October 30, 1973. "Which was more real, the waking or the dream?" An attempt to define reality. Peter Matthiesson.

CHAPTER SIX

Definition

Definition is the rhetorical pattern a writer uses when writing with the intent to clarify the meaning of a word or term. Often the definition will be an aside to some other rhetorical task the writer has set out to do. But sometimes the very act of defining an abstract or difficult word such as "love" will give overall rhetorical structure to an entire essay, which is then said to be developed by definition.

In its most formal practice, definition is not commonly found in the works of diarists. On the other hand, it is exactly the kind of pattern we would expect to find in prose written by lawyers and other professionals for whom the exact meanings of words and phrases are important. But even the lonely writer musing to a diary in a solitary place will occasionally wonder what a certain term means or what is entailed by a particular word and will scribble down an informal definition of it.

For example, C. S. Lewis begins his journal about the death of his wife with this sentence: "Nobody told me how much grief is like fear." He then proceeds to tell us the extent and nature of his grief. Anne Morrow Lindbergh, on the other hand, defines marriage as "the wonderful blending of silence and communication, sharing and solitariness, being bored and being stimulated, disputes and agreements, the everyday and the extraordinary, the near and the far—that wonderful blending that makes for the incredible richness, variety, harmoniousness, and toughness of marriage." Mary MacLane unabashedly defines herself as a genius, an oddity, a bundle of emotions, while Peter Matthiesson defines his subject the way we expect a diarist to—indirectly—sketching the meaning of "reality" as he jots down his thoughts about Zen.

For the essayist, definition is a workaday rhetorical pattern that often crops up in essays, even those with another primary intent. Its aim is always to answer the questions "What is it?" or "What does this mean?" When it is necessary to define a word or term, the classic procedure most essayists use—along with dictionary makers—is to place the word in the general category to which it belongs and then to specify how it differs from other words in that category. Here are some examples:

TERM	GENERAL CATEGORY	DIFFERENCE
monarch	ruler	of a principality
to lurk	to move	furtively
brutish	the state of being	stupidly cruel

Placed in full sentences, these definitions specify that a "monarch" is *a ruler* of a principality; "to lurk" means *to move* furtively; and that to be "brutish" is *to be* stupidly cruel. Amplified with examples and anecdotes, these kernel definitions will quickly make clear what each word means.

When penning definitions, writers typically make some predictable mistakes. Commonest of all errors is the circular definition such as one that defines an *instructor* as a "teacher." Since *instructor* is a synonym for *teacher*, this definition is merely circular and adds nothing to our understanding of the word's meaning. A better definition would begin by stating that an *instructor* is "a person whose job is to impart knowledge to others." With appropriate examples and details, we can then make clear what an instructor is and does. When defining, the writer should not only specify what a term is but should also say what it is not. Having elaborated on what an instructor does, you might then contrast the role of the instructor with that of a counsellor, showing how their basic functions differ.

Another common error to avoid is the definition that relies too heavily on the use of figurative language. For instance, to define *love* as the "rainbow of life" gives no clear answer to the question "What is love?" A better definition can be found in Webster's Dictionary, where *love* is defined as "a feeling of warm attachment, enthusiasm, or devotion." By itself, "rainbow of life" is just as mystifying as "love," and to the literal-minded reader, even more baffling.

When writing an essay defining a word or term, always remember that your purpose is to tell your reader exactly what that term or word means, what functions and roles are implied in it, and—if doing so adds clarity—what it is not. The ideal, of course, is to be crisp and clear in the writing, to specify exact meaning without being tedious. But with the definition essay, to overinform your readers is always kinder than to leave them stumped.

MARY MACLANE

Mary MacLane (1881–1929) became an overnight literary sensation with the publication of her diary when she turned twenty. Alternately labeled "obscene," "brilliant," and "mad," the diary sold 80,000 copies in its first month off the press. For the next seven years MacLane spent her time among the intellectuals and bohemians of Chicago, Boston, and New York. Born in Canada and brought up in Minnesota and Montana at the turn of the 19th century, she shows an uncanny intelligence and sense of independence for a girl of nineteen, the age at which she started her fascinating personal journal. Except for a motion picture titled Men I Loved, *in which she starred and for which she wrote the script, she never produced another work of significance after her famous diary. She firmly determined never to marry and claimed only one close friend, Fannie Corbin, a high school English teacher who played the role of her literary mentor. MacLane died in the manner she had feared most—poor and alone in a Chicago hotel room.*

Reading the journal, one cannot escape noticing two characteristics: honesty and resentment. The honesty can be attributed to the MacLane stubborn sense of survival; the resentment to Mary's anger that her sensual nature and deep desire for love were never even remotely fulfilled by her family or her ordinary life in Butte. Her father died when she was still a child, and the other members of her family apparently never understood her odd nature or responded to its needs. The remarkable aspect of the diary is the unstinting honesty with which the author faces her emotions. For instance, in an entry not recorded in the excerpt that follows, she openly admits to loving the sexual urge:

> "I love the sex-passion which is in this witching Body of me. I love to feel its portent grow and creep over me, like a climbing vine of tiny red roses, in the occasional dusks. It is no shame or shadow or sordidness: but beauty and sweetness and light."

Most young women of her day were not so acutely in touch with their own emotions and so able to express them—even in the privacy of a journal—as was this disturbed member of an American family of the northwestern plains.

Butte, Montana

January 13, 1901

1 I of womankind and of nineteen years, will now begin to set down as full and frank a Portrayal as I am able of myself, Mary MacLane, for whom the world contains not a parallel.

2 I am convinced of this, for I am odd.

3 I am distinctly original innately and in development.

I have in me a quite unusual intensity of life. 4

I can feel. 5

I have a marvelous capacity for misery and for happiness. 6

I am broad-minded. 7

I am a genius. 8

I am a philosopher of my own good peripatetic school. 9

I care neither for right nor for wrong—my conscience is nil. 10

My brain is a conglomeration of aggressive versatility. 11

I have reached a truly wonderful state of miserable morbid unhappiness. 12

I know myself, oh, very well. 13

I have attained an egotism that is rare indeed. 14

I have gone into the deep shadows. 15

All this constitutes oddity. I find, therefore, that I am quite, quite odd.... 16

I was born in 1881 at Winnepeg, in Canada. Whether Winnepeg will yet live to be proud of this fact is a matter for some conjecture and anxiety on my part. When I was four years old I was taken with my family to a little town in western Minnesota, where I lived a more or less vapid and lonely life until I was ten. We came then to Montana. 17

Whereat the aforesaid life was continued. 18

My father died when I was eight. 19

Apart from feeding and clothing me comfortably and sending me to school—which is no more than was due me—and transmitting to me the MacLane blood and character, I can not see that he ever gave me a single thought. 20

Certainly he did not love me, for he was quite incapable of loving any one but himself. And since nothing is of any moment in this world without the love of human beings for each other, it is a matter of supreme indifference to me whether my father, Jim MacLane of selfish memory, lived or died. 21

He is nothing to me. 22

23 There are with me still a mother, a sister, and two brothers.

24 They also are nothing to me.

25 They do not understand me any more than if I were some strange live curiosity, as which I dare say they regard me.

26 I am peculiarly of the MacLane blood, which is Highland Scotch. My sister and brothers inherit the traits of their mother's family, which is of Scotch Lowland descent. This alone makes no small degree of difference. Apart from this the MacLanes—these particular MacLanes—are just a little bit different from every family in Canada, and from every other that I've known. It contains and has contained fanatics of many minds—religious, social, whatnot, and I am a true MacLane.

27 There is absolutely no sympathy between my immediate family and me. There can never be. My mother, having been with me during the whole of my nineteen years, has an utterly distorted idea of my nature and its desires, if indeed she has any idea of it.

28 When I think of the exquisite love and sympathy which might be between a mother and daughter, I feel myself defrauded of a beautiful thing rightfully mine, in a world where for me such things are pitiably few.

29 It will always be so.

30 My sister and brothers are not interested in me and my analyses and philosophy, and my wants. Their own are strictly practical and material. The love and sympathy between human beings is to them, it seems, a thing only for people in books.

31 In short, they are Lowland Scotch, and I am a MacLane.

32 And so, as I've said, I carried my uninteresting existence into Montana. The existence became less uninteresting, however, as my versatile mind began to develop and grow and know the glittering things that are. But I realized as the years were passing that my own life was at best a vapid, negative thing.

33 A thousand treasures that I wanted were lacking.

34 I graduated from the high school with these things: very good Latin; good French and Greek; indifferent geometry and other mathematics; a broad conception of history and literature; peripatetic philosophy that I acquired without any aid from the high school; genius of a kind, that has always been with me; an empty heart that has taken on

a certain wooden quality; an excellent strong young woman's-body; a pitiably starved soul.

With this equipment I have gone my way through the last two years. But my life, though unsatisfying and warped, is no longer insipid. It is fraught with a poignant misery—the misery of nothingness.

I have no particular thing to occupy me. I write every day. Writing is a necessity—like eating. I do a little housework, and on the whole I am rather fond of it—some parts of it. I dislike dusting chairs, but I have no aversion to scrubbing floors. Indeed, I have gained much of my strength and gracefulness of body from scrubbing the kitchen floor—to say nothing of some fine points of philosophy. It brings a certain energy to one's body and to one's brain.

But mostly I take walks far away in the open country. Butte and its immediate vicinity present as ugly an outlook as one could wish to see. It is so ugly indeed that it is near the perfection of ugliness. And anything perfect, or nearly so, is not to be despised. I have reached some astonishing subtleties of conception as I have walked for miles over the sand and barrenness among the little hills and gulches. Their utter desolateness is an inspiration to the long, long thoughts and to the nameless wanting. Every day I walk over the sand and barrenness.

And so, then, my daily life seems an ordinary life enough, and possibly, to an ordinary person, a comfortable life.

That's as may be.

To me it is an empty, damned weariness.

I rise in the morning; eat three meals; and walk; and work a little, read a little, write; see some uninteresting people; go to bed.

Next day, I rise in the morning; eat three meals; and walk; and work a little, read a little, write; see some uninteresting people; go to bed.

Again I rise in the morning; eat three meals; and walk; and work a little, read a little, write; see some uninteresting people; go to bed.

Truly an exalted, soulful life!

What it does for me, how it affects me, I am now trying to portray....

To-day

It is the edge of a somber July night in this Butte-Montana. The sky is overcast. The nearer mountains are gray-melancholy. And at this point I meet Me face to face.

47 I am Mary MacLane: of no importance to the wide bright world and dearly and damnably important to Me.

48 Face to face I look at Me with some hatred, with despair and with great intentness.

49 I put Me in a crucible of my own making and set it in the flaming trivial Inferno of my mind. And I assay thus:

50 I am rare—I am in some ways exquisite.

51 I am pagan within and without.

52 I am vain and shallow and false.

53 I am a specialized being, deeply myself.

54 I am of woman-sex and most things that go with that, with some other *pointes*.

55 I am dynamic but devastated, laid waste in spirit.

56 I'm like a leopard and I'm like a poet and I'm like a religieuse and

57 I'm like an outlaw.

58 I have a potent weird sense of humor—a saving and a demoralizing grace.

59 I have brain, cerebration—not powerful but fine and of a remarkable quality.

60 I am scornful-tempered and I am brave.

61 I am slender in body and someway fragile and firm-fleshed and sweet.

62 I am oddly a fool and a strange complex liar and a spiritual vagabond.

63 I am strong, individual in my falseness: wavering, faint, fanciful in my truth.

64 I am eternally self-conscious but sincere in it.

65 I am ultra-modern, very old-fashioned: savagely incongruous.

66 I am young, but not very young.

67 I am wistful—I am infamous.

68 In brief, I am a human being.

I am presciently and analytically egotistic, with some arresting dead-feeling genius. 69

And were I not so tensely tiredly sane I would say that I am mad. So 70 assayed I begin to write this book of myself, to show to myself in detail the woman who is inside me. It may or it mayn't show also a type, a universal Eve-old woman. If it is so it is not my purport. I sing only the Ego and the individual....

Speculations

1. In this journal, the author attempts to define herself, to state who she is. Do you agree with her assessment of herself as "odd" (paragraph 1)? Support your answer with examples from the journal.

2. What does the author mean when she says (paragraph 26) "I am a true MacLane?"

3. In paragraph 28, the author makes the following statement: "When I think of the exquisite love and sympathy which might be between mother and daughter, I feel myself defrauded of a beautiful thing rightfully mine, in a world where for me such things are pitiably few." In view of the diary entries you have read, what advice would you give members of Mary MacLane's family in order to improve the relationship? What advice would you give Mary MacLane?

4. In what ways does the author reveal some youthful immaturity, and in what ways maturity beyond her years? Provide specific examples.

5. What aspects of this entry do you consider typical of journal writing?

Spin-offs for writing

1. Write an essay in which you write an objective description of Mary MacLane, taking into account her intellect, her character, and her daily activities.

2. Using Mary MacLane's journal as a model, write a definition of yourself—assessing your mind, your emotions, your relationships, and your lifestyle. Your essay must answer the question, "Who am I?"

ANNE MORROW LINDBERGH

Anne Morrow Lindbergh (b.1906) is best known in the United States for being the wife of Charles Lindbergh, American aviator and popular hero, who in 1927 made the first solo nonstop transatlantic flight in the Spirit of St. Louis, *now permanently on exhibit at the Smithsonian Institute. The famous couple was married in 1929, but their fame brought a major tragedy, the kidnapping and murder of their little boy, adding an element of sorrow to their storybook romance. The subsequent publicity drove them to England, where Anne found some solace in writing. An inveterate diarist, she observed tirelessly and scrupulously every detail connected with the many flights she took with her husband in his airplane. The results were published in two books,* North of the Orient *(1935) and* Listen! The Wind *(1938). When Charles Lindbergh's anti–World War II speeches earned him the reputation of being a Nazi collaborator, Anne Lindbergh publicly supported him, but at least one journal entry reveals that she suffered secret doubts about the wisdom of his stand. Among her published works are a book about her own philosophy of the role of women,* Gift from the Sea *(1955);* The Unicorn and Other Poems *(1956); a novel,* Dearly Beloved *(1962); and a volume of essays,* Earth Shine *(1969). Her journals and letters were published in* Bring Me a Unicorn *(1972),* Hour of Gold, Hour of Lead *(1973),* Locked Rooms and Open Doors *(1974), and* War Within and Without *(1980), from which the following entry was excerpted.*

This journal entry is surprising when it is juxtaposed with the popular view that the Lindbergh marriage consisted of those glamorous and romantic elements women desire. After all, Charles Lindbergh was handsome and acclaimed by most Americans as the perfect hero. Yet, Anne Morrow Lindbergh's journal reveals that her marriage, like all solid marriages, was woven of two fabrics—happiness and unhappiness. The entry that follows was written at the height of World War II, during a time when Charles Lindbergh, referred to as "C.," had to be away from home to work in Detroit as a consultant for Ford's bomber plant. This continual separation motivated Anne, the wife, to contemplate the real meaning of marriage.

April 8, 1942

1   C. is come and gone again. The three days when he was here were so full and intense it seems they weighed more than the days before or after. And it is difficult to record them. They had that kind of pre-marriage intensity and preciousness that is difficult to capture. With the dull pain of departure—like a threatening thunderstorm—over an afternoon. The light is more beautiful on an afternoon like that, the green more green, the earth more vivid. But it is an unreal light.

2   Those days are not marriage. They are being in love, but not the casual give and take, the wonderful blending of silence and communication, sharing and solitariness, being bored and being stimulated,

disputes and agreements, the everyday and the extraordinary, the near and the far—that wonderful blending that makes for the incredible richness, variety, harmoniousness, and toughness of marriage.

Marriage is tough, because it is woven of all these various elements, the weak and the strong. "In love-ness" is fragile for it is woven only with the gossamer threads of beauty. It seems to me absurd to talk about "happy" and "unhappy" marriages. Real marriages are both at the same time. But if they are *real* marriages they always have this incredible *richness* for which one is eternally joyful and grateful.

It is strange, I can conceive of "falling in love" over and over again. But "marriage," this richness of life itself, I cannot conceive of having again—or with anyone else. In this sense "marriage" seems to me indissoluble.

It would be impossible to cover all we talked of. I am sorry, as it seems to me so vital, and almost to carry the seeds of all our life and (real conversations do this) our problems. But I can only jot down to remember and think about.

Of C.'s job—working in Ford's new bomber plant. I get the sense that he feels it is new work and challenging and absorbing, and this is good.

But he is thinking of me, now his own war-future is temporarily settled. What will my war-future be? Shall I stay here with the children and write? Or shall I move to Detroit and join in his life there?

Another husband would assume that I would come with him to Detroit, but he sees my side too clearly. He wants so much for me. He wants me to live my own life. He wants this so passionately that it angers him when he sees anything frustrating it. Household duties, cooks that can't cook, nurses that won't leave me alone. Friends and family obligations which take my time. Depressions which rob me of confidence. I think almost all our quarrels arise from this passionate desire of his to see me freed to fulfill what there is in me.

And to all these questions what do I say? I cannot give quick pat answers. The questions go too deep. I know I am naturally passive—or at least seem to be—am inclined to let life come, rather than go to meet it. C. is impatient for the answers. I can only work them out slowly—with much quiet and solitude and patience and no sense of urgency. How explain to a man that when a woman is expecting a child, that is the only question she sees clearly and the only answer she can give. One cannot see beyond the child—or only with great difficulty. One can force oneself to give *intellectual* answers—but the only answer one really FEELS is the child.

10 My intellectual answers are—No, that I cannot sit in an ivory tower during the war, that I want to share his life and home, if I can. That my present war-work is having a child. That I believe my writing must always be "marginal" in its attack. But that life itself should be participating. That one can "participate" in giving and caring for children, in feeding and nourishing and loving one's husband and home.

11 If I can build the right kind of nourishing home for him in Detroit I want to **go** there. If he can get more from escaping here to sea and beauty and peace and quiet, then I want to stay here, with perhaps occasional trips to Detroit on my part.

12 When it comes to writing, the questions go too deep for intellectual answers. I must, as Rilke said, "live the questions first" and then perhaps someday come to the answers. But this spiritual pilgrimage I cannot yet explain to anyone and it is not yet clear. I feel very isolated, very alone in it. But I find parallels to it in the thoughtful and the sensitive, the artists, everywhere. It is in Auden's long poem[1] and again in *Flight to Arras*.

13 I have not yet written out the afternoon with Sue—four hours of conversation after weeks and weeks of thought alone. It was a lovely day. We touched so much, deeply and lightly.

14 Sue and I talked about Americans and Romanticism, of books and of the war, of mysticism and of nurses, of wrinkles, of gardening and of marriage, of cooks and of eternity, of children. It was very satisfying. The thread that has spread out the most in my mind is Americans and Romanticism.

15 Almost every young person is a Romantic Idealist. Certainly I was—and am still, in a sense. There has always been a "dream figure" in my life—not always a person, of course. But some people learn to accept life and that it is better than "the dream." At least I got married and have had children.

16 I told C., speaking of this conversation (we were talking of idealizing people), and C. said, "You can't meet your heroes if you feel that way about them." And I said, "Well, I don't know—I didn't lose my dream by marrying it!" He said, "That's the nicest thing you ever said to me."

---

[1] "New Year Letter" (January 1, 1940)

But I said it the wrong way round really. For I didn't marry my "dream." C. wasn't my "dream." I never idealized him before I met him. It wasn't the hero I loved in him. It was the man—the man who has never disappointed me. I had my "dreams," too, very different from C. That was what all the struggle was about, giving up my "dreams" for this flesh-and-blood man—whom I loved, God knew.

I sometimes feel it is the one thing I deserve credit for, the one thing I am intensely proud of, that I had the courage and the wisdom to give up my "dream" for real life, to realize that "life" was better than "dreams" and that C. was life.

Speculations

1. According to the author, what difference exists between a love affair and a marriage? Do you agree with her contrast? Why or why not?
2. Why is it that the author can conceive of falling in love repeatedly but of being married only once? What is your view of this subject?
3. Why is the question of whether the author should go to Detroit with her husband or remain where she is so difficult to answer? What elements are involved? What advice would you offer?
4. What do you suppose Charles Lindbergh meant when he said to his wife, "You can't meet your heroes if you feel that way about them"?
5. Define the term *hero*. Whom do you consider the greatest hero of your time? Why? List his/her characteristics.

Spin-offs for writing

1. Write your own definition of marriage, including what marriage is not and examples of the ingredients that make for a solid marriage.
2. Using your college or local library as a source, write a paper in which you pass judgment on Charles Lindbergh's stand during World War II. You will need to study the views of those supporting him as well as those opposing him; then draw your own conclusions.

C. S. LEWIS

Clive Stapel Lewis (1898–1963) was an English author admired equally for his literary insights and his clear exposition of Christian beliefs. His career was divided between being a fellow and tutor of English at Magdalen College, Oxford, and serving as professor of Medieval and Renaissance literature at Cambridge. He was a prolific writer. Among his most important works are The Allegory of Love *(1936), an analysis of romantic love during the Middle Ages;* The Screwtape Letters *(1942, rev. 1961), a satire on the theme of redemption;* A History of English Literature in the Sixteenth Century; *the* Chronicles of Narnia *(1950), an allegorical fantasy; many works of literary criticism;* Surprised by Joy *(1954), a highly personal exploration of religious experience; and* A Grief Observed *(1961) from which the following excerpt is taken.*

To the puzzlement of many close friends, C. S. Lewis, so respected as an advocate of Christianity, parted from his first wife and married an American divorcee, Joy Gresham, the "H." of his journal. Soon after their secret civil ceremony in 1956, Joy was diagnosed as having terminal cancer. A few months later, they were married in a religious hospital bedside ceremony and their marriage was made public. Although Joy's cancer seemed in remission for some months, she died on July 13, 1960, causing Lewis to be shattered by his bereavement. Soon after his wife's death, Lewis began to keep a journal to express his grief in order to live through it. What follows is one of the most gripping definitions of grief—recognizable in its concrete details by anyone who has suffered the loss of a deep love.

July, 1960

1. No one ever told me that grief felt so like fear. I am not afraid, but the sensation is like being afraid. The same fluttering in the stomach, the same restlessness, the yawning. I keep on swallowing.

2. At other times it feels like being mildly drunk, or concussed. There is a sort of invisible blanket between the world and me. I find it hard to take in what anyone says. Or perhaps, hard to want to take it in. It is so uninteresting. Yet I want the others to be about me. I dread the moments when the house is empty. If only they would talk to one another and not to me.

3. There are moments, most unexpectedly, when something inside me tries to assure me that I don't really mind so much, not so very much, after all. Love is not the whole of a man's life. I was happy before I ever met H. I've plenty of what are called 'resources'. People get over these things. Come, I shan't do so badly. One is ashamed to listen to this voice but it seems for a little to be making out a good case. Then comes a sudden jab of red-hot memory and all this 'commonsense' vanishes like an ant in the mouth of a furnace.

On the rebound one passes into tears and pathos. Maudlin tears. I almost prefer the moments of agony. These are at least clean and honest. But the bath of self-pity, the wallow, the loathsome sticky-sweet pleasure of indulging it—that disgusts me. And even while I'm doing it I know it leads me to misrepresent H. herself. Give that mood its head and in a few minutes I shall have substituted for the real woman a mere doll to be blubbering over. Thank God the memory of her is still too strong (will it always be too strong?) to let me get away with it.

For H. wasn't like that at all. Her mind was lithe and quick and muscular as a leopard. Passion, tenderness and pain were all equally unable to disarm it. It scented the first whiff of cant or slush; then sprang, and knocked you over before you knew what was happening. How many bubbles of mine she pricked! I soon learned not to talk rot to her unless I did it for the sheer pleasure—and there's another red-hot jab—of being exposed and laughed at. I was never less silly than as H's lover.

And no one ever told me about the laziness of grief. Except at my job—where the machine seems to run on much as usual—I loathe the slightest effort. Not only writing but even reading a letter is too much. Even shaving. What does it matter now whether my cheek is rough or smooth? They say an unhappy man wants distractions—something to take him out of himself. Only as a dog-tired man wants an extra blanket on a cold night; he'd rather lie there shivering than get up and find one. It's easy to see why the lonely become untidy; finally, dirty and disgusting.

Meanwhile, where is God? This is one of the most disquieting symptoms. When you are happy, so happy that you have no sense of needing Him, so happy that you are tempted to feel His claims upon you as an interruption, if you remember yourself and turn to Him with gratitude and praise, you will be—or so it feels—welcomed with open arms. But go to Him when your need is desperate, when all other help is vain, and what do you find? A door slammed in your face, and a sound of bolting and double bolting on the inside. After that, silence. You may as well turn away. The longer you wait, the more emphatic the silence will become. There are no lights in the windows. It might be an empty house. Was it ever inhabited? It seemed so once. And that seeming was as strong as this. What can this mean? Why is He so present a commander in our time of prosperity and so very absent a help in time of trouble?

I tried to put some of these thoughts to C. this afternoon. He reminded me that the same thing seems to have happened to Christ:

'Why hast thou forsaken me?' I know. Does that make it easier to understand?

9 Not that I am (I think) in much danger of ceasing to believe in God. The real danger is of coming to believe such dreadful things about him. The conclusion I dread is not 'So there's no God after all,' but 'So this is what God's really like. Deceive yourself no longer.'

10 Our elders submitted and said 'Thy will be done.' How often had bitter resentment been stifled through sheer terror and an act of love—yes, in every sense, an act—put on to hide the operation?

11 Of course it's easy enough to say that God seems absent at our greatest need because He *is* absent—non-existent. But then why does He seem so present when, to put it quite frankly, we don't ask for Him?

12 One thing, however, marriage has done for me. I can never again believe that religion is manufactured out of our unconscious, starved desires and is a substitute for sex. For those few years H. and I feasted on love; every mode of it—solemn and merry, romantic and realistic, sometimes as dramatic as a thunderstorm, sometimes as comfortable and unemphatic as putting on your soft slippers. No cranny of heart or body remained unsatisfied. If God were a substitute for love we ought to have lost all interest in Him. Who'd bother about substitutes when he has the thing itself? But that isn't what happens. We both knew we wanted something besides one another—quite a different kind of something, a quite different kind of want. You might as well say that when lovers have one another they will never want to read, or eat—or breathe.

13 After the death of a friend, years ago, I had for some time a most vivid feeling of certainty about his continued life; even his enhanced life. I have begged to be given even one hundredth part of the same assurance about H. There is no answer. Only the locked door, the iron curtain, the vacuum, absolute zero. 'Them as asks don't get.' I was a fool to ask. For now, even if that assurance came I should distrust it. I should think it a self-hypnosis induced by my own prayers.

14 At any rate I must keep clear of the spiritualists. I promised H. I would. She knew something of those circles.

15 Keeping promises to the dead, or to anyone else, is very well. But I begin to see that 'respect for the wishes of the dead' is a trap. Yesterday I stopped myself only in time from saying about some trifle 'H. wouldn't have liked that.' This is unfair to the others. I should soon be using 'what H. would have liked' as an instrument

of domestic tyranny; with her supposed likings becoming a thinner and thinner disguise for my own.

I cannot talk to the children about her. The moment I try, there appears on their faces neither grief, nor love, nor fear, nor pity, but the most fatal of all non-conductors, embarrassment. They look as if I were committing an indecency. They are longing for me to stop. I felt just the same after my own mother's death when my father mentioned her. I can't blame them. It's the way boys are.

I sometimes think that shame, mere awkward, senseless shame, does as much towards preventing good acts and straightforward happiness as any of our vices can do. And not only in boyhood.

Or are the boys right? What would H. herself think of this terrible little notebook to which I come back and back? Are these jottings morbid? I once read the sentence 'I lay awake all night with toothache, thinking about toothache and about lying awake.' That's true to life. Part of every misery is, so to speak, the misery's shadow or reflection: the fact that you don't merely suffer but have to keep on thinking about the fact that you suffer. I not only live each endless day in grief, but live each day thinking about living each day in grief. Do these notes merely aggravate that side of it? Merely confirm the monotonous, tread-mill march of the mind round one subject? But what am I to do? I must have some drug, and reading isn't a strong enough drug now. By writing it all down (all?—no: one thought in a hundred) I believe I get a little outside it. That's how I'd defend it to H. But ten to one she'd see a hole in the defence.

It isn't only the boys either. An odd by-product of my loss is that I'm aware of being an embarrassment to everyone I meet. At work, at the club, in the street, I see people, as they approach me, trying to make up their minds whether they'll 'say something about it' or not. I hate it if they do, and if they don't. Some funk it altogether. R. has been avoiding me for a week. I like best the well brought-up young men, almost boys, who walk up to me as if I were a dentist, turn very red, get it over, and then edge away to the bar as quickly as they decently can. Perhaps the bereaved ought to be isolated in special settlements like lepers.

To some I'm worse than an embarrassment. I am a death's head. Whenever I meet a happily married pair I can feel them both thinking. 'One or other of us must some day be as he is now.'

At first I was very afraid of going to places where H. and I had been happy—our favourite pub, our favourite wood. But I decided to do it at once—like sending a pilot up again as soon as possible after he's had a crash. Unexpectedly, it makes no difference. Her absence is no more emphatic in those places than anywhere else. It's not local at all. I suppose that if one were forbidden all salt one wouldn't notice it much more in any one food than in another. Eating in general would be different, every day, at every meal. It is like that. The act of living is different all through. Her absence is like the sky, spread over everything.

22 But no, that is not quite accurate. There is one place where her absence comes locally home to me, and it is a place I can't avoid. I mean my own body. It had such a different importance while it was the body of H's lover. Now it's like an empty house. But don't let me deceive myself. This body would become important to me again, and pretty quickly, if I thought there was anything wrong with it.

Cancer, and cancer, and cancer. My mother, my father, my wife. I wonder who is next in the queue.

23 Yet H. herself, dying of it, and well knowing the fact, said that she had lost a great deal of her old horror at it. When the reality came, the name and the idea were in some degree disarmed. And up to a point I very nearly understood. This is important. One never meets just Cancer, or War, or Unhappiness (or Happiness). One only meets each hour or moment that comes. All manner of ups and downs. Many bad spots in our best times, many good ones in our worst. One never gets the total impact of what we call 'the thing itself'. But we call it wrongly. The thing itself is simply all these ups and downs: the rest is a name or an idea.

24 It is incredible how much happiness, even how much gaiety, we sometimes had together after all hope was gone. How long, how tranquilly, how nourishingly, we talked together that last night!

25 And yet, not quite together. There's a limit to the 'one flesh'. You can't really share someone else's weakness, or fear or pain. What you feel may be bad. It might conceivably be as bad as what the other felt, though I should distrust anyone who claimed that it was. But it would still be quite different. When I speak of fear, I mean the merely animal fear, the recoil of the organism from its destruction; the smothery feeling; the sense of being a rat in a trap. It can't be transferred. The mind can sympathize; the body, less. In one way the bodies of lovers can do it least. All their love passages have trained them to have, not identical, but complementary, correlative, even opposite, feelings about one another.

26 We both knew this. I had my miseries, not hers; she had hers, not mine. The end of hers would be the coming-of-age of mine. We were

setting out on different roads. This cold truth, this terrible traffic-regulation ('You, Madam, to the right—you, Sir, to the left') is just the beginning of the separation which is death itself.

And this separation, I suppose, waits for all. I have been thinking of H. and myself as peculiarly unfortunate in being torn apart. But presumably all lovers are. She once said to me, 'Even if we both died at exactly the same moment, as we lie here side by side, it would be just as much a separation as the one you're so afraid of.' Of course she didn't *know*, any more than I do. But she was near death; near enough to make a good shot. She used to quote 'Alone into the Alone.' She said it felt like that. And how immensely improbable that it should be otherwise! Time and space and body were the very things that brought us together; the telephone wires by which we communicated. Cut one off, or cut both off simultaneously. Either way, mustn't the conversation stop?

Unless you assume that some other means of communication—utterly different, yet doing the same work, would be immediately substituted. But then, what conceivable point could there be in severing the old ones? Is God a clown who whips away your bowl of soup one moment in order, next moment, to replace it with another bowl of the same soup? Even nature isn't such a clown as that. She never plays exactly the same tune twice.

It is hard to have patience with people who say 'There is no death' or 'Death doesn't matter'. There is death. And whatever is matters. And whatever happens has consequences, and it and they are irrevocable and irreversible. You might as well say that birth doesn't matter. I look up at the night sky. Is anything more certain than that in all those vast times and spaces, if I were allowed to search them, I should nowhere find her face, her voice, her touch? She died. She is dead. Is the word so difficult to learn?

Speculations

1. In his attempt to define grief, the author compares grief to several other feelings. What are they and what is the purpose served by these comparisons? What comparison of your own might you add to the list?
2. How does the author's grief affect his relationship with God? Do you find his reaction reasonable or would you suggest a more appropriate response? Explain your answer.
3. What hope can you offer a person who has suffered the agonizing loss of a loved one? Describe the process of healing as you understand it.

4. In paragraph 18, the author asks the question, "Are these jottings morbid?" Answer his question and offer reasons for your position.

5. What did H. mean when she said "Alone into the Alone"? (See paragraph 27.) How does this phrase affect your view of death?

Spin-offs for writing

1. Taking a different approach from Lewis's journal, write a definition of joy, based on some jubilant or ecstatic experience in your life.

2. Write an essay exploring the effect on you of some immense loss you have suffered—a pet, a precious belonging, or a person dear to you. The loss does not necessarily have to involve death. Write as if confiding in your journal.

PETER MATTHIESSEN

Peter Matthiessen (b. 1927) is an American novelist, naturalist, journalist, and explorer. Born in New York City, he has lead a life of various adventures, from diving and fishing commercially to being captain of a charterboat. His participation in the worldwide search for the great white shark culminated in his book Blue Meridian *(1971) and in the film* Blue Water, White Death. *As a naturalist explorer, he undertook expeditions to remote places like the Amazon jungles, the Canadian Northwest Territories, the Sudan, New Guinea, and Nepal. Matthiessen found his spiritual roots in Zen Buddhism, about which he writes with lyrical beauty. Among his best-known works are six novels:* Race Rock *(1955),* Partisans *(1956),* Raditzer *(1962),* At Play in the Fields of the Lord *(1965),* Far Tortuga *(1989), and* Killing Mister Watson *(1990). His nonfiction includes* The Tree Where Man Was Born *(1972),* The Snow Leopard *(1979),* In the Spirit of Crazy Horse *(1984), and* Nine-Headed Dragon River *(1986), from which the following excerpt is taken.*

In his attempt to experience the whole of existence and find his spiritual roots, the author made a pilgrimage to Nepal, where he spent time in a religious center and climbed parts of the Himalayas. There, in the freezing heights of the pure mountain air, he was able to experience moments of freedom from intellectual and physical bondage that led to a feeling of wondrous harmony with the universe. What he learned convinced him that the ancient Hindus were right in believing that we in the West do not see the universe as it really is. We see only maya, an illusion—the collective "magic show" that gives common ground to our own kind. What we need is to widen our perceptions and stop elevating divinity above the common miracles of every day. In other words, divinity resides in a snowflake as much as in theology.

September, 1973

The weathers change, the clouds blow in mists across the mountain pond. I pick blueberries in the waiting meadow. At twilight, a wild wind spins the lake, and rain and thunder come as sesshin[1] begins.

Each morning after work period, I slip the canoe from the bank and drift along the lake. In the stillness of the trees, red autumn leaves of the swamp maple float on a black mirror. After three days of sesshin, my eye is opening, and all things in nature stand forth in four dimensions, clear and ringing. On the dark bottom of the lake, a pale newt, belly up, lies side by side with a pale leaf, all color gone.

Now a beaver, like a spirit of the lake, splits the surface with its coarse-haired head as water pours from the blunt snout—*slap!* All is

---

[1] **sesshin**—a Zen meditation retreat, usually lasting from three to seven days.

still again. Where the spirit vanished, a circle is spreading out across the world.

4 Days pass, and the beavers draw near. Are they drawn to a stillness in the canoe that was not there before? The ringing and luminosity of the first days of sesshin seem to have vanished, as if an intensity had gone, or is it that I grow accustomed to fresh ways of seeing and take it now for ordinary perception? Before sesshin, the mountain is the mountain; then the mountain seems extraordinary, more than the mountain; today the extraordinary and the ordinary are not different, and the mountain is the mountain once again.

5 In the night window of the zendo, a full moon appears among the clouds that cross the eastern ridge. Now the moon goes. A white moth comes out of the night. The white moth goes.

6 In zazen,[2] one is one's present self, what one was, and what one will be, all at once. I have a glimpse of the Mahayana teaching known as nondiscrimination, perceiving that this black cushion, candle flame, cough, belch, Buddha, incense smell, wood pattern on the floor, pine branch, sharp pain—and also awareness of these phenomena, of all phenomena—are all of equal significance, equal value. And the next day, what resolves in my mind like a soft soap bubble swelling and soundlessly bursting is that "my" mind and all minds everywhere are manifestations of One Mind, Universal Mind, like myriad birds flying as one in a swift flock, like so many minute coral animals, in the sway of tides on a long reef, not the same and yet not different, feeding as one great creature with a single soul.

7 The stars grow colder, and each morning a mist shrouds the lake until Indian summer sun burns it away. At the north end a feeding beaver lifts its forepaws from the water, calmly observing, and the silent hickories are observing, too, in red-gold light. The canoe slips ashore on the far bank, and I swim out naked into the shining mist.

8 A heavy rain at night, clear blue at dawn. Sesshin passes. In greatest contentment, ease, simplicity, I wash lettuce by the waterfall.

9 Before going away, I sit by the lake with Eido-roshi, enjoying the fair white clouds that cross the mountains. "Who is it that is looking at the clouds?" he says. "Do you know who?" I shake my head. Laughing, we lie back in the warm grass and watch these clouds that have never been anywhere else in all the world.

---

[2] **zazen**—Sitting meditation

October 20, 1973

To the north, high on the mountain's face, has come in view the village called Rohagaon. The track passes along beneath wild walnut trees. The last leaves are yellowed and stiff on the gaunt branches, and the nuts are fallen; the dry scratch and whisper of sere leaves stir a vague melancholy of some other autumn, half remembered. The wildwood brings on mild nostalgia, not for home or place but for lost innocence—the paradise lost that, as Proust said, is the only paradise. Childhood is full of mystery and promise, and perhaps the life fear comes when all the mysteries are laid open, when what we thought we wanted is attained. It is just at the moment of seeming fulfillment that we sense irrevocable betrayal, like a great wave rising silently behind us, and know most poignantly what Milarepa meant: "All worldly pursuits have but one unavoidable and inevitable end, which is sorrow: acquisitions end in dispersion; buildings, in destruction; meetings, in separation; births, in death." Confronted by the uncouth specter of old age, disease, and death, we are thrown back upon the present, on this moment, here, right now, for that is all there is. And surely this is the paradise of children, that they are at rest in the present, like frogs or rabbits.

October 21, 1973

The trail meets the Suli Gad high up the valley, in grottoes of bronze-lichened boulders and a shady riverside of pine and walnut and warm banks of fern. Where morning sun lights the red leaves and dark, still conifers, the river sparkles in the forest shadow; turquoise and white, it thunders past spray-shined boulders, foaming pools, in a long rocky chute of broken rapids. In the cold breath of the torrent, the dry air is softened by mist; under last night's stars this water trickled through the snows. At the head of the waterfall, downstream, its sparkle leaps into the air, leaps at the sun, and sun rays are tumbled in the waves that dance against the snows of distant mountains.

Upstream, in the inner canyon, dark silences are deepened by the roar of stones. Something is listening, and I listen, too: who is it that intrudes here? Who is breathing? I pick a fern to see its spores, cast it away, and am filled in that instant with misgiving: the great sins, so the Sherpas say, are to pick wildflowers and to threaten children. My voice murmurs its regret, a strange sound that deepens the intrusion. I look about me—who is it that spoke? And who is listening? Who is this ever-present "I" that is not me?

The voice of a solitary bird asks the same question.

14 Here in the secrets of the mountains, in the river roar, I touch my skin to see if I am real; I say my name aloud and do not answer.

15 By a dark wall of rock, over a rivulet, a black-and-gold dragonfly zips and glistens; a walnut falls on a mat of yellow leaves. Seen through the mist, a water spirit in monumental pale gray stone is molded smooth by its mantle of white water, and higher, a ribbon waterfall, descending a cliff face from the east, strikes the wind sweeping upriver and turns to mist before striking the earth. The mist drifts upward to the rim, forming a halo in the guarding pines.

October 30, 1973

16 At daybreak, when I peek out at the still universe, ice fills my nostrils; I crouch back in my sleeping bag, cover my head.

17 At dawn the camp is visited by ravens. Then a cold sun rises to the rim of the white world, bringing light wind.

18 This morning we shall carry three more loads up to Kang La, and then three more. That will make nine; there are fourteen altogether. To avoid the bitter cold, we wait until the sun touches the slopes, then climb hard to take advantage of the snow crust, reaching the pass in an hour and a half. In the snowbound valleys to the north, still in night shadow, there is no sign of our companions, no sign of any life at all.

19 The sherpas start down immediately; they, too, seem oppressed by so much emptiness. Left alone, I am overtaken by that northern void—no wind, no cloud, no track, no bird, only the crystal crescents between peaks, the ringing monuments of rock that, freed from the talons of ice and snow, thrust an implacable *being* into the blue. In the early light, the rock shadows on the snow are sharp; in the tension between light and dark is the power of the universe. This stillness to which all returns is profound reality, and concepts such as soul and sanity have no more meaning here than gusts of snow; my transience, my insignificance are exalting, terrifying. Snow mountains, more than sea or sky, serve as a mirror to one's own true being, utterly still, utterly clear, a void, an emptiness without life or sound that carries in itself all life, all sound. Yet as long as I remain an "I" who is conscious of the void and stands apart from it, there will remain a snow mist on the mirror.

20 A silhouette crosses the white wastes below, a black coil dangling from its hand. It is Dawa Sherpa carrying tump line[1] and headband,

---

[1] **tump line**—a strap or sling attached to the chest or forehead and used to support a load borne on the bearer's back

yet in this light a something moves that is much more than Dawa. The sun is roaring, it fills to bursting each crystal of snow. I flush with feeling, moved beyond my comprehension, and once again, the warm tears freeze upon my face. These rocks and mountains, all this matter, the snow itself, the air—the earth is ringing. All is moving, full of power, full of light.

In a dream I am walking joyfully up the mountain. Something breaks and falls away, and all is light. Nothing has changed, yet all is amazing, luminescent, free. Released at last, I rise into the sky. . . . This dream comes often. Sometimes I run, then lift up like a kite, high above earth, and always I sail transcendent for a time before awaking. I *choose* to awake, for fear of falling, yet such dreams tell me that I am a part of things, if only I would let go, and keep on going. 21

In recent dreams, I have twice seen light so brilliant, so intense, that it "woke me up," but the light did not continue into wakefulness. Which was more real, the waking or the dream? 22

Speculations

1. Does Matthiessen succeed in defining reality? If yes, what is it? If not, why not? Explain your answer.

2. The author's journal covers time from early September to late October—almost two months. What indicates the passing of time? What dominant impression is constant in the author's description?

3. What point is the author making in paragraph 10? Summarize it in one sentence. Do you agree with the author? Explain your answer.

4. How does the author make his descriptions of nature come to life? Provide examples of what you mean.

5. How does Matthiessen's definition differ from that of Mary MacLane (see pp. 166–181)? Take special notice of attitude and purpose.

Spin-offs for writing

1. Define reality in terms of a personal experience that for you reaches to the core of existence and reveals its essential meaning.

2. Write an essay describing some aspect of nature that has overwhelmed you with either awe, fear, or love. Use vivid details (and even figurative language if it comes naturally to you).

Student Journal—Definition

Jo. J. Oli

October 3, 1992

I am sitting in my room trying to forget the past year. All I can think about is the way he held me when we were together, and how his arms felt around my waist . . . the smell of Tide in his collar. Now, after a year of the most beautiful times I ever had, I have to put him behind me and forget what could have been. Our love affair was painfully one-sided. I gave him all I had, and he gave me his best, a best that was never as good as it should have been or could have been. What do I mean when I say his "best"? I mean a real effort to make a relationship work. People often go through life without realizing what it takes to make a relationship work. I think I now understand the full meaning of the term *love relationship*. My mind wanders to the time we first met. . . .

Monster and I (that's what I used to call him affectionately) met September 9, 1991. That day seemed like it would never end. I fell in love with him at first sight. I couldn't sleep all night; I only thought of him. We started dating shortly after that. We saw each other occasionally, but on a limited basis. I admit, he warned me from the start that he did not want a girlfriend at this point in his life. He told me that he could not give any part of himself to a serious relationship because circumstances in his life did not allow him to make a commitment. He told me so many things in his life were so wrong that he could not devote any part of himself to me. Yet, I decided to challenge him. I did not believe that he could be so shut out to love. I thought that if I gave him more love than anyone could ever ask for, he would come around. After all, I was head-over-heels crazy about him. All I could think about every morning I awoke was my Monster. All I could think about every night I didn't see him was my Monster.

Things just weren't the same on his end. The closer I tried to get to him, the more he warned me to keep my distance. Every time I tried to show him a little more love, he clutched up and froze me out of his heart. I did more for this man than I ever did for any friend I've had. When he ended up on a hospital bed after a mix-up with some medication he took, I was the only one who tracked him down and found him in the emergency room. In the midst of finals week I spent the weekend with him to make sure he was okay. I helped him recover and showed him that my love was endless. My love is still endless, except for the barriers he built.

My Monster had a fear of closeness. He never allowed anyone near his heart long enough to know its tenderness. He was afraid of getting hurt. When I showed him that I could love him more than life itself without hurting him, he did not understand. He pushed me away and said time after time that he just was not ready. I saw the love of my life slip away from me slowly, but there was absolutely nothing I could do. The man that could drive up my pulse rate with a single kiss was closing up like a Venus fly trap. "I can't commit to anyone," he said. "I love you," he said, but he could not tolerate a close emotional relationship. At first I thought I simply didn't appeal to him enough, but he assured me that that was not the case. He insisted that if he could ever get involved with anyone, it would be me, but his fears just would not let him.

The more he pulled away, the more I moved toward him. I piled acts of kindness on him. I swore undying love and loyalty. But none of this helped. He was too blind to appreciate something he did not expect. I struggled for a year to keep our relationship working. By the end of the year, all I could think was that I wanted to spend the rest of my life with Monster. But, he couldn't even see a month ahead in his future. The only person that had any room at all in his future was himself.

Slowly, I found myself resenting him for not trying hard enough. I used to think that if he would give a little effort to accept my love, he would be able to overcome his fear of intimacy. I tried as hard as I could. I will never look back and regret not having tried hard enough because I know what I did was more than anyone had ever done or would ever do for him. But I finally came to a point of acceptance. I told myself that I could not go on giving my everything to a man who could not even give back half. There was no balance in our emotional bond. I told myself I would throw myself off a cliff for him, but I could not allow those feelings of commitment to grow because I had no cooperation.

Tonight, I acknowledge that it takes more than one person to make a love affair. I had done the loving, but Monster had been a mere participant. I now accept the fact that even though he was probably the ultimate love of my life, and even though there will never be anyone I will love as much as him, I must let go. We never reached the kind of intimacy necessary for two people to bond with each other. Yes, we had a mutual caring and affection, but he would not allow us to get any further than that. I realize now that a real love relationship means mutual desire, willingness, and caring. Without these elements the most precious gem is but a pebble.

I didn't sleep a wink the day I met Monster. I don't think I will sleep a wink tonight . . . we broke up today.

7.
COMPARISON / CONTRAST.

May 20, 1851. "There is, no doubt, a perfect analogy between the life of a human being and that of the vegetable. . . ." A comparison between human and vegetables. Henry David Thoreau.

October 25, 1914. "While waiting outside the Albert Hall, an extraordinarily weird contrast thrust itself before me. . . ." A contrast between two women seen on the streets of London. W. N. P. Barbellion.

May 10, 1925. "I lunched today, here in Prescott, at the Palace restaurant which in bygone days, twenty years ago, was the Palace Saloon. . . ." A contrast between a famous saloon, then and now. Henry Fountain Ashurst.

March 7, 1944. "If I think now of my life in 1942, it all seems so unreal." A comparison/contrast between the life she led when she was free and her life after going into hiding from the Nazis. Anne Frank.

CHAPTER 7

Comparison / Contrast

Comparison/contrast is a method of thinking as commonly found in the streets as in essays. To compare means to point out similarities; to contrast means to specify differences. Though they are often introspective, diary writers—like the rest of us—are just as likely to dabble in comparisons or contrasts of ideas, people, or objects they encounter. For example, Henry Thoreau's careful observation of nature inspires the comparison in his diary between plants and people. Another diarist in this chapter, W. N. P. Barbellion, contrasts two encounters he had in London; the first with a beautiful young mother he met on his way to Albert Hall; the next with "a wretched soul of some thirty summers" playing the violin and singing in a hideous voice as she begged alms from concertgoers. Henry Fountain Ashurst, a former United States senator, contrasts a saloon in Prescott, Arizona, as it was in his youth with the way it is now. And Anne Frank, scribbling in her annex hideout from the Nazis in Amsterdam, compares her life when she was free with her life now that she is in hiding.

The comparison/contrast essay often attempts to specify in a systematic way the likenesses or differences that a writer perceives between two items. And it is always based on a criterion that is either stated or implied. For example, if you declare that Jane is more statuesque than Mary, physical difference is the implied basis of your contrast. If you state that George is a despicable fraud whereas Malcolm is the soul of honesty, you are contrasting on the implied basis of morality or ethics. A comparison of Stalin and Hitler might uncover similarities in their desire for control, cruelty to people, and belief in a messianic mission. A contrast between the novel and film versions of *Gone with the Wind* might choose to focus on differences in dramatic impact, character development, and historical accuracy. In any event, you cannot simply contrast or compare without using some common measures against which you match up your subjects. A solid beginning to any comparison/contrast essay, then, is to carefully select some significant criteria against which you can compare or contrast your subjects.

One nearly foolproof method of doing this is to head up two columns with the subjects being compared/contrasted. Next, write down in an extreme left-hand column the criteria you will use. After that, simply fill in the blanks and cover each point in your essay. Here is how your diagram might look for an essay comparing/contrasting the Republican and Democratic party platforms:

REPUBLICANS   DEMOCRATS

Abortion
Fiscal philosophy
Foreign policy

Fill in the stated position of each party on the issue listed and you will have a chart that sketches, in broad outlines, the differences between the two platforms on your selected criteria. Add examples and you have basically outlined your complete essay.

There are other practical strategies for writing comparisons or contrasts. First, be sure to deal with both sides of the question. Don't dwell at length on one side and then expect your reader to fill in the other side. For example:

> *A naive person is not the same as an innocent person. A naive person is stupidly childish and can easily be duped.*

This contrast is skimpy and woefully incomplete. Here is a better version:

> *A naive person is not the same as an innocent person. A naive person is stupidly childish and can easily be duped whereas an innocent person is one who is free from corruption and untainted by evil. One characteristic is related to intelligence, the other to experience.*

Second, use transitions that clarify your comparison or contrast. Here is a list of some of the most commonly used transitions:

FOR COMPARING	**FOR CONTRASTING**
similarly	whereas
likewise	in contrast to
a likeness between	on the other hand
also	instead of
much in common	however

Comparison/contrasts are usually organized in one of two basic patterns: within paragraphs (alternating method) or between paragraphs (block method). The first method is used by Thoreau to draw a comparison between plant and human life; the second, by W. N. P. Barbellion to contrast the two women he observed in London. Neither pattern is better than the other, although for lengthy and complex comparison/contrasts you will probably find it easier to organize your ideas in successive paragraphs. However, using one pattern over another is mainly a matter of writer preference.

HENRY DAVID THOREAU

Henry David Thoreau (1817–1872) was an American writer and naturalist. Born in Concord, Massachusetts—a citizen of Boston and its environs all of his life—he has come to represent the classic New England character that has greatly influenced thinking in the United States. Thoreau was a tireless champion of individual freedom and of the philosophy that greed for material goods brings no happiness. While studying at Harvard, he become an admirer of Ralph Waldo Emerson, who became his mentor and advisor. In 1845, Thoreau moved to an isolated area near Walden Pond, where he built himself a cabin and lived alone for more than two years. His goal was to have only those material goods absolutely necessary to life and in that way he could judge whether life at its core was good or bad. His experience was meticulously recorded in a journal, later on titled Walden. *For a while he worked in his father's pencil factory, did some surveying, and taught grammar school. But most of his time was spent observing nature and writing the results of his observations in his journals. In 1849 Thoreau spent a night in jail for refusing to pay a poll tax that supported the Mexican War, to which he was a conscientious objector because he felt that it represented an extension of slavery. The result of this experience was "Civil Disobedience," an essay still influential today among political dissidents who see civil disobedience as a means of protesting a government's unfair laws. Among Thoreau's other published works are* A Week on the Concord and Merrimack Rivers *(1849),* Excursions *(1863),* The Maine Woods *(1864),* Cape Cod *(1865), and* A Yankee in Canada *(1866).*

Thoreau spent long hours observing plants and trees, learning their Latin as well as English names, and describing them with detail in his journal. Often he used his knowledge for practical purposes, spelling out in writing which tree woods were the most flexible or most durable for building houses or furniture. It is said that he had such respect for his natural environment and held such an intimate relationship with it, that he would apologize to a tree if he had neglected it. But Thoreau is at his best when he applies his knowledge of botany to philosophical speculation, as he does in the following journal entry, where he draws an extended analogy between plants and human beings.

1 **May 20. Tuesday.** There is, no doubt, a perfect analogy between the life of the human being and that of the vegetable, both of the body and the mind. The botanist Gray says:—

2 "The organs of plants are of two sorts:—1. Those of *Vegetation*, which are concerned in growth,—by which the plant takes in the aërial and earthy matters on which it lives, and elaborates them into the materials of its own organized substance; 2. Those of *Fructification* or *Reproduction*, which are concerned with the propagation of the species."

So is it with the human being. I am concerned first to come to my *Growth*, intellectually and morally (and physically, of course, as a means to this, for the body is the symbol of the soul), and then to bear my *Fruit*, do my *Work*, *propagate* my kind, not only physically but *morally*, not only in body but in mind.

"The organs of vegetation are the *Root*, *Stem*, and *Leaves*. The *Stem* is the axis and original basis of the plant."

"The first point of the stem preëxists in the embryo (*i.e.*, in the rudimentary plantlet contained within the seed): it is here called the radicle." Such is the rudiment of mind, already partially developed, more than a bud, but pale, having never been exposed to the light, and slumbering coiled up, packed away in the seed, unfolded [*sic*].

Consider the still pale, rudimentary, infantine, radicle-like thoughts of some students, which who knows what they might expand to, if they should ever come to the light and air, if they do not become rancid and perish in the seed. It is not every seed that will survive a thousand years. Other thoughts further developed, but yet pale and languid, like shoots grown in a cellar.

"The plant . . . develops from the first in two opposite directions, *viz.* upwards [to expand in the light and air] to produce and continue the stem (or *ascending axis*), and downwards [avoiding the light][1] to form the root (or *descending axis*). The former is ordinarily or in great part aërial, the latter subterranean."

So the mind develops from the first in two opposite directions: upwards to expand in the light and air; and downwards avoiding the light to form the root. One half is aërial, the other subterranean. The mind is not well balanced and firmly planted, like the oak, which has not as much root as branch, whose roots like those of the white pine are slight and near the surface. One half of the mind's development must still be root,—in the embryonic state, in the womb of nature, more unborn than at first. For each successive new idea or bud, a new rootlet in the earth. The growing man penetrates yet deeper by his roots into the womb of things. The infant is comparatively near the surface, just covered from the light; but the man sends down a tap-root to the centre of things.

The mere logician, the mere reasoner, who weaves his arguments as a tree its branches in the sky,—nothing equally developed in the roots,—is overthrown by the first wind.

---

[1] (The bracketed portions are Thoreau's.)

10 As with the roots of the plant, so with the roots of the mind, the branches and branchlets of the root "are mere repetitions for the purpose of multiplying the absorbing points, which are chiefly the growing or newly formed extremities, sometimes termed *spongelets.* It bears no other organs."

11 So this organ of the mind's development, the *Root*, bears no organs but spongelets or absorbing points.

12 Annuals, which perish root and all the first season, especially have slender and thread-like fibrous roots. But biennials are particularly characterized by distended, fleshy roots containing starch, a stock for future growth, to be consumed during their second or flowering season,—as carrots, radishes, turnips. Perennials frequently have many thickened roots clustered together, tuberous or palmate roots, fasciculated or clustered as in the dahlia, pæony, etc.

13 Roots may spring from any part of the stem under favorable circumstances; "that is to say in darkness and moisture, as when covered by the soil or resting on its surface."

14 That is, the most clear and ethereal ideas (Antæus-like) readily ally themselves to the earth, to the primal womb of things. They put forth roots as soon as branches; they are eager to be soiled. No thought soars so high that it sunders these apron-strings of its mother. The thought that comes to light, that pierces the empyrean on the other side, is wombed and rooted in darkness, a moist and fertile darkness,—its roots in Hades like the tree of life. No idea is so soaring but it will readily put forth roots. Wherever there is an air-and-light-seeking bud about to expand, it may become in the earth a darkness-seeking root. Even swallows and birds-of-paradise *can* walk on the ground. To quote the sentence from Gray entire: "Roots not only spring from the root-end of the primary stem in germination, but also from any subsequent part of the stem under favorable circumstances, that is to say, in darkness and moisture, as when covered by the soil or resting on its surface."

15 No thought but is connected as strictly as a flower, with the earth. The mind flashes not so far on one side but its rootlets, its spongelets, find their way instantly on the other side into a moist darkness, uterine,— a low bottom in the heavens, even miasma-exhaling to such immigrants as are not acclimated. A cloud is uplifted to sustain its roots. Imbosomed in clouds as in a chariot, the mind drives through the boundless fields of space. Even there is the dwelling of Indra.

16 I might here quote the following, with the last—of roots: "They may even strike in the open air and light, as is seen in the copious aërial rootlets by which the Ivy, the Poison Ivy, and the Trumpet Creeper

climb and adhere to the trunks of trees or other bodies; and also in Epiphytes or Air-plants, of most warm regions, which have no connection whatever with the soil, but germinate and grow high in air on the trunks or branches of trees, etc.; as well as in some terrestrial plants, such as the Banian and Mangrove, that send off aërial roots from their trunks or branches, which finally reach the ground."

So, if our light-and-air-seeking tendencies extend too widely for our original root or stem, we must send downward new roots to ally us to the earth.

Also there are parasitic plants which have their roots in the branches or roots of other trees, as the mistletoe, the beech-drops, etc. There are minds which so have their roots in other minds as in the womb of nature,—if, indeed, most are not such?!

Speculations

1. Where does Thoreau state the main point of his journal entry? How effective is this placement? Explain your answer.

2. Thoreau chooses what is called the alternating method of comparison; that is, he alternates back and forth, comparing specific aspects of plants with those of human beings. What are Thoreau's bases of contrast between plants and humans? Does the contrast seem logical? Explain your answer.

3. According to Thoreau, what are the dangers human beings must avoid in their mental growth? List them and comment on their validity as a danger to society. Provide examples of thinkers that fit Thoreau's descriptions.

4. The author suggests that we achieve a balance between mental (intellectual and moral) growth and physical growth. (See paragraph 3.) How would you suggest achieving this balance? Provide some practical advice.

5. What characteristics of style does the author use? Is it typical of the journal writing you have read so far? Give examples to support your answer.

Spin-offs for writing

1. Write an essay in which you compare or contrast one of the following pairs: 1) two of your best friends, 2) two places you often visit, 3) two feelings that often overcome you.

2. Using Thoreau's journal as a springboard, write an essay in which you draw an analogy between some aspect of nature and human experience.

W. N. P. BARBELLION

W. N. P. Barbellion [pseudonym for Bruce Frederick Cummings] (1889–1919) is among a small group of literary figures whose fame is based on private records they kept of their daily lives. Published as The Journal of a Disappointed Man (1919), Barbellion's diary has drawn attention and praise for three reasons: it offers some excellent descriptions of nature; it reveals deep insight into the author's innermost thoughts; and it tells of the author's great courage in the face of a crippling disease that affected him physically as well as emotionally. Born in North Devon, England, the son of a well-known journalist, Barbellion grew up in a cultured and literary environment. By the time he was fourteen, he had decided to become a naturalist and he succeeded amazingly well in this career despite his lack of formal training. He was eventually appointed to the staff of the Natural History Museum at South Kensington, London. His chronic ill health forced him to retire in 1917 and to spend the rest of his brief life improving his journals. In addition to The Journal of a Disappointed Man, he also wrote Enjoying Life (1919), a book of essays and short stories, and A Last Diary (published posthumously in 1920).

In a letter to his brother, Barbellion wrote, "I have been to the top and to the bottom, very happy and very miserable. But don't think I am whining. I prefer a life which is a hunt, and an adventure rather than a study in still life...." The brief contrast that follows seems to be a paradigm of the life he described to his brother since it deals with two contrasting images—the top and the bottom.

October 25, 1914

A Woman and a Child

1   On the way to the Albert Hall came upon the most beautiful picture of young maternity that ever I saw in my life. She was a delightfully girlish young creature—a perfect phoenix of health and beauty. As she stood with her little son at the kerb waiting for a 'bus, smiling and chatting to him, a luminous radiance of happy, satisfied maternal love, maternal pride, womanliness streamed from her and enveloped me.

2   We got on the same 'bus. The little boy, with his long hair and dressed in velvet like little Lord Fauntleroy, said something to her—she smiled delightedly, caught him up on her knees and kissed him. Two such pretty people never touched lips before—I'm certain of it. It was impossible to believe that this virginal creature was a mother—childbirth left no trace. She must have just budded off the baby boy like a plant. Once, in her glance, she took me in her purview, and I knew she knew I was watching her. In travelling backwards from Kensington Gardens to the boy again, her gaze rested on

me a moment and I, of course, rendered the homage that was due. As a matter of fact there was no direct evidence that she was the mother at all.

The Albert Hall Hag

While waiting outside the Albert Hall, an extraordinarily weird contrast thrust itself before me—she was the most pathetic piece of human jetsam that ever I saw drifting about in this sea of London faces. Tall, gaunt, cadaverous, the skin of her face drawn tightly over her cheekbones and over a thin, pointed, hook-shaped nose, on her feet brown sandshoes, dressed in a long draggle-tailed skirt, a broken-brimmed straw hat, beneath which some scanty hair was scraped back and tied behind in a knot—this wretched soul of some thirty summers (and what summers!) stood in the road beside the waiting queue and weakly passed the bow across her violin which emitted a slight scraping sound. She could not play a tune and the fingers of her left hand never touched the strings—they merely held the handle.

A policeman passed and, with an eye on the queue, muttered audibly, 'Not 'arf,' but no one laughed. Then she began to rummage in her skirt, holding the violin by the neck in her right hand just as she must hold her brat by the arm when at home. Simultaneously sounds issued from her mouth in a high falsetto key; they were unearthly sounds, the tiny voice of an articulating corpse underneath the coffin lid. For a moment no one realised that she was reciting. For she continued to rummage in her skirt as she squeaked, 'Break, break, break, on thy cold gray stones, O sea,' etc. The words were scarcely audible tho' she stood but two yards off. But she repeated the verse and I then made out what it was. She seemed ashamed of herself and of her plight, almost without the courage to foist this mockery of violin-playing on us—one would say she was frightened by her own ugliness and her own pathos.

After conscientiously carrying out her programme but with the distracted, uncomfortable air of some one scurrying over a painful task—like a tired child gabbling its prayers before getting into bed—she at length produced from her skirt pocket a small canvas money bag which she started to hand around. This was the climax to this harrowing incident—for each time she held out the bag, she smiled, which stretched the skin still more tightly down over her malar prominence and said something—an inarticulate noise in a very high pitch. 'A woman,' I whispered to R——, 'she claims to be a woman.' If any one hesitated a moment or struggled with a purse she would wait patiently with bag outstretched and head turned away, the smile vanishing at once as if the pinched face were but too glad of the opportunity of a rest from smiling. She stood there, gazing absently—two lifeless eyes at the bottom of deep socket holes in a head which was almost a bare skull. She was perfunctorily carrying out an objectionable task because she could not kill the will to live.

6   As she looked away and waited for you to produce the copper, she thought, 'Why trouble? Why should I wait for this man's aid?' The clink of the penny recalled her to herself, and she passed on, renewing her terrible grimacing smile.

7   Why didn't I do something? Why? Because I was bent on hearing Beethoven's Fifth Symphony, if you please. . . . And she may have been a well-to-do vagrant—well got up for the occasion—a clever simulator? . . .

Speculations

1. What sociological comment does the journal entry make? What aspects revealed are still prevalent today? Cite examples.
2. The contrast is organized according to the block method, using the first part of the journal entry to fully describe the high-class woman and then the second part to fully describe the low-class woman. What advantage does this method have for this particular journal entry?
3. What figurative language is used in the contrast? (Cite specific examples.) What effect is created?
4. In the end, how does the author react to the woman begging? What is your judgment of his reaction?
5. Which of the two portraits seems the more vivid, more realistic, more effective? Give reasons for your answer.

Spin-offs for writing

1. Using the block method of focusing on one subject at a time and drawing a conclusion at the end, write a contrast of two human beings or of two animals with whom you are thoroughly familiar. Follow Barbellion's example of supplying vivid details.
2. Write an essay in which you contrast the life of the wealthy in your city with that of the poor, using the following bases for the contrast: homes, clothing, food, and jobs. As part of your contrast, analyze why the contrast exists.

HENRY FOUNTAIN ASHURST

Henry Fountain Ashurst (1874–1962) served as the United States senator from Arizona for five successive terms, beginning in 1911. Before his election to this public office, he had been a ranch hand, lumberjack, and hod carrier. Largely self-educated, he became a newspaper reporter and eventually a lawyer. As chairman of the Indian Affairs Committee, he was a Wilsonian in his political philosophy and consistently criticized the Republican administration—their programs, their policies, and their presidential appointments. Known as an eloquent orator and a dapper dresser, he often appeared on the Senate floor in a black-braided coat, striped trousers, wing collar, and corded eyeglasses. His speeches were models of grandiose oratory—packed with Latin maxims and literary references. From June 1910 to July 1937, Ashurst kept a diary, which was published in 1962 under the title A Many Colored Toga.

The brief entry that follows reminisces nostalgically about the glorious past of a gambling saloon in its turn-of-the-century heyday. The reader cannot be sure that the author actually visited the saloon twenty-five years earlier or whether he is simply imagining what it was like based on the descriptions of others who did see it. What is striking is the contrast between the glamorous, exciting hall of the past and the dingy Chinese restaurant it had become in 1925.

Prescott

May 18, 1925

I lunched today, here in Prescott, at the Palace Restaurant which in bygone days, twenty years ago, was the Palace Saloon, then operated by three expert sports: Messrs. Bob Brow, Ben Belcher, and Barney Smith. At that time, at a long mahogany bar defended by a footrail of shining brass, bartenders clad in snowy linen, graceful as Sir Roger de Coverly,[1] served ale, porter, gin rum, brandy, lager beer, and old whiskies.

In the cafe in the rear of the saloon were then served Lucullan viands. There Bacchus reigned, and champagnes of choicest flowers, which painted landscapes even in sterile brains, went roaring down thirsty throats. There Venus smiled and fleet-footed Mercury was often dazzled by the bales of crisp currency and the clink of golden coin at the gambling tables. The whirr of the roulette ball, the thud of the dice at the crap-games which were as clods falling upon the coffin-lid of fortune, and the rattle of ivory poker-chips were then to be

---

[1] Sir Roger de Coverly—Rakish country squire featured in Joseph Addison and Richard Steele's 18th-century *Spectator* magazine.

heard above the dulcet notes of the wingless angels who warbled all night long in that house of joy and tears.

3   The back bar then gleamed like a ledge of jewels as its cut glass and silver and ebony were reflected by huge mirrors. There lawyer, tourist, "tenderfoot," merchant-prince, sportsman, savant, public-official, hard-rock-miner, cowboy, and remittance man mingled on equal terms. In that house, remorse sometimes fastened its fangs into men's souls, or fed itself upon the husks of their blighted hopes; there earnings were squandered—diced away in a night—there noble resolves were broken by those persons who entered into the domain of vice through the beautiful gate of temptation. Like enchanted fruit in the dwelling of a sorcerer, the objects of admiration lost their attraction and value as soon as grasped, and all that remained was regret for the time lost in their pursuit. The tear of sympathy welled quickly to the gambler's rayless eyes, and the hands of the proprietors of the Palace were horns of plenty, for not only were their hearts warm and their impulses generous, but the fixed principle of their code was that "jinx" and "hoodoo" kept away from him who *never* turned deaf ear to needy persons.

4   Now the great hall is tenantless save for the wraiths of frequenters of long ago. Spiders have festooned the back bar with cobwebs; dust now begrimes the tables where once the bets were laid. The gambler of that day has "cashed in" all his chips and has entered that vast realm where aces, kings, and queens alike are counted as deuces. The battalions of Bacchus are shattered, the singers are silent—their songs perished twenty years ago—and the restaurant is now conducted by a Chinaman named Dong.

Speculations

1. What organization does the author use for his contrast—block or alternating? Why do you suppose he chose that format?

2. Does the brevity of the second description make it inferior to the first? Why or why not?

3. In paragraph 2, what do the references to Lucullan, Bacchus, Venus, and Mercury contribute?

4. In your opinion, which of the two saloons offers the greater benefit to society? If you were an entrepreneur, which one would you prefer to finance? Give reasons for your answer.

5. In what aspect is this contrast similar to the contrast by Barbellion on pp. 198–200? In what aspect do the contrasts differ?

Spin-offs for writing

1. Reversing Ashurst's purpose, think of a scene in your past that was ugly, neglected, dilapidated and contrast that scene with its modern improvement. Be sure to use vivid details and use the block method of contrasting.

2. Write an essay deploring the neglect of a certain run-down area of your city or hometown. Include the reasons for the dilapidation.

ANNE FRANK

Anne Frank (1929–1945) was a German-born Dutch girl known throughout the world for The Diary of a Young Girl, *her fascinating record of adolescence in German-occupied Amsterdam during World War II. The diary gives a clear picture of the Nazi anti-Semitism that developed under Hitler and led to the Holocaust. Anne's diary is an amazingly candid self-portrait as well as an analysis of family relationships. Moreover, it depicts with exceptional maturity the universal problems of young people as they try to find their moral place in a crumbling world. In 1942, Anne's father, Otto Frank, fearing the persecution of the Nazis, went into hiding with his family in the annex of an Amsterdam warehouse he owned with some business partners. There the Franks and four friends hid for over two years. During this difficult confinement, Anne continued her education under her father's tutelage and wrote the equivalent of two books, including her diary, some short stories, fables, and an unfinished novel. Anne never saw the publication of her much-acclaimed diary, for she died of typhoid fever in the Bergen-Belsen concentration camp. Of the eight people who went into hiding, only Otto Frank survived.*

Life in the annex was strained with petty quarrels and childish tensions, arising from the fears and anxieties caused by the terrifying circumstances in which the eight "prisoners" were forced to exist. The experience changed the author from carefree innocence to mature insight, as revealed in the entry that follows. Notice that Anne addressed her diary as "Dear Kitty," as if writing to her best friend.

Tuesday, 7 March, 1944

1 Dear Kitty,

2 If I think now of my life in 1942, it all seems so unreal. It was quite a different Anne who enjoyed that heavenly existence from the Anne who has grown wise within these walls. Yes, it was a heavenly life. Boy friends at every turn, about twenty friends and acquaintances of my own age, the darling of nearly all the teachers, spoiled from top to toe by Mummy and Daddy, lots of sweets, enough pocket money, what more could one want?

3 You will certainly wonder by what means I got around all these people. Peter's[1] word "attractiveness" is not altogether true. All the teachers were entertained by my cute answers, my amusing remarks, my smiling face, and my questioning looks. That is all I was—a terrible flirt, coquettish and amusing. I had one or two advantages, which kept me rather in favor. I was industrious, honest, and frank. I

---

[1] Peter van Pels, a young boy in hiding with Anne. They fell in love while in the annex.

would never have dreamed of cribbing from anyone else [I would never have refused anyone who wanted to crib from me]. I shared my sweets generously, and I wasn't conceited.

Wouldn't I have become rather forward with so much admiration? It was a good thing that in the midst of, at the height of, all this gaiety, I suddenly had to face reality and it took me at least a year to get used to the fact that there was no more admiration forthcoming.

How did I appear at school? The one who thought of new jokes and pranks, always "king of the castle," never in a bad mood, never a crybaby. No wonder everyone liked to cycle with me, and I got their attentions.

Now I look back at that Anne as an amusing, but very superficial girl, who has nothing to do with the Anne of today. Peter said quite rightly about me: "If ever I saw you, you were always surrounded by two or more boys and a whole troupe of girls. You were always laughing and always the center of everything!"

What is left of this girl? Oh, don't worry, I haven't forgotten how to laugh or to answer back readily. I'm just as good, if not better, at criticizing people, and I can still flirt if . . . I wish. That's not it though, I'd like that sort of life again for an evening, a few days or even a week; the life which seems so carefree and gay. But at the end of that week, I should be dead beat and would be only too thankful to listen to anyone who began to talk about something sensible.

I don't want followers, but friends, admirers who fall not for a flattering smile but for what one does and for one's character.

I know quite well that the circle around me would be much smaller. But what does that matter, as long as one still keeps a few sincere friends?

Yet I wasn't entirely happy in 1942 in spite of everything; I often felt deserted, but because I was on the go the whole day long, I didn't think about it and enjoyed myself as much as I could. Consciously or unconsciously, I tried to drive away the emptiness I felt with jokes and pranks. Now I think seriously about life and what I have to do. One period of my life is over forever. The carefree schooldays are gone, never to return.

I don't even long for them any more; I have outgrown them, I can't just only enjoy myself as my serious side is always there.

12 I look upon my life up till the New Year, as it were, through a powerful magnifying glass. The sunny life at home, then coming here in 1942, the sudden change, the quarrels, the bickerings, I couldn't understand it, I was taken by surprise, and the only way I could keep up some bearing was by being impertinent.

13 The first half of 1943: my fits of crying, the loneliness, how I slowly began to see all my faults and shortcomings, which are so great and which seemed much greater then. During the day I deliberately talked about anything and everything that was farthest from my thoughts, tried to draw Pim[2] to me; but couldn't. Alone I had to face the difficult task of changing myself, to stop the everlasting reproaches, which were so oppressive and which reduced me to such terrible despondency.

14 Things improved slightly in the second half of the year, I became a young woman and was treated more like a grownup. I started to think, and write stories, and came to the conclusion that the others no longer had the right to throw me about like an india-rubber ball. I wanted to change in accordance with my own desires. But *one* thing that struck me even more was when I realized that even Daddy would never become my confidant over everything. I didn't want to trust anyone but myself any more.

15 At the beginning of the New Year: the second great change, my dream.... And with it I discovered my longing, not for a girl friend, but for a boy friend. I also discovered my inward happiness and my defensive armor of superficiality and gaiety. In due time I quieted down and discovered my boundless desire for all that is beautiful and good.

16 And in the evening, when I lie in bed and end my prayers with the words, "I thank you, God, for all that is good and dear and beautiful," I am filled with joy. Then I think about "the good" of going into hiding, of my health and with my whole being of the "dearness" of Peter, of that which is still embryonic and impressionable and which we neither of us dare to name or touch, of that which will come sometime; love, the future, happiness and of "the beauty" which exists in the world; the world, nature, beauty and all, all that is exquisite and fine.

17 I don't think then of all the misery, but of the beauty that still remains. This is one of the things that Mummy and I are so entirely different about. Her counsel when one feels melancholy is: "Think of all the misery in the world and be thankful that you are not

---

[2]Pim—nickname for Anne's father, Otto Frank.

sharing in it!" My advice is: "Go outside, to the fields, enjoy nature and the sunshine, go out and try to recapture happiness in yourself and in God. Think of all the beauty that's still left in and around you and be happy!"

I don't see how Mummy's idea can be right, because then how are you supposed to behave if you go through the misery yourself? Then you are lost. On the contrary, I've found that there is always some beauty left—in nature, sunshine, freedom, in yourself; these can all help you. Look at these things, then you find yourself again, and God, and then you regain your balance. 18

And whoever is happy will make others happy too. He who has courage and faith will never perish in misery! 19

Yours, Anne

Speculations

1. In comparing herself before and after 1942, the author indicates that she has changed. What word captures her change? Do you believe that she might have achieved the same level of change without being forced into hiding? Give reasons for your answer. Where does she clarify that she is contrasting two parts of her life?

2. What universal longing does paragraph 8 express? To what do you attribute this longing?

3. What sign of maturity is revealed in paragraph 14? How important do you consider this characteristic? Do you find it important for yourself and for your friends?

4. What difference in outlook exists between Anne and her mother. Which outlook do you consider more conducive to serenity? Support your answer with reasons and examples.

5. Of the blessings listed in Anne's prayer (see paragraph 16), which do you consider the most important to a life of genuine fulfillment? Give reasons for your answer.

Spin-offs for writing

1. Write an essay in which you contrast yourself ten years ago with what you are today. Consider such bases of contrast as material desires, self-centeredness, or goals.

2. Write an essay developing the idea behind this quotation from Anne Frank's diary: "I don't want followers but friends, admirers who fall not for a flattering smile but for what one does and for one's character."

Student Journal—
Comparison / Contrast

Pimo Mancia

November 18, 1992

I am vexed, really vexed. In fact, it's good to have a journal in which to blow off steam. I just returned from my class in U.S. History, taught by Professor B. I had looked forward to taking this class because my high school training was in El Salvador, where we did not study the details of North American historical events or trends. I felt sure that the lives of the pilgrims, the relationship of the colonies with the Indians, and the Civil War would make for fascinating class discussions and dramatic lecturing. I was thrilled with the thought of learning about Custer's "last stand," about the social intrigues during colonial days, about Benjamin Franklin's popularity during his ambassadorship to France, and about the heroism of Abraham Lincoln. But so far all we have done in this class is sit and listen to long-winded lectures, read from dog-eared notes in a monotonous voice. We have spent what seems like an eternity on the Federalist Papers as the basis of the U.S. Constitution. We also listened to boring explanations of the difference between the Federalists, led by Alexander Hamilton, and the Anti-Federalists, led by Thomas Jefferson. While I know that it is important to understand these political philosophies, why does the teacher have to be so arid and tedious? Why can't he move around the room, get excited, and gesture energetically so that we don't fall asleep? Why can't he ask us questions or set forth a proposition that we would either support or reject? U.S. History should involve us. We should form strong opinions about a conservative government that supported the rich landowners versus a more liberal government that wanted to empower the workers. But no, our teacher prefers to hear himself pontificate about the Constitution, and present lists and lists of laws, such as the Alien and Sedition Acts, the Embargo Act, and the Essex Junto—whose meaning I shall have to review before our next test. I'll have to memorize the dates, too, because this teacher is a stickler for dates.

What gets me is that I know teaching does not have to be that dull. I know it because my World Mythology teacher, Ms. R., is so different from Professor B. She is a combination of actress and scholar. Her own love of mythology oozes out of every pore in her body. She dances about the room, showing us paintings, writing on the chalkboard, and challenging us to think, think, think. For instance, in order to get across the ancient Egyptian belief in a hereafter where everyone is judged systematically, she had us re-enact the Judgment Hall of Maati in the underworld. One student had to play the part of the deceased who is to be judged, another the part of Anubis who leads the deceased into the hall, where Osiris, played by yet another student, is seated in anticipation of the judgment. Another student had to play the role of the Goddess of Truth, whose feather is weighed in a balance against the heart of the deceased to see how honest he is. Another student played the monster called Eater of the Dead, crouching next to the deceased in order to jump on him and destroy him the moment he lies. I was chosen to be Thoth, the clerk of Maati, whose job it was to record the events going on. The most important role was that of Osiris, seated in an imaginary shrine of fire, ready to pass judgment on the deceased, either allowing him to pass on into eternal life because he was good, or having him destroyed forever because he was evil. The rest of the class pretended to be among the fourteen gods who attend this ceremony. The student playing the role of the deceased had to face Osiris and speak these words: "I know thy name and I know the name of the fourteen gods. I have been purged of all evil. . . ." At some point, of course, Eater of the Dead pretended that the deceased had lied, so he jumped on him, causing the class to roar with laughter. This dramatic exercise was then followed by a serious discussion about the whole idea of a final judgment and a hereafter. We then tried to see how this Egyptian theology had influenced modern Christianity with its belief in a book of life in which all deeds are recorded, a final judgment, and a hell or paradise.

I'll bet ten years from now I'll remember the Hall of Maati, but I doubt if I will have a clue about the Embargo Act.

8.
EXAMPLES.

January 12, 1765. "I had eyed a singular lady some time. She was very debauched. But I took a fancy to her." Courting in Italy. James Boswell.

January 14, 1808. "Of all our acquaintances in Brunswick, the only really intelligent one is Jacobsohn." Examples of the kinds of people he met in Brunswick, Germany. Stendhal.

June 28, 1921. "There's no doubt that certain incidents are symbolic." An extended example of a certain symbolic incident in his life. Siegfried Sassoon.

March 11, 1975. "Everyone wants to go home." A Chronicle of life in a nursing home. Joyce Mary Horner.

CHAPTER 8

Examples

All writers, even diarists, use examples to support their assertions. The moment you scribble down in your diary, "I am worn out from today's struggles," you are inclined to immediately add examples: "I couldn't balance my checkbook; I lost five pages of my Sociology 101 report by not pushing the 'save' button on my computer; and besides, I am coming down with a sore throat." In the writings of nearly every profession can be found a similar urge to support assertions with examples. Physicians use examples to explain what symptoms patients must look for; ministers use them as anecdotes in sermons; and lawyers use them to establish legal precedents. Adding a concrete example to strengthen the meaning of an idea is a universal rhetorical technique.

As the excerpts in this chapter show, it is also a technique commonly practiced by diarists. Here we see James Boswell confessing, through several examples, to his rakish and unrestrained pursuit of alluring women. Stendhal's journal provides some amusing examples of the kinds of people he met in Brunswick, Germany. On a more somber note, Joyce Mary Horner offers some moving examples of the longings of aged inmates in a convalescent hospital, while Siegfried Sassoon cites an extended example to symbolically illustrate the changes that have taken place in his life.

The effective use of examples in all kinds of writing is governed, as are most rhetorical choices, largely by common sense. One mistake beginning writers often make is to cite as an example a passage that repeats rather than proves the intended point. Here is an example:

A good writer is one on whom nothing is lost. For example, he will let nothing get by him and will meticulously take account of his surroundings.

Using the phrase "for example" does not automatically make what follows an example. A real example is always more specific than the point it is cited to prove. Here is an improved revision:

A good writer is one on whom nothing is lost. For example, if he were to discover a shell at his feet while taking a stroll along the beach, he would notice the shell's bluish green luminescence, its curved surface—polished like a smooth shirt button—and its inner space filled with sand and the smell of the sea.

Common sense also tells us that any example cited should always be clearly connected to the idea it is intended to support. Penning a brief introduction that sets the context for the example is usually the best way to establish this connection, as the following paragraph fails to do:

> *Bright blue eyes are "shimmering ponds." The summer withers away "like maple leaves in autumn." The music envelopes you "like a cloud of heady perfume." The first example is a metaphor; the second, a simile; and the third a personification.*

Notice how the paragraph is improved when the writer begins with the main point and connects it with a brief introduction to the examples that follow:

> *Even prosaic people, who have never written a poem, use figurative language in their daily conversations. Bright blue eyes are "shimmering ponds." The golden summer is said to wither away "like maple leaves in autumn." Music is felt to envelope the listener "like a cloud of heady perfume." The first example is a metaphor; the second, a simile; and the third a personification.*

Virtually every rhetorical mode—from narration to argumentation—will occasionally cite examples. And commonly used to introduce them are the following phrases:

For example
For instance
A case in point is
Let me illustrate
The following instance proves this point

However, not all examples need to be methodically introduced or mechanically connected to the idea they are intended to support. Sometimes just the context of the writing will already make it clear why an example is being cited:

> *The culture of victimization is largely responsible for the $117 billion spent annually on insurance to protect against litigation, but the phenomenon extends, of course, far beyond the courts. It is a major theme in race relations and in the feminist critique of society. It has spawned a new academic discipline, victimology. It provided unerring fodder for the morbidly voyeuristic audiences of television talk shows and is responsible for a virtual genre of books that have titles like* The Cinderella Complex, The Casanova Complex, The Soap Opera Syndrome, Adult Children of Alcoholics, Beyond Codependency, Beyond Acceptance, *and* Obsessive Love: When Passion Holds you Prisoner, *and explore the compulsions, maladies, syndromes, and presumptions that purportedly prevent people from assuming control of their lives. Without it, a good percentage of the*

125,000 psychologists, therapists, and counselors who form the country's gargantuan therapy industry would be out of work.

John Taylor, "Don't Blame Me."

It is so evident from the context what the examples support that the insertion of a mechanical connection would seem clumsy.

JAMES BOSWELL

James Boswell (1740–1795) was a Scottish author much criticized and ridiculed by the literati of his day for being sycophantically eager to associate with all of the great men of that time. In 1763 he met Samuel Johnson, whom he immortalized in his work The Life of Samuel Johnson, LL.D., *considered a masterpiece of minute biographical detail. So skillful was Boswell's work, that Johnson's fascinating conversations, as recorded by Boswell, are perhaps more important today than Johnson's own literary output. Certainly, as a result of Boswell's genius, no man is better known to his readers than Johnson. Boswell has been judged by many modern critics to be the greatest biographer of all time. However, in his day, the praise was sparse and the besmirching constant. For instance, Macaulay declared him a "bore," "servile and impertinent, shallow and pedantic, a bigot and a sot, bloated with family pride," and generally a pompous fool. However, to imagine that Boswell was merely a hanger-on to the celebrated Johnson is quite erroneous. When he was on the Continent, Boswell became close friends with many distinguished men of his time, such as Jean Jacques Rousseau, François Voltaire, and the Corsican freedom seeker, General Pascal Paoli, about whom he wrote his* Account of Corsica, The Journal of a Tour to That Island: and Memoirs of Pascal Paoli *(1768). Boswell's other works include,* The Journal of a Tour of the Hebrides with Samuel Johnson, LL.D. *(1785), and numerous other journals, now housed at Yale University.*

It is only in the last half century that Boswell has come to be appreciated for the vital and talented man that he was. In studying him as a personality, we find two characters emerging—the meticulous intellect and the shameless libertine. It is this second side that is reflected in the entries that follow. We have chosen them because of their amusing and exaggerated raciness. These journal entries, too, reveal the real Boswell. In fact, for those who know Boswell only as an unrelenting biographer, this material will round out the picture. Boswell was twenty-five years old and traveling on the Continent when the events of his journal took place. The entries are written in Turin, the capital of Piedmont, in the northwestern part of Italy.

Saturday, 12 January, 1765

I called this morning on Gray, who lived at the Academy. I found there Mr. Needham of the Royal Society, whose acquaintance I much wished for.[1] When I hear of such a man's being in a place where I arrive at, I go immediately and make him the first visit, although I stand upon the very pinnacle of punctilios with the British in general. I found him a learned, accurate, easy man. He said he

---

[1] John Turberville Needham, Roman Catholic priest and man of science, was at this time serving as governor to the eldest son of Viscount Dillon. He propounded a theory of spontaneous generation, and his microscopic observations of animalcula roused great excitement at the time. He was a friend of Buffon, who described his work in the *Natural History.*

followed just the study which pleased him at the time, and went on calm and moderate, finding every part of knowledge add to the general stock. We talked of vanity, which I defended, and owned I felt a good deal. "Yes," said he, smiling, "you never hear of a great man but you would wish to be him. I am not so, for I have observed the condition of such men. I love fame only as an ingredient in happiness." This idea pleased me much. I then went to the King's museum where Signor Bartoli showed me a very curious collection of antiquities and natural curiosities. He then showed me His Majesty's library, which is truly noble.

2 I dined with Billon[2] at the Auberge d'Angleterre. My landlord at the Bonne Femme had endeavoured to impose upon me. I was enraged at the rogue, and determined to change him. I called up the landlord of this inn, who hates the other fellow. "Sir, are you a friend or relative of the landlord of the Bonne Femme?" "No, Sir." "Dare I speak ill of him to you?" "Yes, Sir," "Well, then, he's a rascal, and I should like to come to your house." The fellow was confounded and pleased, and having been lectured by Billon, he made a reasonable price with me.[3] We had another French officer with us, a lively young fellow. We were mighty gay. But I was in feverish spirits.

3 At night I sat a long time in the box of Mme. B., of whom I was now violently enamoured. I made my declarations, and was amazed to find such a proposal received with the most pleasing politeness. She however told me, "It is impossible. I have a lover" (showing him), "and I do not wish to deceive him." Her lover was the Neapolitan Minister, Comte Pignatelli, in whose box she sat. He was a genteel, amiable man. He went away, and then I pursued my purpose. Never did I see such dissimulation, for she talked aloud that I should think no more of my passion, and the *piémontais*[4] around us heard this and said without the least delicacy, "A traveller expects to accomplish in ten days as much as another will do in a year." I was quite gone. She then said to me, "Whisper in my ear," and told me, "We must make arrangements," assuring me that she had talked severely to persuade people that there was nothing between us. She bid me call upon her next day at three. This was advancing with rapidity. I saw she was no very wise personage, so flattered her finely. "Ah, Madame, I understand you well. This country is not worthy of you. That is true" (like a mere fool). "You are not loved here as you ought to be." Billon

---

[2] Captain Billon a French officer to whom Boswell had been introduced by a friend.
[3] Boswell's Accounts show that six days' food and lodging at the Bonne Femme cost him about £3 (about $4.00 at 1993 exchange rates), and nine days at the Auberge d'Angleterre about £3.6 (approximately $5.00).
[4] a person from Piedmont

came and repeated gross bawdy. This was disgusting. When I got home I was so full of my next day's bliss that I sat up all night.

Sunday 13 January. By want of sleep and agitation of mind, I was quite feverish. At seven I received a letter from Mme.——— telling me that people talked of us, and forbidding me to come to her or to think more of the "plus malheureuse de femmes." This tore my very heart. I wrote to her like a madman, conjuring her to pity me. Billon came and went out with me in my coach. He told me I had lost her merely by being an *imprudent* and discovering my attachment to all the world. I had wrought myself up to a passion which I was not master of. I saw he looked upon me as a very simple young man; for amongst the thorough-bred libertines of Turin to have sentiment is to be a child. I changed my lodgings. She wrote to me again. I wrote to her an answer more mad than my former one. I was quite gone. At night I saw her at the opera. We were reserved. But I told her my misery. She said, "C'est impossible." I was distracted. I forgot to mention that I have paid her one visit.

[Boswell to the Countess Burgaretta. Original in French][5]

Turin, Sunday 13 January, 1765

I have no words, Madame, to tell you how your letter has pierced my heart. I have been so agitated by that passion you have inspired in me that I have not slept half an hour all night. The thought never left me of the happiness which was to be mine today at *"a quarter past three."* And now comes your cruel letter, forbidding me to come today to your house.

Madame, I am wholly yours. You may dispose of me as it shall please you, but consider that a worthy man's happiness should be a matter of consequence to a woman such as I have the honour to conceive you to be. Your conduct has roused hopes which it will cost me the bitterest regret to abandon. O Madame, you are generous! Think, I entreat you, of your unhappy lover who is tortured by his passion for you and dares to ask your pity as his due.

Madame, with your brilliance, with your knowledge of the world, you can find means to console this lacerated heart. Grant me, I entreat you, an assignation this evening at any hour when you can be alone. Reflect. Let your humanity speak. I am unwilling to see you

---

[5]This and the following letters to Mme. Burgaretta and Mme. Skarnavis were first printed, together with Geoffrey Scott's translations, in the fifth volume of Colonel Isham's privately printed *Private Papers of James Boswell*. Scott's versions are used here with slight changes. The letters to these two ladies are printed from Boswell's copies.

in company: I cannot do so without confusion and torment. Dear Madame, adieu. Answer me unless you wish to kill me.

[Boswell to the Countess Burgaretta. Original in French]

Turin, 13 January, 1765

8 Forgive me, Madame, if the pain and stupefaction caused by the blow of your first letter prevented me from paying attention to your commands for its return. Here are both your letters.[6] I have kissed them a thousand times, laden though they are with so much cruelty. They come from you: that is enough. Torments, from your hand, are to me precious. Baneful and delicious madness! O Love! Most adorable of women, my heart and my soul exist but for you.

9 You call yourself unhappy. Great Heavens! What can I do? Command me, Madame: you will see whether I am attached to you or not.

10 Yesterday evening we came to an explanation. I made you an unreserved avowal of my passion for you. You were good enough to tell me that your situation is a delicate one and that "the most careful arrangements would be necessary." I can be blamed for nothing but an excess of passion which almost deprives me of power to conceal it; and I believe, Madame, that this is why you hesitate to display your generosity to an unhappy foreigner who throws himself at your feet and pleads for pity.

11 But, Madame, if the utmost deference and discretion of conduct may yet earn some reward of gratitude, I shall not cease to flatter myself with hopes of your favour. My happiness, my life, depend on you. Persist in your cruelty, and I cannot answer for the consequences of the most violent passion man ever felt. You do not refuse me your friendship. O Madame! Dear and kind Countess! Give me a proof of your compassion. In granting that, you will grant all that my unhappy stars permit me to obtain. I shall do what I can to calm myself. I shall leave Turin full of sadness, but also full of gratitude. We shall correspond; and I, wherever I am, shall remain yours. Once more, my dear Madame, I beseech you think seriously. Write me a word or two before the opera; calm me as much as you can. I shall have the honour to be in your opera box for as brief a time as you command. I shall be all obedience; and always, always yours.

12 **Monday 14 January.** Night before last I plainly proposed matters to Mme. St. Gilles. "I am young, strong, vigorous. I offer my services as a duty, and I think that the Comtesse de St. Gilles will do very

---

[6] Boswell does not seem to have kept copies of them.

well to accept them." "But I am not that kind of woman." "Very well, Madame, I shall believe you." I thought to take her *en passant*.[7] But she was cunning and saw my passion for Mme. B_____, so would not hazard with me.

This morning I waited on Mr. Needham, who read me a defence of the Trinity which was most ingenious and really silenced me. I said, "Sir, this defence is very good; but pray what did you do before you thought of it?" He replied that he submitted to it as a mystery. He said the Catholic religion was proved as a general system, like the Newtonian philosophy, and, although we may be perplexed with partial difficulties, they are not to shake our general belief. He said the world would very soon be divided into Catholics and Deists. He threw my ideas into the orthodox channel. But still I recalled Rousseau's liberal views of the benevolent Divinity, and so was more free. Needham said that a man whose melancholy hurt his rational powers could hardly be accountable for his moral conduct. He consoled me.

After dinner I called on Norton and Heath, two English gentlemen. I did not know what to say to them. I liked the opera much tonight, and my passion was already gone. Honest Billon said, "If you want to make love, I can find you a girl." I agreed to this by way of cooling my raging disposition to fall in love. At night Mme. St Gilles seemed piqued that I pursued her no longer, and, suspecting that I was enchained by Mme. B_____, she said, "Really, you are a little mad. You get notions, and your head turns. I'll tell you: I think you have studied a great deal. You ought to go back to your books. You should not follow the profession of gallant or you will be terribly taken in. Be careful of your health and of your purse. For you don't know the world." Although my former love-adventures are proof enough that it is not impossible for me to succeed with the ladies, yet this abominable woman spoke very true upon the whole. I have too much warmth ever to have the cunning necessary for a general commerce with the corrupted human race.

[Boswell to the Countess Burgaretta. Original in French]

Turin, Monday 14 January, 1765

I entreat you, Madame, to return me the two letters which I have had the honour to write you. Act towards me with the same generosity that I have shown you. Today I feel better. My passion abates; and for that reason I still have hopes that you will make the *arrangements* of which you spoke.

---

[7] in passing

16 *Tuesday 15 January.* Wrote all the morning. After dinner saw the King's palace, where are a number of very excellent pictures. I was shown the King's own apartment. I took up his hat and cane, but found them neither lighter than silk nor heavier than gold. In short, they could not be distinguished from the hat and stick of uncrowned mortals. I was much pleased with his closet, where he had a *prie-dieu*[8] and a good many books of devotion. His Majesty is truly pious.

17 I then went to Billon's, who had a very pretty girl for me with whom I amused myself. I then went to another ball at the Théâtre de Carignan. I tired much. Billon had promised to have a girl to sleep with me all night at his lodgings. I went there at eleven but did not find her. I was vexed and angry.

18 *Wednesday 16 January.* Billon and another French officer dined with me. We were well. I then called on Needham, who explained his philosophical opinion of transubstantiation, by which I was convinced that it was not absurd. He and I then went and waited on the French Ambassadress. After which I went to Mme. St. Gilles', where I was quite disgusted. I went home very dull. What a strange day have I had of it![9]

19 *Thursday 17 January.* All the forenoon I wrote. After dinner I took Bartoli to air in my coach. We went and saw the Bernardines' library. I was gloomy but patient. At night I was again at a ball. I was calm, pensive, and virtuous. Sabbati,[10] Secretary to the French Ambassador, talked a good deal with me, and said, "You are a man from another century." I had eyed a singular lady some time. She was very debauched. But I took a fancy to her. Sabbati presented me to her. I said, "Mme. S____,[11] this is the fifth evening that I have tried to make your acquaintance." She seemed gay and pleased.[12]

20 *Friday 18 January.* I passed the morning at home, but was so sadly dissipated that I could do no good. While I was at dinner, an Augustine monk came and asked charity. He said he had been twenty-seven years *religiosus et semper contentus*.[13]

---

[8] Praying stool

[9] The memorandum covering this day adds: "This day pause; swear solemn behaviour. Madness is no excuse, as you can restrain it. No girls or you're poxed. Swear this, and no more imaginary enjoying; it weakens. Be calm."

[10] Honoré Auguste Sabatier de Cabre.

[11] Maria Anna Theresa Skarnavis (Boswell's spelling of Scarnafis, the Piedmontese version of the name) was the wife of Filippo Ottone Ponte, Count of Scarnafigi, who was appointed on 27 January Minister to Portugal from Sardinia. He was later Ambassador to France. Mme. Skarnavis was about seven years older than Boswell.

[12] The memorandum elaborates a little here: "Gave her arm going out. Asked you, 'Do you live close by?' 'Auberge d'Angleterre.' Perhaps she'll send."

[13] religious and always content

I then went to Billon's, where I had a pretty girl. I was disgusted with low pleasure. Billon talked of women in the most indelicate manner. I then went to Mme. Burgaretta's, where I found two more swains. She grumbled and complained of a headache; and she dressed before us, changing even her shirt. We indeed saw no harm; but this scene entirely cured my passion for her. Her *femme de chambre*[14] was very clever, and when the Countess was dressed, carried away her morning clothes in a little barrel. At the opera I sat in the box of Mme. S____, who was soft and gentle, and seemed to like my compliments. I was at Mme. St. Gilles' in good spirits, and went home pretty much content.

[Boswell to the Countess Burgaretta. Original in French]

Turin, 18 January, 1765[15]

Pray, Madame, allow me to tell how grateful I am to you for all the kindnesses you have extended to a stranger. You have, I trust, no fault to find with my conduct ever since I pledged myself to the strictest discretion. You do not know the value of your Scotsman. There is no suffering he will not endure for the lady he worships. Madame, you will forgive me if my sincere passion compels me to ask you, with all deference, to tell me, yes or no, whether you will be able to receive me before I leave.

I will confess, Madame, that I find myself so much indebted to M. P____ that I should have scruples against doing him an offence. But I believe, Madame, that you have no ties with him which preclude generosity to another. If that is indeed so, I entreat you to make me the happiest of mortals, and I shall cherish an undying memory of the goodness of your heart. Of my discretion you have already made proof. Reflect on this, and answer me.

Your brother is my friend.[16]

Saturday 19 January. Here have I stayed a week longer than I intended, partly from love, partly to see a grand opera which is to be performed tomorrow. After dinner I sat some time with Needham, who told me he was in orders as a Catholic priest and had always lived with conscientious strictness. He said he had many severe struggles to preserve his chastity, but had done so, and was now quite serene and happy. He had also been distressed with a lowness

---

[14] chamber maid

[15] Scott dated this letter 12 January 1765 and placed it first in the series. However, the memorandum covering this day reads: "Short card to Burgaretta; thank and say it *injuste* to Pignatelli."

[16] Mme. Burgaretta's brother has not been identified.

of spirits which impedes devotion. Thomas à Kempis complains of a *siccitas animi*.[17] I was amazed to find a man who had such parts and had seen so much of the world, and yet so strict as worthy Needham. I talked of the eternity of Hell's torments, which he defended as the continual shade which must be in the universe, which wicked beings ought justly to form. He said too that the pains would be in proportion to the offences, and that perhaps to exist with a certain degree of pain was better than to be annihilated.

26 At the opera I sat in Mme. S____' box, and fairly told her my love, saying that I could not leave Turin, being entirely captivated by her. She seemed propitious.[18] Mme. St. Gilles, deservedly balked of my services, was not a little angry. She was impudent enough to tell about that I had made a bold attack upon her. I did not like to hear this joke.

27 *Sunday 20 January.* The Comte Pignatelli, Envoy from Naples, had given me some letters of recommendation for different places. I was struck with this piece of politeness, and waited upon him this morning. He was indisposed, and abed, where he had a neat little desk on which he wrote. We chatted very agreeably, and agreed in abusing the *piémontais*, who are indeed a good-for-nothing mongrel race, ignorant and trifling. I said a man of genius made such a figure here as Voltaire would do in a society of people that valued themselves upon cutting pens, and despised those who cut worse than they did. At the opera I again sat by Mme. S____. She advised me to go, and rather to think of such a scheme when I should return. She would not allow me any the least liberty.

28 Last night the new opera was played, called *The Conquest of Mexico*. The decorations were superb, and some of the music very good, but not so well as the last opera, which was by old Sassone.[19]

29 Sabbati and I talked again tonight. He said everything great and spirited was carried on by prejudices early implanted. He said a jealous man was most easily deceived. Last night I had taken *congé*[20] of Mme. St. Gilles, so went no more near her. This evening I went to a ball given by some bourgeois at my inn. I danced one or two min-

---

[17] A dryness of the soul.
[18] In the memoranda Boswell records the conversation (in French): "BOSWELL. 'I cannot go away. Why leave what is most dear to me?' MME. SKARNAVIS. 'I cannot make up my mind.' BOSWELL. 'I shall tell you without flattery, the women here have neither taste nor sentiment. I saw you. I tried to make your acquaintance, &c. Will you allow me a visit?' MME. SKARNAVIS. 'Yes. You may command me,' &c. She was truly *kind*."
[19] The "new opera," *Montezuma*, was composed by Francesco di Majo; the "last opera," probably *L'Olimpiade*, by Johann Adolph Hasse, generally known as *Il Sassone* (the Saxon).
[20] leave

uets, and thought to do them honour. But the good bourgeois gave me broad hints not to keep them from the floor.

Monday 21 January. Never was mind so formed as that of him who now recordeth his own transactions. I was now in a fever of love for an abandoned being whom multitudes had often treated like a very woman of the town. I hesitated if I should not pass the winter here and gravely write to my father that really a melancholy man like myself so seldom found anything to attach him that he might be indulged in snatching a transient pleasure, and thus would I inform him that an Italian Countess made me remain at Turin. Was there ever such madness? O Rousseau, how am I fallen since I was with thee! I wrote a long letter to Mme. S____, entreating her pity and all that.[21] Her answer was that if she had known my letter was of such a nature, she would not have opened it. She had told me plainly her mind at the opera. Pedro, my stupid *valet de place*,[22] brought me this shocking word-of-mouth message. I saw that amongst profligate wretches a man of sentiment could only expose himself.

After dinner I went to Needham, and was consoled with learned and solid conversation. We went to the opera together, and sat in the middle of the parterre, from whence I never stirred but was quite independent. I enjoyed fully the entertainment. Needham talked of the religious orders, particularly of the Trappe, and explained them in so philosophical a manner that I had much solemn satisfaction.

After the opera Norton and Heath insisted I should go home with them and sup. I went, like a simpleton. They carried me into a low room of their inn, where they romped with two girls and gave me a most pitiful supper. This, now, was true English. I had now and then looked from the parterre to Mme. S____, but did not go to her box. I determined to set out next morning for Milan.

[Boswell to the Countess Skarnavis. Original in French]

Turin, Auberge d'Angleterre, 21 January 1765

Permit me, Madame, to write to you, for it is thus that I can best express to you the nature of my feelings towards you. I shall express them very briefly, without timidity and without restraint.

You are already aware that I feel for you the strongest of passions. I glory in it, and make no complaint of all I suffer. I shall not again

---

[21] One of the stock phrases of Bayes in the Duke of Buckingham's *Rehearsal*.
[22] In a descriptive list which Boswell kept of his *valets de place*, he characterizes Pedro as "old, small, and feeble."

repeat my ardent professions. You have no doubts on that head; if you have, it is from an excess of suspicion. I have heard many tales of you. I believe none. I am determined to believe none. No, Madame, I adore you, and nothing could avail to weaken that adoration.

35 Yesterday evening I told you I was consoling myself with hopes of your goodness. Your answer, both tender and cruel, was, "It is far better to go away." You gave me the most cautious advice. But you refrained from telling me it would be impossible to win your favour. I implore you, Madame, to reflect seriously, and to use no evasions with a romantic lover who deserves quite other consideration than one gives to the kind who may be had any day. Madame, I venture to affirm that never have your charms been more worthily felt than by me. If you accord me the supreme happiness, you will be showing yourself generous to an excellent man who would be attached by gratitude to you for the rest of his life. You are in perfect safety with me. You can rely on my honour in every respect. Our characters, Madame, are alike. Yes, I am sure of it. We have the liveliest ideas, which we express only by our glances. We have a modesty which nothing can destroy. Assuredly we are not novices in love. Nevertheless, with exquisite delicacy you prevent my touching your hand; and I, if I hear mention of Mme. Skarnavis, find myself blushing. Ah! when we abandon ourselves to pleasures under the veil of darkness, what transports, what ecstasy will be ours! Pardon me, Madame, I am greatly agitated. I place myself under your protection: dispose of me as you see fit. If you tell me, "Sir, think no more of that happiness; 'tis impossible,"—if you say that, I shall hear you with distress, I shall tear myself away from Turin, I shall leave on the instant.

36 But if I am not disagreeable to you, if your generous heart prompts you to say, "Stay: I am one who can value a true passion at its worth," you cannot conceive, Madame, how keenly I shall be touched. O love! baneful and delicious madness,[23] I feel you, and am your slave.

37 I well know, Madame, that I ought to remain long here to earn the great boon which I entreat. But just now I am not my own master. For the rest of my stay, I shall be entirely yours. I shall mix no more with the world. For all save you I shall have left Turin. I have tried to explain myself, Madame; it is for you to reflect and decide. It is a singular case. Have a care. Dear and amiable Countess, let your

---

[23] "O Amour! Folie funeste et délicieuse!" Boswell was thrifty of his fine phrases: he had used this a week before in his second letter to Mme. Burgaretta. Seven months later he used the thought expressed in the opening sentences of this letter to Mme. Skarnavis to begin one to Mme. Sansedoni.

humanity speak. Let us see if you can rise superior to low prejudices and tell your true thoughts.

Turin, 21 January 1765

It shall be between ourselves. Oh, you have nothing to fear! 38

Reflect—and in a few hours' time give me your reply. I shall send to get it. You have told me what you would do in my case; I well know what I should do in yours. Have a care, Madame, there is here something important at stake. I tremble, but I have hopes. Heaven bless you. 39

Tuesday 22 January. Needham and Gray breakfasted with me. I was quite easy and genteel. I sent to Mme. S____ and begged she would return me my letter. She bid the valet say that she had thrown it in the fire. Here was the extreme of mortification for me. I was quite sunk. Worthy Needham bid me continue to lay up knowledge, and took an affectionate leave of me, hoping we should meet again. 40

I set out at eleven. As I went out at one of the ports, I saw a crowd running to the execution of a thief. I jumped out of my chaise and went close to the gallows. The criminal stood on a ladder, and a priest held a crucifix before his face. He was tossed over, and hung with his face uncovered, which was hideous. I stood fixed in attention to this spectacle, thinking that the feelings of horror might destroy those of chagrin. But so thoroughly was my mind possessed by the feverish agitation that I did not feel in the smallest degree from the execution. The hangman put his feet on the criminal's head and neck and had him strangled in a minute. I then went into a church and kneeled with great devotion before an altar splendidly lighted up. Here then I felt three successive scenes: raging love—gloomy horror—grand devotion. The horror indeed I only *should* have felt. I jogged on slowly with my *vetturino*,[24] and had a grievous inn[25] at night. 41

Speculations

1. What would be your reaction to a friend or acquaintance who would act in the manner confessed by Boswell? Would you be tolerant? Repelled? Amused? Judicious? Explain your reaction.
2. Paragraphs 8 and 9 are declarations of passion and love. What is the writer's tone? How seriously should he be taken?

[24] driver
[25] a bad inn

3. In between his love affairs, Boswell holds some serious conversations with his friend Needham. They discuss such theological subjects as the Trinity, the doctrine of transubstantiation, and the torments of hell. What do these conversations contribute to the journal?
4. Who are the women with whom Boswell is taken? How many are there? What does the number tell us about the quality of the relationship with each?
5. What other activities, beside socializing, interest Boswell? How important do you consider these activities today?

Spin-offs for writing

1. Write an imaginary journal entry about a fascinating encounter you have had with a person from a foreign country or a different city or town than yours. Use examples to add interest to your account.
2. Write an essay in which you use three or four examples of the kinds of women (or men) you consider attractive. Be sure to supply a context that makes the examples relevant.

STENDHAL

Stendhal [pseudonym of Marie Henri Beyle] (1783–1842) was a French novelist whose psychological insights place him among the greatest fiction writers in the French language. Because of his hatred for his father and the Jesuit environment of his home in Grenoble, he moved to Paris as a young man and worked there in the Ministry of War, becoming a dragoon in Napoleon's army. His personal life was taken up with a variety of amorous interests that often seemed to overwhelm him. One of his major and most unhappy love affairs provided the background for On Love *(1822), a psychological analysis of love, predating Freud. Stendhal's first novel,* Armance *(1827), was ignored or scorned by the critics; however, his next novel,* The Red and the Black *(1831), in which red symbolized the army and liberalism and black symbolized the church and repression, was hailed as a masterpiece, especially in England. Typical of Stendhal's characters is the novel's hero, Julien Sorel, who is a passionate youth with his own unconventional moral code. Stendhal's other great novel,* The Charterhouse of Parma *(1839), is set in Italy and is about the relentless pursuit of happiness in the form of love and power. Stendhal read widely and filled numerous journals with his thoughts and observations. The following autobiographical works were published long after his death:* The Life of Henri Brulard *(1939),* Memoirs of Egotism *(1949), and* The Private Diaries of Stendhal *(1954), from which the following excerpt is taken.*

As was the custom for well-connected European youths, Stendhal at twenty-five spent some time in 1808 traveling around Europe in order to further his education and broaden his outlook on life. Part of his travels included a stay in Brunswick, an industrial city in West Germany, about ninety miles southeast of Hamburg. There he got acquainted with several people, whom he described and analyzed in his diary.

January 14, 1808

1. Of all our acquaintances in Brunswick, the only really intelligent one is Jacobsohn. Together with intelligence, he has all the finesse of the Jew he is, and two million.

2. A great deal of imagination of the oriental kind; but he doesn't speak French well, and his vanity is too unguarded. By flattering his vanity at the baths of Helmstedt, they made him spend two thousand écus. By handling him properly, you could make him spend ten, but in his household he's miserly like a Jew.

3. Herr von Siestorpf, master of the hounds, intelligence No. 2.

4. A man of sixty, 80,000 francs income. A physiognomy expressing finesse and malice. Badhearted; he's never given financial aid

to anyone. He ordered a telescope from a poor young artist of Brunswick (Herr von Siestorpf is a very great enthusiast for this sort of endeavor); he was to have given the poor young man 200 écus; when it was finished, he would no longer give him more than sixty.

5 They say he was little affected by the death of his only son, who died at the age of twenty-four, and disapproved of the latter's love for a natural daughter of the Duke of Brunswick, I believe, but having the title of countess, lady of honor, received at Court, etc. A hard man with no consideration for misfortune. Somewhat resembles a boar.

6 No. 3. Herren von Münchhausen, Ambassador; von Strombeck, Councilor.

7 These two men combined would make two charming men. They have a merit that is quite different the one from the other. Herr von Münchhausen, a man of high society, a pitiless chatterbox, is forever recounting fairly diverting anecdotes. Puts himself forward a bit too much, is always reminding you indirectly that he was present when Prince Heinrich, M. de Boufflers, M. de Nivernais, etc. said such-and-such an amusing thing. An income of 36,000 francs, life annuities for the most part. Miserly and unkempt to the last degree. Placing his whole happiness, his whole existence in decorations, ribbons, badges, etc. At bottom, a man of the Court.

8 A good musician, playing the harmonica, piano, etc. well, having published music. All told, a specimen of the upper society man. Fifty-five years old.

9 All of which is the contrary of Herr von Strombeck, who looks like an apothecary. Heavy, ponderous and slow-witted; and yet ideas, which are neither sound nor accurate, on the subject of virtue and governments. A good friend, a very fond father, a good son, a good brother. Loving the arts, having a little knowledge of astronomy, well educated but lacking the philosophic spark, unable to unify his ideas. HIS LOVE FOR ♀.[1] Thirty-five years old, and an income of 12,000 francs.

10 His wife is a mother, nothing more. A perfect nullity, mildness, virtue, but ghastly sluggishness; a German woman as much as it's possible to be one.

11 Herr von Bothmer, Grand Chamberlain. Is sixty-six years old. If he were only forty, we should undoubtedly have placed him as No. 1. Ravenous appetite, eating as much meat as three ordinary men. Knows six languages, has composed some nice German dramatic

---

[1] symbol for female

compositions. Has the literary taste that prevailed in Germany under Frederick the Great. The great Germans—Goethe, Wieland, Klopstock, Bürger, Herder, Schiller—have changed that.

Herr von Bothmer is no longer anything more than a shade of what I believe he used to be. He has nothing to live on but his salary, 6,000 or 7,000 francs; he's commander of the Protestant branch of the Teutonic Order. He's kindly through philosophy and also, I believe, through tenderheartedness; and, he deliberately sings everybody's praises with an appearance of candor, which makes everybody delighted. Has a great love for Frau von Marenholtz, his daughter, an accomplished coquette who completely captivates Brichard. 12

Father of a witless savage, a genuine military man, excessively strong, well fitted to disgust any man thinking of following the profession of arms. This son, named Ferdinand, didn't want Brichard and me to call him that. 13

Herr von Bothmer doesn't have liberal and settled ideas about anything. He's a mediocre and amiable little philosopher. Jacobsohn, on the contrary, is really the most intelligent man here. No one would have any doubt about it if only he knew French passably. 14

Speculations

1. In his description of Jacobsohn, to what technique does the author resort? Does he seem justified?

2. What is your impression of Herr von Siestorpf as described by Stendhal? How would you treat such a person if he were in your circle of acquaintances?

3. Why does the author suggest that Messrs. von Münchhausen and von Strombeck would make one excellent man if packaged together? What two contemporary or historical public personalities would fit the same description? If you could take on the characteristics of another person and add them to yourself, what would these characteristics be?

4. In paragraph 12, what is the difference between being kindly "through philosophy" and being kindly "through tenderheartedness"? If you had to choose, which would you prefer?

5. All of the men described are listed as intelligent. What "handicap" keeps Mr. Jacobsohn from being quickly and fully acknowledged as the most intelligent of the men described? Is this judgment justified? Why or why not?

Spin-offs for writing

1. Using your own ability to analyze character and disposition, provide several examples of people whom you consider intelligent. Follow Stendhal's technique of being ruthlessly observant and honest.

2. Choose a person who, if given the chance, could make a difference in our society. State the most prominent feature of that person's character and provide an extended illustration of the feature. For instance, you might choose Bill Clinton for his relentless and compulsive energy, illustrating this feature with some anecdote from his presidency.

SIEGFRIED SASSOON

Siegfried Sassoon (1886–1965) was an English poet and novelist. An officer during World War I, he was decorated for heroism; yet, ironically, his poetry was known for its satirical and shockingly graphic treatment of trench warfare and for its attacks on the hypocrisy of treating combat in war as a glorious kind of patriotism. Despite his own bravery, Sassoon deplored the grim brutality of war and its accompanying waste. He felt that the only proper attitude toward war was that of the pacifist. His poetry included The Old Huntsman *(1917),* Counter-Attack *(1918),* Satirical Poems *(1926),* Vigils *(1935), and* Sequences *(1957). He wrote a fictional semi-autobiographical trilogy:* Memoirs of a Fox-hunting Man *(1928),* Memoirs of an Infantry Officer *(1930), and* Sherston's Progress *(1936). Segments of his private life were recorded in the* Siegfried Sassoon Diaries, 1920–1922 *(1981), from which the following entry is taken.*

While sitting with a friend in a half-empty concert hall, listening to an eighteenth-century German quintet played by a group of ladies, and being bored by the mediocrity of the performance, the author inspects the performing musicians and suddenly recognizes an old friend of his mother's who used to teach his brothers the violin. Somehow this sudden appearance of a past association recalls vividly the whole of his former life, which was so different from his life in the present.

June 28, 1921

There's no doubt that certain incidents are symbolic. This evening showed me an epitome of certain changes in my life. This sort of thing can happen at any time, if one meets people who belong to one's definite *past* when one is with someone (or doing something) belonging to the immediate present and the unresolved future. Tonight seemed poignant because Mother was in it: and she belongs neither to the past nor the present. I ought to say that she belongs to both; but it wouldn't be true.

I must be careful not to exaggerate the significance of such events, but this evening contained a swift and lucid condensation of several years. It was complete and inevitable, as though it were the result of long rehearsal and preparation.

I had arranged to spend the evening with Gabriel (whom I'd not seen since June 3rd). Being in an economizing mood, I decided to give the Russian Ballet a miss. (If I'd wholly acquiesced in the G. atmosphere, I'd have gone to the Ballet, and there'd have been nothing to write about.) But I decided on a compromise evening— the sort I'd spend if I were alone. And of course everything miscarried.

4   I got a couple of press-tickets from Turner for a concert at Steinway Hall. I hoped that the concert would be soothing and sensible. There was to be a Schubert quintet. I knew nothing about the musicians taking part in the performance.

5   Immediately after dinner (the usual dreary affair at the Reform) I took G. to the concert. We arrived a few minutes late, and sat down in the back row of the stalls. The hall was less than half-filled, and the audience looked stodgy and dowdy. (I remembered that I'd not been to Steinway Hall since 1912, when I heard Buhlig play there.)[1]

6   A perfunctory eighteenth-century German quintet was being played by some ladies. The first violin wore a small round hat; the others were bare-headed; this produced an incongruous and amateurish effect, as though they'd just 'dropped in' for a bit of music.

7   The performance was devoid of authority and precision, and the tone was without resonance. I was at once aware of an oppressive feeling; I realised that I was already acutely 'bored'. The man next me was reading a magazine! Gabriel resigned himself to a dull evening, not yet knowing how I'd behave.

8   I inspected the performing ladies. They were all of them very much in earnest; doing their utmost to achieve an efficient 'rendition', and apparently enjoying the music more than their audience. The lifeless classical suite proceeded; and then the unexpected thing occurred. I was startled! But not by the music. I recognized among the performers an old friend of my mother's, a very nice woman who used to teach my brothers the violin. I'd known her all my life. And there she sat, bowing away in her dignified style, as I've so often seen her do, in sonatas by Handel and Corelli.

9   This spectacle, and her immediate association with a familiar and rather tedious type of music, recalled the whole of my early life in a most vivid way. I glanced at G., who was leaning back with his eyes closed. *He* had no connection with my life until thirty-two months ago.

10 Mother always disliked and distrusted G. She still talks about him as 'that hopeless creature', and I only took him to Weirleigh three times, ending in the summer two years ago. Mother intuitively recognized that he didn't belong to her world. His half-frivolous and wholly pleasure-loving temperament repelled her (as it often repels me).

[1] Richard Buhlig, American pianist (1880–1952).

The next moment I caught sight of Mother, sitting half-a-dozen rows 11
in front of us, with her countrified black hat and bleached-looking
white hair.

I didn't know that she was in London. She had come, of course, 12
because her old friend was playing in the quintet. Pity stabbed my
heart as I recognized her. There was a gulf of more than six rows of
seats between us. She belongs now to a different life from mine, a
remote worn-out life from which I've escaped into the adventurous
uncertainties and perplexities of active experience. Mother seemed
indigenous to the mechanical serenity of the dull classical music. I
could anticipate every phrase, as I can when she talks about the
weather and the servants and the doings of relatives. I knew exactly
how each movement would end. I'd heard it all before, or something
very similar. And here it was being indifferently rehearsed before a
stodgy audience.

It was a futile echo of something which had long ceased to interest 13
me, like the village cricket-club and the political reactions of the
local gentry. I'd prefer to be harrowed by dissonances of Schönberg
and Stravinsky, or exasperated by the dogmatic socialism of a reactionary labour-leader.

If I'd been alone I'd have moved up and spent the rest of the evening 14
with Mother. But I was with G. already. G. represents green chartreuse and Epstein sculpture. Mother is G. F. Watts and holy communion. They can't be mixed.

And I foresaw exactly how Mother's hostility would stiffen and 15
how frigidly when she was confronted by G. I should only have
spoilt her evening if I'd emerged from that back row. The largo
ended with pompous and harmonious dignity. Mother began to applaud. I left the hall hastily, followed by G. who was immensely relieved at being allowed to escape so early.

Out on the pavement, in the cool cloudless evening, I stared at the 16
yellow sky, took a deep breath, and decided to go on to see Pavlova
dance at the Queen's Hall—ballet time—something lively would be
a pleasant contrast. G. was delighted.

The past receded, as Mother will recede when she is dead and I have 17
other things to think about. That sounds brutal and callous: but it
is true.[2] We left the past in that stuffy hall, lulled by academic

---

[2] No; it is not true. But it *felt* true when I wrote the words. 14.9.26.S.S. And since she died she seems nearer than ever—a spiritual reality. 26.3.49.S.S.

eighteenth-century music badly performed. Poor old Mother. But what else could I do?

18 The Pavlova show was a failure. Queen's Hall stalls were crowded with suburban-looking people, vulgar but enthusiastic. The dances were tawdry; the music was meretricious and obviously 'popular'. In spite of Pavlova's exquisite technique, the 'show' was the Nijinsky Ballet debased to suit the palate of the Ballad Concert public.

19 And Firbank[3] was there. We encountered him at the bar, during an intermission, flushed and florid, fantastic and dishevelled, grasping a dark-brown brandy-and-soda in his wobbly hand.

20 He is one of the things that amuse G. 'Simply too marvelous!' He belongs to the life into whose fringes I am drawn by my 'friendship' with G. He is the type of man that G. would have become if he'd never met me. A talented drunken freak without enough strength of character to steer him through the shoals of intellectual Bohemia.

Speculations

1. The author insists that his experience at the concert symbolized his entire past. How, in your view, was this connection made? Trace the process of how it happened?

2. What do you think the author means when he writes that he prefers the "dissonances of Schönberg and Stravinsky" to the music his mother enjoys, and he would rather be "exasperated by the dogmatic socialism of a reactionary labour-leader" than to listen to the "political reactions of the local gentry"? (See paragraph 13.) Do you see similar differences between yourself and your parents? If so, what are they?

3. Why do you suppose the author's mother never liked the author's friend Gabriel? Is this attitude typical or atypical? Give reasons for your answer.

4. Would a friend like Gabriel appeal to you and would you seek to establish a close friendship with such a person? Why or why not? What, if anything, might he contribute to your life and what might he destroy? Be specific in answering these questions.

5. In your opinion, how does one's taste in literature, music, painting, and other arts affect one's lifestyle? Supply examples to support your point of view.

---

[3]Ronald Firbank, eccentric novelist (1886–1928).

Spin-offs for writing

1. Write an essay in which you provide an illustration of how an event in your life changed your attitude or your taste.
2. Describe your closest friend and give examples of how that friend is a good or bad influence on your life.

JOYCE MARY HORNER

Joyce Mary Horner (1903–1980) was an American poet and novelist, born in England, who spent twenty-four years of her life as a member of the English faculty at Mount Holyoke College in Massachusetts, retiring from this post in 1969. In 1930 she published an article in the Smith College Studies in Modern Languages *on women novelists and their connection with the feminist movement—a work that predated the actual feminist movement by forty years. In 1974 she took a serious fall while in a hospital for tests, and this accident aggravated her already serious and crippling arthritis, forcing her to leave the home she shared with her close friend and colleague Elizabeth Green, and move into a convalescent hospital. While in the hospital, she began to keep a journal in which she drew some witty and touching portraits of those around her. This journal also reveals her deep love for literature, the arts, and politics and is inspiring in the way it shows how someone with diminished physical abilities can still lead a richly-textured life of the mind and spirit. In addition to many poems, Joyce Mary Horner published two novels,* The Wind and the Rain *(1943) and* The Greyhound and the Leash *(1949).*

What follows is a realistic picture of the lives people lead in nursing homes, where they are forced to confront their physical and mental frailties and the erosion of time as they face the reality of approaching death. While the author is neither maudlin nor melancholy, she does provide dramatic examples of the difficulties arising from getting old. But her point of view is always good humored, courageous, and sympathetic.

March 11 [1975]

1 Everyone wants to go home. Perhaps that says too much. Everyone "wants out." Or there may be some who are beyond wanting as much as that. But the woman who calls "Martha" over and over, the woman who calls "Eileen," want what they used to have and sometimes think they can get it if they call loud enough. (The woman who calls "Eileen" or "Irene" sometimes wants less than that. She wants someone to untie her and asks anyone who passes. Sometimes she'll say "Man, bring a hammer," but it's still to be untied. I wonder if she ever contemplates the next step after being untied; if she can.) As I write I hear a man across the hall say, "I couldn't go anywhere. I don't know where my folks are. I know where they were." That is the situation of many. One of the men in the room opposite owns a house quite near and it is empty, except for a cat whom his sister feeds. His roommate, who is 92 and very ready to be "going on 93," is as nearly reconciled as anyone I have met, the last of his family and with a certain pride in survival, in his able-bodiedness (he can take quite long walks in the right weather), in his appetite. He is deaf

and cannot see to read, facts probably overlooked by people like me who think "if I could walk like that, I'd go home." . . .

April 29

In a way both days I wrote nothing down were high days. Sunday, I walked with the walker on the cement walk at the front in a strong, rather cold wind and felt as if I were climbing a mountain. The sun was in and out, the sky blue and grey, the clouds going by fast—an English day. But I wasn't thinking of anything but that I was walking in a wind and managed it.

Yesterday my moment of achievement came when I got out of my chair without help—I haven't been able to repeat it. But oddly another high moment came when I was sitting under the hair dryer with Elizabeth and Millie, and drinking tea and looking out at the still bare trees against another grey-blue sky. It surprises me that it is possible to feel that kind of exhilaration when one is past seventy. Each time I feel it may be the last, but that is partly superstition, partly habit. Partly common sense.

Read the *New Republic* and the world returned. Having read T.R.B. and others on Vietnam, I read Frank Kermode on the perilous state of the arts in London—the taxes, the terrible prices, and the threat of extinction. As he says, no one wants the Old Vic to be turned into a Bingo hall.

Today the hired men are taking people for routine rides in wheelchairs. (It is possible they are volunteers, as any of them might be retirement age. One looks like a church deacon.) I think any way of getting out is good, but do not want that sort of professional jaunt. I walked my three cement blocks in the coolish sun. . . .

June 27

I noted that several of the ninety-year-olds enjoyed their food yesterday more than I did and could eat cucumbers and sauerkraut and onions and peppers better than I could. Not worth being 90 for, though, even if one acquired their appetites. Miss Z. next to me, who *is* 90 and has all her faculties, said she felt 90 was quite enough. One woman at the end of the table who did not eat made plaintive noises all the time, but she does the same thing even when her daughter is wheeling her in a wheelchair. Mrs. Sullivan at another table was still calling out "Martha," and once in a while someone would tell her, "Martha's at work, Kathleen." Miss Z. said, "Does one ever get used to these sounds?" I suppose the answer is yes and no. One cannot hear them for some time and then they sweep over one again, not a *memento mori* but a memento of how it is, not being able to die. . . .

July 3

7   There was much good in yesterday, including the fact that my knees worked better—better than today. I managed to get outside twice, mostly in the company of the old benchers. One who is 95 told me he'd lost his wife ten years ago after sixty-five years of marriage. "And when you lose your wife. . . ." he said and couldn't go on. I couldn't say much that he could hear. He wears a religious medal and, no doubt, waits upon the good Lord's time for him. I come nearest to conversation with Mr. O., who at least knows a bird when he sees one, and is always gentle and courteous, but he too is going deaf, as no doubt I shall go. Mr. H. went to mass for the first time since he came here. Mr. O. said, "Mister's gone to mass. I can't believe it. He's told the priest he didn't want to see him at all. He said, 'I know where I'm going!'" But he suddenly went. Out of doors, a perfect summer day.

8   Today another perfect summer day, when I felt for a short time what may be the height of bliss for a septuagenarian with crippled knees. The place was only just round the corner from here, in the shade with a wind blowing, among ferns, and on clover, with long grasses across the road blowing as I have always loved to see grasses blow, whether in a hayfield, cornfield, or on a walk as at the Malvern cottage. And of course in the meadow in Maine. I remember how my first summer in Maine was full of the sense of "days bound each to each," etc. Eating out of doors in the company one loves has been a constant pleasure in my life. Once there was talk on a ship—the old, slow, Baltimore Mail Line—of making the passengers get together and each tell the high moment of his summer vacation. Fortunately it never happened, but I remember telling the young woman I saw most of on that nice slow voyage that I thought mine was biting into a macaroon on Brighton beach—one of those many days of a long sunny summer when G. and S. lived at Brighton and we had sun, sea, tea (bought in a teapot in a little hut) so many times. The macaroon moment must have been an apotheosis. Like an adolescent I must say, "I have had this" and not, "I must pay for this." Or even, "I am paying." . . .

July 30 (or 31—I think I've got a day out in my calendar)

9   I keep on being struck by the fact that the people who wait on us are working for very little. They grumble, but also laugh, as they push their mops and cleaners around in the corridor. They have children

whose teeth have to be corrected, and things stolen and this or that expense for the car. Often with the women, their husbands are unemployed or part-time. Others, since the governor's threat of laying off state employees, go in fear for their wives or husbands. This is the Middle America Nixon used to talk about and which he (only now it's Ford) is gradually strangling. They are the ones—except for those already unemployed—who take it first. Elizabeth and I will be caught in it a little later, most of our friends later still. After all, I was young when I worked for next to nothing in the Depression and even so I still went home—once I came back with 75 cents in my pocket. It is the middle-aged ones here I feel most sorry for, old enough to be tired, young enough to have children who still depend on them, though I am sorry for the young nurses too whose husbands have been to college and can't get jobs and the humiliation of dependence, not just because they're men.

Visited Miss K., whose birthday it turned out to be and I think it was good for both. We had a subject—Nixon in the *Atlantic* book review—but got ourselves in round the edges. She is almost certain she is losing the sight of the second eye. This was followed by a wonderful surprise visit from Elizabeth and the complete relaxation of being at home with someone who knows all about one, as deep as one goes. . . .

August 31

It can't be possible that August too is gone. Last August I think I'd just got the sling off my arm, but was full of hope.

What a strange spectacle it must have been yesterday to see Miss K. and me at the ends of her telephone hearing aid (a great device for conversation) reciting in concert "To be or not to be." We got most of it but I still forget about "the spurns that patient merit of the unworthy takes." She remembered it better than I did. We then recited "Thou wast not born for death, immortal bird." I don't know what her roommate thinks. She behaves as if we were not there. The gods—the kind in "The Lotus-Eaters"—would laugh. Is it a way of convincing ourselves we are still the same person? Anyhow I found it exhilarating, though rejecting the bare bodkin as beyond my powers, and postponing it even if I could use it—and, of course, if I had one. And rejoicing over "the insolence of office."

Reading further in the *Harvard Advocate*, I realized, what I had not known, that Auden's death was the perfect one—he died in his sleep after a poetry reading that was a success. What more could one ask? Jo once said that Professor Saunders had a perfect death, sitting in his chair reading the *N. Y. Times*; my uncle Ernest, known in the family as a "scamp" (and that's a word I have not heard for decades), had another kind—he was out in the early morning, picking mushrooms....

September 22

14 I am torn between not wanting the summer to go and wanting Elizabeth to come back. Today very disappointing because warm, and yet cloudy with a shower just when I wanted to go out. From all points of view it is so hard getting out these days and it makes me wonder how I can stand the winter.

15 We have a new inmate called Dotty, which seems an unhappy name for one who is mental in a fey kind of way, with a high voice and laugh and a way of uttering high birdlike sounds. Last night we think she must have untied herself and when she was being tied up again, took to shouting, "Help, help, police." She kept it up a long time. Since we've lost Martha Danielson with her ring of names, to the West Wing, we haven't had anyone who raised so much noise. There is Mrs. P. who calls, "Nurse," or "Jimmy," or "Rich-ard," persistently, but she knows, I believe, what she's doing. She just wants attention. Well, I want more than I get since Sarah left.

16 There is a man here (young for here, though he has a grandchild; his daughters look young—girls, and all much alike, including the grandchild) who is dying slowly. His family comes in numbers and there are always some sitting outside his door. I think it is cancer of the throat he has and he is kept under drugs most of the time. One niece, a nun not in the uniform of the order, comes often. I wonder if she prays for his death. I get the impression of a large, religious and very devoted family. In an old picture they'd be on their knees round his bed. Here they obey rules and sit in the drab, antiseptic corridors while one goes in. I never have spoken to any of them, but two of his sisters who are well-dressed matrons, sociable, hair well-cared for, etc.—they come every day too. But it is the slim dark girls who wring the heart....

September 23

17 Elizabeth's card about the wild flowers by the beach, somewhere in Maine or New Brunswick, moved me to tears not so much of nostalgia as of *desire*. That is one of my ideal landscapes and no one should live too close to it—one should come upon the beach, with its rocks and wild roses and any sea birds and driftwood. No Daniel Hoffmans to try and tell you it's private.

Cheered up in very low spirits by reading that the Willits–Hallowell Center at Mt. H. promises one "unabated happiness." I thought that was solely within the jurisdiction of heaven.

September 24

A nurse this morning complained that she kept on getting the same patients, one who was always taking her clothes off, one who screamed, "Police!"—and one who fought and bit and scratched. It is hard on these young women. But terrible to think of being reduced to biting and scratching and screaming. And not to be able to say, "There but for the grace of God," as it may happen to oneself, with or without the grace of God.

I suppose the man who is dying so slowly, and I am sure painfully in the hours he can't have the drug, is an example of what one would choose in preference to the hospital method of keeping the body alive. (There's a suit on this in Penna.—or N.J.—at the moment, the parents begging or indeed suing the hospital to let their daughter die, when she is in a coma, and there is no hope of recovery.) I'd still take this way, but it is unbearable for them all that his body clings to life.

September 25

Woke to rain, with the promise of more. There goes my picnic with the Potters. Today Paul has his operation and Connie will be with him. Half the reading group in hospitals, one way or another, the other half on the road in Canada. But we got the G Minor Quintet on *Morning Pro Musica*—I think that would have to be one of my six desert island records, a game they used to play on the BBC. I always marvel that anything can have so much of the sense of tragedy of life in it and rise above it in the last movement. The music was all good this morning—I find I've enjoyed the Chopin series and especially the Preludes.

September 26

The man (Mr. Moriarty) died a few minutes ago. It was strange to realize it by the fact that all of the watchers went away—I'd watched them come in at different times for so long and just now happened to look and see them all going away together, two sisters, two young girls, and an older woman, probably his wife. Someone has been here day and night for what seems a long time—it's been their life and they'll miss it at first. Without knowing them at all, except for an exchange of greetings with the sisters, I have found the whole thing moving, unlike all the other deaths while I've been here. There was something very sad in the little group going away in silence, while up and down the corridor different radios and TVs uttered different sounds, a total din.

September 27

23 Today a very low point—weather, feelings inside, asthma, minor minimal disappointments, like failing to get my letter to Elizabeth in Nova Scotia and the facts that Bertile did not think my Brighton poem worth commenting on—perhaps it is for the family circle. Having begun to be interested in writing again, I should school myself to the idea, probably the reality, that what I write does not belong to the times.

24 Listened to a long conversation between Jimmy and Mrs. Hill on the chaos in the kitchen and over the serving of trays that is a result of the new management. And I'd been so much aware of the chaos in the nursing service as compared with, say, the summer. And of course all this coincides with the weather that is not summer, floods of rain, rivers rising, the apple crop spoiling. Summer's over.

Flood warnings out until 2 A.M. Several streets closed.

June 18

25 My anniversary. I have lived here two years and survived, though not without scars and deterioration. (I was deteriorating before the accident, however.) This morning after hearing Elizabeth was coming out for a picnic and then getting the Academic Overture on the radio, I felt extraordinarily alive, while yesterday I felt shut in impenetrable gloom, changing only to a kind of desperation when I spilled a glass of milk over everything. I almost cried over the spilt milk—it was too much. A climax of absurdity and littleness. . . .

July 11

26 There are many things I've meant to put down, but laziness grows and I suppose the taking things for granted, as if this were the normal world. I read less, write less—though more, I suspect, than most people here—enjoy sitting out better than anything, in the shade of warm days with a breeze stirring, sounds of wood thrush and occasional cardinal, very occasionally the smell of pine.

27 Nevertheless there have been events this week. One was a select dinner for about thirty people, with steak and champagne. It was select, in that all the people there were *compos mentis*. It was an extraordinary **mixture** as regards clothes, however—some in hospital nightgowns, even in 1776 type—some in lacy, chiffony, old-lady type of

things. I wore a cotton dress and my roommate something quite impressive from Angotti's. The food was good, so much above the standard that it's hardly worth comparing them, but the whole thing just missed being festive.

Another event was the arrival yesterday of the wedding party of my roommate's grandniece. The bride and bridesmaids very charming, also the bride's mother in a range of summery colors to match the day. Marian was bowled over by it. It was probably good for everyone to see them—so much youth and freshness, hope and flowers—their floating stuffs, garden party hats, and the perfection of summer weather, the kind every bride must desire.

A sad event was the departure of Jean, the nurse who has been here all the time I have, the one who lends me books and whose high spirits—singing and dancing in the halls—I have partly lived on. Yet she has no easy life.

Background to all this, the sounds from the next room, a Miss T. who calls out incessantly for everything, necessities and trifles, in a faint voice the nurses very rarely hear. "Oh! please come nurse. Louisa. Roger. Boys and girls. Oh! please help me"—then she cries, with the forced tears of a child wanting attention. Then her roommate joins in, "Crybaby," she says. "Get me out of here," says Miss T. over and over, and once a voice very much stronger than Miss T.'s, "Nurse. Come and get this woman off my neck."

July 13

My birthday, the third here and the saddest. The first, though I had to be lifted into the chair, was by far the most festive—champagne under the trees on a hot day and all the Reading Group and Jo sitting there, when I turned round at the bottom of the ramp and saw them. Then I had no doubt I'd get home, though I did not think it would be soon. The second was not strictly speaking here; I had it at home and the same people were there, but I got the cake and the Happy Birthday singing here the next day, to my surprise. Today was a day of cold, gloomy weather, no rain but no sun either—or just gleams now and then. I was still depressed from my visit to the dentist and the knowledge that the tooth that is bothering me can't be saved—and what is that going to lead to? But there was a very good letter from Susan, and one from Bertile with a charming French card of snowdrops—esperance, etc.—and a surprise one from Julia who recreated the prize-giving day at Wells Cathedral School most vividly—as she said, the essence or cliché of all summer prize-givings. Julia renews my youth, but not for long. Several people have told me I don't look 73 and I am glad of it, but Oh! God, today I feel it—73 and falling to pieces, knees, teeth, and insides. I wonder how Lord Clark, whom I still think of as Sir Kenneth, my exact twin at so great a distance, has passed his 73rd birthday?

32 The hospital gave me another hairbrush. . . .

March 28 [1977]

33 Yesterday, when someone opened the door, a cat came in, not one of the wild ones who live outside but someone's pet who had strayed. It was a flower of a cat, all the things I like, pansy-tiger markings and a round face and big paws. It stirred all the ailurophile in me as I was allowed to pet it a few moments, to loud purrings and beautiful cat gestures. I thought of the hermit who gave up all but his cat.

34 My watch is running down, along with my knees. I can buy a new watch and shall have to. At the same time I hanker after a new dress, which seems folly. What is that Hardy poem, "When I behold my face / And view my wrinkled skin" and at the moment my downtrodden-looking hair. Yet I still want a new dress. Renouncing the world is hard.

35 Poor L.M. distressed this morning because they wouldn't let her telephone her mother in the grave. She knew the number to call too.

36 Today for the first time I felt my legs were not going to make it back to my room. Today also my watch finally stopped.

Speculations

1. In your opinion, what are the worst problems of the patients described by Horner? In other words, which problems do you see as being most inhibiting to a normal life? Give reasons for your choice.

2. In paragraph 2 the author refers to some high moments of the past two days. Do you agree with her that these were high moments? Why or why not?

3. Reread paragraph 8; then answer this question: What was the high point of a vacation that you remember? Why was the experience so wonderful? Supply as many details as come to your mind.

4. In paragraph 16, the author wonders if a certain patient's niece, a nun, is praying for her uncle's death. After reviewing the condition of this old man, what would your opinion be if the niece really had been praying for his death? What is your opinion of assisted suicide? Under what circumstances, if any, do you agree that it should be used?

5. What plans or suggestions would you put forward in order to make life as pleasant, rewarding, and purposeful as possible in convalescent hospitals? Try to formulate a week's plan. Think in terms of abating physical pain, keeping the patients mentally or socially alert, and facilitating human communication among the patients.

Spin-offs for writing

1. Focusing on some organization or institution to which you belong—such as church, college, club, or workplace—write an essay describing the organization or institution and provide three or four vivid examples of the kinds of people who also belong to it.
2. Write an essay in which you show either the good or the bad side of physician-assisted suicide. Use examples to strengthen your point of view. These examples can illustrate what might happen, or they can be true-life examples.

Student Journal—Examples

Katie Unterman

December 30, 1992

I woke up this morning to the unpleasant electronic beeps of my alarm clock and wondered why I couldn't just sleep until my natural biological clock got me out of bed. Getting up, I noticed all the textbooks on my shelves and suddenly couldn't understand why people would consider them more important than the trees that had made them. After an hour's reflection, I fell into a depression. I felt disenchanted with the monotony of my life and the hypocrisy of society, and I longed for anything to make things seem worthwhile.

In *Walden*, Henry David Thoreau wrote, "I went to the woods because I wished to live deliberately, to front only the essential facts of life, and see if I could not learn what it had to teach, and not, when I came to die, discover that I had not lived." Like Thoreau, I wanted to learn what life had to teach, and if Thoreau could find spirituality in the woods, I could at least give it a try.

I have passed by O'Melveny Park a number of times since moving to the hills of the San Fernando Valley in 1985, but until today I had never stopped to appreciate the beauty of that untouched world. O'Melveny Park is located in Granada Hills, in the northern-most part of the Valley. Most of it is undeveloped mountain land (at least, undeveloped in society's eyes), familiar only to a few dedicated hikers. I remember hearing about a fire there a few years ago, but when I visited the park I saw no signs of the fire.

I arrived at the park at about noon, with the sun directly overhead and a few random clouds scattered in the sky. I brought nothing with me except a pen and notebook for recording my thoughts, as I did not want to spoil the park's natural beauty with anything from the outside world. The land was flat where I entered, and I spotted some other people who had also decided to journey to the park that day. None of them noticed my presence. I stood on a grassy knoll, absorbing everything around me. To the left of me there was a small grove of orange trees, behind me more flatland, and everywhere else, mountains.

As I walked towards the orange grove, I heard the warbling of different birds calling out, responding to one another. Birds have a freedom which man, somewhere in the evolutionary process, discarded and forgot; the freedom to soar above the ground and see the world from different perspectives. Most people stay in the same place most of their lives, the same city, the same few miles, living the same routine every day.

I picked an orange from a low branch, peeled it, and squeezed the juice into my mouth. The sweetness trickled from my lips, drops of ambrosia from an orange more savory and juicy than any I had ever bought in a market.

After exploring the orange grove and roaming the flatlands for a few minutes, I became disenchanted because of the contamination and abuse of nature around me. A three-foot-high white wooden fence that surrounded the grassy area was covered with graffiti. A majestic, mature oak tree had names and initials carved on its trunk. Its drooping branches reached out as if it were begging me to help. I pictured a time, maybe 100 years ago, when the entire grassy area had been a forest, where plants grew freely and prospered and no human had ever set foot within miles of them. Now, many of the plants were dying, choking from the pollution, and I doubted that society would ever do anything to try to relieve them.

I felt that far from experiencing nature in its whole, I was merely savoring the "pseudo-nature" society had decided to serve me. I saw what others had decided to do with the park's wildlife; I saw the graffiti and the dying plants; and I knew that I would have done something quite different.

I looked north, towards the mountains, and realized that they were what I had really come to explore. Stretching as far as I could see were green and brown hills, towering over me, untouched and untamed. I gradually made my way to the first of the hills, for although I was eager to explore them, I did not want to hurry and overlook anything. Too often we hurry through our daily routines without noticing everything around us. If only people slowed their lives down just a bit, they would notice much they never knew existed.

I began to ascend the mountain via a dirt path apparently made by some other curious explorers before me, but I soon found myself straying from the conformity of the path. Before long I was pushing my way through the trees and shrubs, on the trail nature had made for me. As I ducked under a tree branch or stepped around patches of bright yellow wildflowers, I felt I was seeing nature in its entirety, and a feeling came over me that no man-made park had ever before given me. I felt as if inside of me was a part of every tree, leaf, and flower; in turn, a piece of me was in every one of them. I felt more inner harmony and serenity than ever before in my life.

With every step I took, deeper and deeper into the mountain foliage, I was certain that no human had ever before touched the same spot. After steadily climbing upwards for about twenty minutes, I reached a small clearing of flat dirt on a ledge of the hill. Looking out, I could see for miles—straight rows of identical red-roofed houses, a crowded freeway almost to the point of gridlock, the brown and green mountains at the other end of the valley, and peeking out from behind the mountains, a layer of muddy brown smog. The smog hung ominously over the valley, turning the sky into a muddy ocean. But from that altitude I could view the unblemished blue sky beyond the smog, and I realized that from the depths of the valley I had always assumed that the sky I saw was of its true color and had never realized how much cleaner and fresher a sky could be. Then I realized that most people living in the valley below would never see the sky as I was seeing it, and that they would continue looking up and calling that muddy color "blue".

Impressed as I was with the view, I had come to the park to get away from society, so I proceeded upward through the underbrush of the mountain. Before long I heard a soft noise, the sound of water rushing over rocks in a stream. I followed the noise, stepping all around until the sound of the water became louder. After about five minutes, I finally pushed back the right branch and found it—a rocky creek with dark green moss growing on both banks. The stream was only about one foot wide and, after prodding the bottom with a stick, I judged the depth to be even less. Yet despite the shallowness of the stream, I could not see its bottom. Since I could not find any signs of fish or any other creatures living in the water, I concluded that society had left its mark there too. Even that stream, so remote and unassuming, was left a victim of society's toxic imprint.

But the soft rushing of the water was soothing, so I sat down on the bank, took out my diary, and began recording my thoughts. And so I am now, near the end of my day spent the way Thoreau would have. It has already begun to get dark, and the beginnings of a beautiful orange and pink sunset are in the sky. I can hear the rhythmic chirpings of crickets and the faint rustlings of rabbits in the brush behind me. I can hear the sound of the water in the stream, continuously rushing over the rocks.

9. Argument.

12th March, 1902. "However much one loves this man whom people regard as a *genius*, to do nothing but bear and feed his children, sew, order dinner, apply compresses and enemas and silently sit there dully awaiting his demands for one's services, is sheer torture." A personal argument. Sophia Tolstoy.

27th June, 1940. "France did not fight." An argument on why the French didn't and couldn't stop the German advance on Paris during World War II. William Shirer.

January 30, 1964. "One thing I know for certain: Unlike most of the members of Hitler's intimate circle, I did not have a crippled psyche." Why he served Hitler. Albert Speer.

22nd November, 1980. "The campaign is on, and I will be part of every part of it—and I will always be out of place." An argument for what the politician should be and do. Mario Cuomo.

CHAPTER 9

Argument

Although it is the most public of all rhetorical patterns because it is the one that always presumes an opposition, argumentation is paradoxically fairly common in the writings of diarists. Indeed, reflection in a journal or diary often leads naturally to internal debate and therefore to argument even within the solitary self. A diarist will write: "I hate war; yet, the world must be protected against persecution by tyrants." Or, "Today the newspaper reported another drive-by shooting; surely some action must be taken to stop such senseless killing." Or, "I wish Dr. Jenkins would quit his long-winded lectures about equipotentialism and would instead analyze individual psychological problems that plague our lives." Each assertion is an arguable one that can lead to vigorous self-debate in a diary. Lacking an external audience, such solitary arguments are likely to be waged honestly, with little or no conscious deception.

Excerpted in this chapter are several examples of arguments conducted within the pages of a diary. Sophia Tolstoy, wife of Leo Tolstoy, the famous Russian novelist, argues that she is tired of serving genius and resents being a slave to a selfish man idolized by the world. In his diary, written during World War II, the American journalist William Shirer argues that France never really fought back during the German attack on Paris. Albert Speer, Armaments Minister and architect to the Nazi regime, argued in his postwar diary that he was different from others in Hitler's inner circle because his psyche, unlike theirs, was not diseased. Finally, Mario Cuomo, Governor of New York, writes a reasoned argument supporting the proposition that a politician must never lose sight of his major goal—to live well and serve well.

While the private diarist may argue with an inner self, the ultimate goal of the public arguer is to influence a reader to some personal point of view, using techniques that will vary with the audience and subject. It is self-evident that the techniques that might work to induce your five-year-old brother to give you a bite of his candy bar will not succeed in persuading your scientific peers that the universe is infinite. The wily debater therefore always comes to the argumentative table armed with the weapons most likely to work against a particular opponent. Here are some of the common tactics and ploys for waging a successful argument.

1. Tailor your arguments to your audience. Written or oral, all arguments consist of pleas and evidence. And most audiences have some

interest in the issue that predisposes them to favor one side or the other. If your pleas are tailored to the particular needs and presumptions of your audience, they are likely to exert a strong appeal. On the other hand, pleas that misjudge the personal stake the audience thinks it has in an issue are likely to fall on deaf ears. For instance, an argument in favor of rebuilding inner cities to create new businesses will appeal more to developers looking for new building sites than to homeowners concerned about the overcommercialization of their neighborhoods. On the other hand, an argument in favor of establishing a neighborhood watch might find instant reception among these homeowners. Effective arguments are always tailored to appeal to specific audiences.

2. The pragmatic arguer will avoid debates that cannot be settled by logic and evidence, or arguments that are already decided in the public consciousness. For instance, the proposition that abortion is murder cannot be proved or disproved because it is based on the belief that fetuses have human souls. But since the existence or nonexistence of a soul cannot be settled by either scientific proof or reasoned logic, arguments about it inevitably end up being circular. Similarly, some beliefs are so solidly entrenched in our social consciousness that they cannot be dislodged. For instance, the libertarian argument that schools, the police, firestations, hospitals, roads, and waterworks should be owned and run by private citizens has never been successful because the overwhelming majority of citizens accept the principle of government management of these facilities and institutions. To argue against a generally accepted belief is usually a waste of energy. The exception to this pragmatic advice is the issue that has become a matter of personal conscience. Indeed, many accepted beliefs that history has proven to be profoundly wrong have been righted by passionate believers arguing from conscience. Slavery is one such issue; school segregation is another. Matters of personal conscience aside, for pragmatic and academic debate you should always choose an argument that is defensible by logic, facts, and evidence.

3. Rely mainly on evidence to prove your point, bearing in mind that merely to assert an opinion is not to prove it. For example, let us suppose that you have made this startling statement: "The so-called Golden Age of Greece was in actuality a dark age of human misery." Your readers will immediately demand proof of such a heretical charge. The evidence from the fourth century B.C. is indeed available. Skeletons dating back to the Age of Pericles, the famous Athenian orator and general, uncovered recently by archeologists, reveal that the inhabitants of that "golden age" were plagued by disease, poor hygiene, malnutrition, and improperly healed injuries. Six out of every ten bodies excavated had hideously decayed teeth. Over half of the skeletons studied showed signs of tuberculosis, malaria, anemia, leprosy, and syphilis. Many had improperly healed broken bones and bore evidence of severe malnutrition. Thirty-five was the average age of the excavated remains at the time of death, revealing a picture quite different from the idyllic lifestyle celebrated in the heroic Greek epics.

Remember, however, that all evidence is not equally reliable or trustworthy. Some basic rules can guide your evaluation of evidence:

- *Use evidence taken only from reputable sources.* For instance, the information about life an Athenian society during the Golden Age comes from archeologist Joseph C. Carter of the University of Texas in Austin, and physical anthropologists Maciej Henneberg and Renata Henneberg from the University of the Witwatersrand in Johannesburg, South Africa. The collaborative research of these scientists was published in the Fall 1992 issue of Research and Exploration, a quarterly journal put out by the National Geographic Society. The evidence can be considered solid since the source is reputable.

- *Verify and check one source against another.* If all of the consulted sources agree, chances are the evidence is good. If they widely disagree, you are on less certain ground. Evidence will necessarily vary on issues still being debated by science. For instance, scientific sources disagree in the assessment of a possible cure for AIDS or even on the scope of the epidemic. With evidence on this subject varying widely, the researcher is forced to exercise discretion in choosing which source to ignore or to cite.

- *Cite only up-do-date or the latest evidence.* Research findings that are fifty years old have most likely since been modified or refuted. For instance, before 1963 quasars were believed to be bright stars within our galaxy; but since then more intense and careful study of the spectra of quasars has concluded that these faint blue celestial objects are possibly eight billion light-years away and outside our galaxy. Usually the latest evidence will be found to be also the most authoritative.

- *Exercise your own judgment and common sense in judging the credibility of experts.* The Book Review Digest *is an excellent reference for critical evaluations of books. Also, you can check the credentials of authors in the various biographical dictionaries or* Who's Who *volumes in specialized subjects, such as* Who's Who in Medicine, Who's Who in American Art, Who's Who in American Politics, Who's Who in Engineering, Who's Who in Music, *and* Who's Who in Australia *or other countries (arranged in alphabetical order).*

- *Be skeptical about statistics.* Most of us tend to believe figures more readily than we do words. "Eighty-five percent of rattlesnake bites are on the hand or arm, proving the risk of playing with rattlers," strikes us as more convincing than "Playing with a rattlesnake is risky business; snakes can bite." Yet writers have been known to *distort or even fabricate statistics. And you should always question the truthfulness of statistics that make giddy claims such as "Every day thousands upon thousands of wives are battered," or "millions of people have become unemployed because of the president's economic policies." Common sense tells us that such statistics are more metaphorical than real. When you do cite statistics, always quote the source. For instance, you might say, "According to a telephone poll of 1,400 adult Americans, taken for Time/CNN on September 22–24, 1992, 62 percent of those responding believed that the quality of our environment is not getting better; only 30 percent believed it was getting better."*

4. Anticipating the opposition in your arguments is a clever way of stealing an opponent's thunder. It may even be tactically smart to concede whatever slight merit you can find in an opposing argument—before you move on to counter or refute it. Here is an example of an argument that acknowledges the opposition and then dismisses it:

We should all stop drinking milk; it was meant for calves, not for human beings. Recent research by the Physicians Committee for Responsible Medicine questions the nutritional value of milk and even suggests that it might be harmful to large numbers of people with allergies. Of course, the dairy industry will disagree, immediately pointing to people's need for calcium, for phosphorus, and for other minerals found in milk. But those minerals can be found in kale juice and in many other products that do not have the harmful allergenic qualities of milk. It is time that we follow the advice of specialists like Dr. Frank Oski, director of pediatrics at the Johns Hopkins University, who invites us to give up drinking milk since its claim to high nutritional value is wrong.

The highlighted sentence, having given a nod to the traditional argument in favor of milk, moves on to counter it with the nutritional wonders of kale juice.

SOPHIA TOLSTOY

Sophia Tolstoy (1844–1920) was best known for being the wife of Count Leo Nikoleyevich Tolstoy, one of Russia's greatest novelists and author of the vast epic, War and Peace *(1869), and the psychological novel,* Anna Karenina *(1877). She was the daughter of Andrei Behrs, a German court physician in Moscow, from whom she inherited her fiery temperament. During his stays in Moscow, Leo Tolstoy fell in love with the Behrs family because of their charming and lively social life, which helped him break out of his hermit's existence. Although he was attracted to all three Behrs sisters, it was Sophia whom he married when he was thirty-four and she eighteen. Much has been written about the stormy relationship of this couple, whose marriage lasted forty-six years and produced numerous children. According to Sophia's diary, the marriage did not turn out to fulfill her dreams of a romantic relationship. In addition to being considerably older than she, Tolstoy was essentially at home in the country, surrounded by peasants, whereas Sophia was city bred and loved the hum and excitement of city life. Her diaries are filled with yearning, bitterness, and emotional outbursts. According to her daughter Alexandra's biography,* Tolstoy: A Life of My Father, *the untimely death of her sons Alyosha and Vanishka placed an unbearable burden on Sophia's delicate psyche and drove her to suicidal depressions. Nevertheless, despite the ups and downs of their marriage, both Leo and Sophia confess a deep love for one another. Eclipsed by her husband's fame as a writer, Sophia's own literary talents were nevertheless considerable. In addition to her famous diary,* My Life *(1922), she also wrote a novel,* Song Without Words *(1898).*

The Lev Nikolaevich of Sophia's diary is of course Leo Tolstoy, whom she had tended to all of her married life. In the entries that follow, we learn that the author—who served as the novelist's secretary, maid, and nurse—has grown bitter and resentful at having, for so many years, subjugated her own interests to Tolstoy's requirements. She wonders if it was fair that she was forced to remain unfulfilled in order to foster and nurture her husband's genius.

1 *March 13, 1902.* It is warmer—13 degrees in the shade—and there was a warm rain. Lev Nikolaevich continues to improve. I am still sitting with him until 5 in the morning; Sasha took my place yesterday and Tanya will do so today.

2 Late yesterday evening I read a translation of an essay by Emerson called 'The Over-Soul.' I could find little new in it: it was all said long ago and much better by the ancient philosophers—amongst other things, the statement that every *genius* is more closely connected to the dead philosophers than to the living members of his

family circle. It is rather a naïve conclusion. Of course it's true that when their material earthly life has fallen away, there remains nothing of these dead philosophers but their written thoughts. So that not only geniuses but we simple mortals, when we read their thoughts, can come into much closer contact with these dead philosophers than with geniuses, even living ones. For living geniuses, until they have thrown off their mortal envelope and passed into history with their works, are created to consume the entire existence of the apparently uncomprehending members of their family circle.

3 For a *genius* one has to create a peaceful, cheerful, comfortable home; a *genius* must be fed, washed and dressed, must have his works copied out innumerable times, must be loved and spared all cause for jealousy, so that he can be calm; then one must feed and educate the innumerable children fathered by this genius, whom he cannot be bothered to care for himself, as he has to commune with all the Epictetuses, Socrateses and Buddhas, and aspire to be like them himself.

4 And when the members of his family circle have sacrificed their youth, beauty—everything—to serve this genius, they are then blamed for *not understanding* geniuses properly—and they never get a word of thanks from the geniuses themselves of course, for sacrificing their pure young lives to him, and atrophying all their spiritual and intellectual capacities, which they are unable to nourish and develop due to a lack of peace, leisure and energy.

5 I have served a *genius* for almost forty years. Hundreds of times I have felt my intellectual energy stir within me, and all sorts of desires—a longing for education, a love of music and the arts ... And time and again I have crushed and smothered all these longings, and now and to the end of my life I shall somehow or other continue to serve my *genius*.

6 Everyone asks: 'But why should a worthless woman like you need an intellectual or artistic life?' To this question I can only reply: 'I don't know, but eternally suppressing it to serve a genius is a great misfortune.' However much one loves this man whom people regard as a *genius*, to do nothing but bear and feed his children, sew, order dinner, apply compresses and enemas and silently sit there dully awaiting his demands for one's services, is sheer torture. And there is never anything in *return* for it either, not even simple gratitude, and there's always such a lot to grumble about instead. I have borne this burden for too long, and I am worn out.

7 This tirade about the way geniuses are misunderstood by their families was provoked by my anger at Emerson and all those who have written and spoken about this question since the days of Socrates and Xantippe.

8 When genuine love exists between a genius and his wife, as there used to be between Lev Nikolaevich and me, she does not need a great mind to understand him, she needs only her loving feelings and the instincts of her heart, and everything will be clear and they will both be happy, as we used to be. I never minded spending my entire life labouring and serving my genius husband, until I read his diaries and saw that he had always blamed *me* for his being so famous. (He had somehow to justify his life of comparative luxury with me.) This happened in the year of my Vanechka's death, when I clung to my husband with my grief-stricken soul—and was cruelly disappointed in my feelings for him.

Speculations

1. In a letter to Sophia, penned in July of 1910, Leo Tolstoy wrote the following: "Your character in recent years has grown more and more irritable, despotic and uncontrolled. The manifestation of these traits of character could not but cool if not the affection itself, at least its expression." How can this statement be reconciled with Sophia's diary entry? What possible explanations can be offered?

2. Raskolnikov, the hero of Fyodor Dostoyevsky's novel, *Crime and Punishment*, proposes a superman theory suggesting that certain geniuses are above the normal system of ethics and justice because their contributions to humanity place them in a category exempt from normal justice. What is your opinion of this theory? For instance, should a literary genius like Tolstoy be free from the responsibilities of fatherhood or marriage in order to pursue his writing, which will be his magnificent gift to society? Give reasons for your answer.

3. What is Sophia's tone in much of the diary? Note, for instance, paragraphs 4–6. Does the tone strengthen or weaken her case?

4. If Sophia were living in today's society and were married to a genius like Leo Tolstoy, would her situation be different from that of her life in the 19th century? Explain your answer.

5. What evidence does Sophia offer in support of her argument that she has been abused? Is the evidence solid or should she have been more selective in her choice of evidence?

Spin-offs for writing

1. Using appropriate examples to support your argument, write an essay in which you support or refute the right of a genius to be above the normal requirements of society.

2. Write an essay in which you either attack the members of your family for throwing roadblocks in the way of your life's goals or praise them for being supportive of your goals.

WILLIAM SHIRER

William Shirer (b. 1904) is an American journalist, historian, and novelist. After graduating from Coe College, Iowa, in 1925, he took a trip to Paris with a friend and loved the city so much that he decided to take a job there with the Paris Tribune. *He quickly formed friendships with other expatriate American writers, such as Harold Stearns, Ezra Pound, Ernest Hemingway, Sinclair Lewis, John Dos Passos, Theodore Dreiser, F. Scott Fitzgerald, and Sherwood Anderson. When Shirer first settled in Paris, he expected to become a poet and novelist, but instead turned to reporting foreign political news. By 1927, when Shirer had covered such important events as Charles Lindbergh's landing at Le Bourget and the Sacco-Vanzetti riots at the American Embassy, he caught the attention of Henry Wales, Chief of Foreign Service for the* Chicago Tribune, *and was asked to become a foreign correspondent for the home paper. In 1937 Shirer moved to Berlin, where he was involved in broadcasting for CBS. While in Berlin he kept a diary, published in 1941 under the title* Berlin Diary: The Journal of a Foreign Correspondent, *1934–1941, which quickly became a bestseller. In 1947 he published a sequel,* End of Berlin Diary. *Among his other works are three novels:* The Traitor *(1950),* Stranger Come Home *(1954), and* The Consul's Wife *(1956). His nonfiction works include* The Rise and Fall of the Third Reich *(1960) and* The Rise and Fall of Adolf Hitler *(1962).*

At the time that Shirer wrote the diary entry that follows, he kept his notes hidden in his hotel room because he was afraid the Gestapo might find them and would shoot him for his critical observations of the Germans. For instance, on June 28, 1940, he reported that the German army in Belgium and in France had been abusing the Red Cross sign and had been using Red Cross ambulances as army oil tanks. The frankness and forthrightness of Shirer's observations have made him one of the most important historians of World War II. The following passage is Shirer's view of how France reacted to the German invasion.

Berlin

June 27

1 To sum up:

2 Make some reservations. That it is too early to know all. That you didn't see all, by any means. And all that.

3 But from what I've seen in Belgium and France and from talks I've had with Germans and French in both countries, and with French, Belgian, and British prisoners along the roads, it seems fairly clear to me that:

4 France did not fight.

If she did, there is little evidence of it. Not only I, but several of my friends have driven from the German border to Paris and back, along all the main roads. None of us saw any evidence of serious fighting.

The fields of France are undisturbed. There was no fighting on any sustained line. The German army hurled itself forward along the roads. Even on the roads there is little sign that the French did any more than harry their enemy. And even this was done only in the towns and villages. But it was only harrying, delaying. There was no attempt to come to a halt on a line and strike back in a well-organized counter-attack.

But since the Germans chose to fight the war on the roads, why didn't the French stop them? Roads make ideal targets for artillery. And yet I have not seen one yard of road in northern France which shows the effects of artillery fire. Driving to Paris over the area where the second German offensive began, an officer from the High Command who had missed the campaign kept mumbling that he could not understand it, that up there on that height, dominating the road and providing wonderful artillery cover with its dense woods, the French must have had the sense to plant a few guns. Just a few would have made the road impassable, he kept repeating, and he would order us to stop while he studied the situation. But there had been no guns on those wooded heights and there were no shell-holes on or near the road. The Germans had passed along here with their mighty army, hardly firing a shot.

The French blew up many bridges. But they also left many strategic ones standing, especially over the Meuse, a great natural defence because of the deepness, the steepness of the valley, and its wooded cover. More than one French soldier I talked to thought it was downright treachery.

At no point in France and at only two or three in Belgium did I see a road properly mined, or, for that matter, mined at all. In the villages and towns the French had hastily thrown up tank-barriers, usually of blocks of stone and rubbish. But the Germans brushed them aside in minutes. A huge crater left by an exploded mine could not have been brushed aside in a few minutes.

D. B. in Paris, having seen the war from the other side, concludes that there was treachery in the French army from top to bottom—the fascists at the top, the Communists at the bottom. And from German and French sources alike I heard many stories of how the Communists had received their orders from their party not to fight, and didn't. . . .

11 Many French prisoners say they never saw a battle. When one seemed imminent, orders came to retreat. It was this constant order to retreat before a battle had been joined, or at least before it had been fought out, that broke the Belgian resistance.

12 The Germans themselves say that in one tank battle they were attacked by a large fleet of French tanks after they had themselves run out of ammunition. The German commander ordered a retreat. After the German tanks had retired some distance to the rear, with the French following them only very cautiously, the Germans received orders to turn about and simulate an attack, firing automatic pistols or anything they had out of their tanks, and executing complicated manœuvres. This they did, and the French, seeing an armada of tanks descend upon them, though these were without ammunition, turned and fled.

13 One German tank officer I talked to in Compiègne said: "French tanks in some ways were superior to ours. They had heavier armour. And at times—for a few hours, say—the French tank corps fought bravely and well. But soon we got a definite feeling that their heart wasn't in it. When we learned that, and acted on the belief, it was all over." A month before, I would have thought such talk rank Nazi propaganda. Now I believe it.

14 Another mystery: After the Germans broke through the Franco-Belgian border from Maubeuge to Sedan, they tell that they continued right on across northern France to the sea hardly firing a shot. When they got to the sea, Boulogne and Calais were defended mostly by the British. The whole French army seemed paralysed, unable to provide the least action, the slightest counter-thrust.

15 True, the Germans had air superiority. True, the British didn't provide the air power they could and should have provided. Yet even that does not explain the French debacle. From what one can see, the effectiveness of the air force in this war has been over-emphasized. One reads of the great mass air attacks on the Allied columns along the roads. But you look in vain for the evidence of it on the roads. There are no bomb craters. True, the German technique was first to machine-gun the troops and then, when they'd scattered to the side of the road, to bomb the *sides* (thus sparing the road when they wanted to use it later). But you also see little evidence of this. A crater here and there along the roadside or in a near-by field—but not enough to destroy an army. The most deadly work of the German air force was at Dunkirk, where the British stopped the Germans dead for ten days.

16 On the whole, then, while the French here and there fought valiantly and even stubbornly, their army seems to have been paralysed as

soon as the Germans made their first break-through. Then it collapsed, almost without a fight. In the first place the French, as though drugged, had no will to fight, even when their soil was invaded by their most hated enemy. There was a complete collapse of French society and of the French soul. Secondly, there was either treachery or criminal negligence in the High Command and among the high officers in the field. Among large masses of troops Communist propaganda had won the day. And its message was: "Don't fight." Never were the masses so betrayed.

Two other considerations:

First, the quality of the Allied and German commanding officers. Only a few weeks ago General Sir Edmund Ironside, chief of the British Imperial General Staff, was boasting to American correspondents in London of the great advantage he had in possessing several generals in France who had been division commanders in the World War, whereas all the German generals were younger men who had never commanded more than a company in the last war. Sir Edmund thought the World War experience of his older generals would tell in the end.

It was an idle boast and no doubt the general regrets it now in the light of what has happened. True, the commanding officers of the German army are, for the most part, mere youngsters compared to the French generals we have seen. The latter strike you as civilized, intellectual, frail, ailing old men who stopped thinking new thoughts twenty years ago and have taken no physical exercise in the last ten years. The German generals are a complete contrast. More than one not yet forty, most of them in the forties, a few at the very top in their fifties. And they have the characteristics of youth—dash, daring, imagination, initiative, and physical prowess. General von Reichenau, commander of a whole army in Poland, was first to cross the Vistula River. He swam it. The commander of the few hundred German parachutists at Rotterdam was a general, who took his chances with the lieutenants and privates, and was in fact severely wounded. All the big German tank attacks were *led* in person by commanding generals. They did not sit in the safety of a dug-out ten miles behind the lines and direct by radio. They sat in their tanks in the thick of the fray and directed by radio and signalling from where they could see how the battle was going.

And as was to be expected from youth, these young generals did not hesitate at times to adopt innovations, to do the unorthodox thing, to take chances.

The great trouble with the Allied command—especially the French—was that is was dominated by old men who made the fatal mistake of thinking that this war would be fought on the same general lines as the last war. The rigidity of their military thinking was fixed somewhere between 1914 and 1918, and the matrix of their minds was never broken. I think this helps to explain why, when confronted by the Germans with a new type of war, the French were unable to adjust themselves to countering it.

22 It wasn't that these tired old men had to adapt themselves to a revolutionary kind of warfare overnight. One of the mysteries of the campaign in the west is that the Allied command seems never to have bothered to learn the lesson of the Polish campaign. For in Poland the German army revealed the tactics it would use in the lowlands and France—parachutists and Stukas to disrupt communications in the rear, and swift, needle-like thrusts with *Panzer* divisions down the main roads through the enemy lines, punching them ever deeper and then closing them like great steel claws, avoiding frontal attack, giving no opportunity for frontal defence along a line, striking far into the enemy's rear before he could organize for a stand. Eight months elapsed between the Polish campaign and the offensive in the west, and yet there is little evidence that the generals of Britain and France used this precious time to organize a new system of defence to cope with the tactics they watched the Germans use in Poland. Probably they greatly underestimated the fight the Polish army put up; probably they thought it had been merely a badly armed rabble, and that against a first-rate army like the French, entrenched behind its Maginot Line, the new style of warfare would beat its head in vain. Had the Maginot Line really extended from Sedan to the sea, this attitude might have been justified. But as the Allies knew, and as the Germans remembered, the Maginot Line proper stopped some miles to the east of Sedan.

23 The second consideration is the fantastically good morale of the German army. Few people who have not seen it in action realize how different this army is from the one the Kaiser sent hurtling into Belgium and France in 1914. I remember my surprise at Kiel last Christmas to find an entirely new *esprit* in the German navy. This *esprit* was based on a camaraderie between officers and men. The same is true of the German army. It is hard to explain. The old Prussian goose-step, the heel-clicking, the "*Jawohl*" of the private when answering an officer, are still there. But the great gulf between officers and men is gone in this war. There is a sort of equalitarianism. I felt it from the first day I came in contact with the army at the front. The German officer no longer represents—or at least is conscious of representing—a class or caste. And the men in the ranks feel this. They feel like members of one great family. Even the salute has a new meaning. German privates salute each other, thus making the

gesture more of a comradely greeting than the mere recognition of superior rank. In cafés, restaurants, dining-cars, officers and men off duty sit at the same table and converse as men to men. This would have been unthinkable in the last war and is probably unusual in the armies of the West, including our own. In the field, officers and men usually eat from the same soup kitchen. At Compiègne I had my lunch with a youthful captain who lined up with the men to get his rations from a mobile "soup cannon." In Paris I recall a colonel who was treating a dozen privates to an excellent lunch in a little Basque restaurant off the avenue de l'Opera. When lunch was over, he drew, with all the care of a loving father, a plan for them to visit the sights of Paris. The respect of these ordinary soldiers for their colonel would be hard to exaggerate. Yet it was not for his rank, but for the man. Hitler himself has drawn up detailed instructions for German officers about taking an interest in the personal problems of their men. One of the most efficient units in the German army at the front is its post office which brings letters and packages from home to the men, regardless of where they are, and which attends to the dispatch of letters and packages from the men home in record time. There are few German soldiers who have not dispatched in the last days silk stockings and perfume home to their families through the free facilities of the army post office.

One reason for the excellent morale of the troops is their realization that they and not the civilians back home are receiving the best treatment the nation can afford. They get the pick of the food and clothing available. In the winter the homes of Germany may not be heated, but the barracks are. The civilians in the safe jobs may not see oranges and coffee and fresh vegetables, but the troops see them every day. Last Christmas it was the soldiers who sent food packages home to their families, and not the reverse. Hitler once said that as a private of the last war he would see to it that the men in the new army benefited by the lessons he had learned. And in this one case, at least, he seems to have kept his promise.

Speculations

1. Where does the author state his proposition? At the time he wrote this diary entry, what kind of reactions would the proposition get from Americans?

2. What evidence does the author produce for his argument? Do you consider the evidence convincing? Why or why not?

3. Once he has offered evidence for his proposition, what does the author do next? Do you agree with him? Why or why not?

4. Shirer indicates that another reason for Germany's success in attacking France was that its generals were young, imaginative, and daring whereas the French generals were old, set in their ways, and civilized but frail. What rebuttal can you offer to Shirer's view? In other words, list the advantages of having older, experienced generals and the disadvantages of having younger and inexperienced ones.

5. Review paragraph 22. What innovations of warfare today did not yet exist in 1940? Do you consider these innovations good or bad? Give reasons for your answers.

Spin-offs for writing

1. Write an essay in which you argue that old-fashioned warfare was more heroic than modern warfare. Use solid evidence to make your point.

2. Marshalling specific examples and facts as your evidence, write an essay arguing that young men make better military leaders than older men.

Or

Marshalling specific examples and facts as your evidence, write an essay arguing that older men make better military leaders than young men.

ALBERT SPEER

Albert Speer (1905–1981) was a German Nazi official, administrator, architect, educator, and author. During World War II he served as one of Hitler's major assistants and confidants—constructing many outstanding buildings and being responsible for German armaments and ammunitions. It was his job to support the Nazi army with guns, aircraft, tanks, and bullets. He also supervised the production of synthetic fuel, which became the source of half of Germany's energy output, To accomplish the task, he used slave labor, On May 23, 1945, after Nazi Germany's surrender, he was arrested and tried at Nuremberg for his war crimes. While admitting that he was guilty of certain crimes, he consistently denied having any knowledge of the Nazi death camps. Nevertheless, he was sentenced to Spandau Prison for twenty years. After his release, he wrote revealingly about the inner workings of Hitler's regime. Among his books on Nazi Germany are these: Inside the Third Reich: Memoirs *(1970) and* Spandau: The Secret Diaries *(1976), from which the following excerpt is taken.*

From his prison in Spandau the author ponders the twists of fate and character that brought his life to ruin. While he acknowledges that he made serious errors in judgment, he insists that he was different from the other war criminals—Hermann Goering, Paul Goebbels, Heinrich Himmler, and others—in that he did not have their kind of crippled psyche.

January 30, 1964. Thirty-one years ago today Hitler took power. In our small Mannheim apartment I listened on the radio to the description of the historic torchlight parade that was marching past Hindenburg[1] and Hitler; I never suspected that I might be playing a part in the new era. I did not even take part in the small victory celebration put on by the Mannheim Party organization.

A few months later I met Hitler by chance. And from that moment on everything changed; my whole life was constantly lived under a sort of high tension. Strange, how quickly I gave up everything that had been important to me up to then: private life with my family, my leanings, my principles of architecture. Yet I never had the feeling that I was making a break, let alone betraying anything I cherished; rather the feeling was one of liberation and intensification, as though only then was I coming to my proper self. In the following period Hitler accorded me many triumphs, acquaintanceship with power and fame—but he also destroyed everything for me. Not only a life work as an architect and my good name, but above all my moral integrity. Condemned as a war criminal, robbed of my freedom for half a lifetime, and burdened with the permanent sense of guilt, I

---

[1] Paul von Hindenburg, president of Germany.

must in addition live in the awareness that I founded my whole existence on an error. All my other experiences I share with many; this one is my own.

3   But is it true that Hitler was the great destructive force in my life? Sometimes it seems to me as though I also owed to him all the surges of vitality, dynamism, and imagination that gave me the sense that I was soaring up above the ground on which everyone else was condemned to stand. And what do I mean when I say he took away my good name? Would I have had any name at all but for him? Paradoxically, I might actually say that this is the one thing he did give me and never again will be able to take from me. It is possible to thrust a person into history, but then no longer possible to push him out of it. I could not help thinking of that recently when I read Grabbe's *Hannibal*. The Punic general has likewise reached the end of all his hopes. Before he takes the cup of poison from his Negro slave, the slave asks what will come after the drink. "We will not fall out of the world; we are in it once and for all."

4   So then I ask myself: Would I like to fall out of history? What does a place in it mean to me, slight though it may be? If thirty-one years ago today I had been confronted with the choice of leading a quiet and respected life as city architect of Augsburg or Göttingen, with a house in the suburbs, two or three decent buildings done a year, and vacations with the family in Hahnenklee or Norderney—if I had been offered all that or else everything that has happened, the fame and the guilt, the world capital and Spandau, together with the feeling of a life gone awry—which would I choose? Would I be prepared to pay the price all over again? My head reels when I pose this question. I scarcely dare to ask it. Certainly I cannot answer it at all.

5   *February 19, 1964.* No entries for more than two weeks. But I have kept pursuing the question I recently set. In the interval there has been something of a shift inside me. Was it really the ambition to enter history that drove me on? This is the question I ask myself now. What really was the determining impetus of my life, the driving force of all my actions? One thing I know for certain: Unlike most of the members of Hitler's intimate circle, I did not have a crippled psyche. I was free of corrosive resentment. That fact also immunized me against Hitler's ideology. I was no antisemite; the racial ideas always seemed to me a crotchet; and I also never thought much of the Darwinistic theory of struggle and killing with which Hitler was obsessed; and finally the whole Lebensraum program was alien to me, much as I too wanted to see Germany big and powerful.

Then what was it actually? First and foremost there was the personality of Hitler, which for a long time exerted a hypnotic and compelling effect upon me. But it was not that alone. Almost as strong, if not stronger, was the sense of intoxication Hitler engendered in me, the tremendous intensification of my confidence in my abilities, and which I soon needed like an addict his drug, Then, during the war, as armaments minister, I noticed for the first time that power also meant something to me, the ordinary ambition to belong among the actors in historic events. I remember when Hitler gave me the assignment to build the Atlantic Wall, a system of fortifications from North Cape to the Pyrenees, what feelings of exultation filled me when my signature could mean the expenditure of billions of marks and direct hundreds of thousands of people to the construction sites. Only in retrospect do I become aware that as an architect at Hitler's side I was also seeking the pleasures of power. 6

Yet I am fairly certain that I was artist enough to have given up all the power in the world without regrets if a single perfect building had been granted me, perfect as the Pantheon, the dome of St. Peter's, or one of Palladio's temple-like mansions. To enter history with such a building—that was the ambition that impelled me. That is why I told Hitler, at the height of the war, at the height of my successes as armaments minister also, that I wanted nothing but to be an architect again. 7

Speculations

1. What is your personal judgment of this man Albert Speer? Do you have any compassion for him or do you consider him beyond sympathy and redemption? Give reasons for your answer.

2. If you were in his position, what answer would you give to the question posed by the author in paragraph 4? Would you be prepared to "pay the price all over again?" Why or why not?

3. What about Hitler's leadership style influenced Speer to follow him? Was Speer's an understandable human response, or was Speer following some incomprehensible, irrational urge within himself?

4. In what specific ways did Speer's psyche differ from the psyches of the other intimate disciples of Hitler? How important to the well being or destruction of a society are the characteristics these other disciples of Hitler revealed?

5. In the final paragraph the author implies that he is first and foremost an artist. What does he mean? What does the implication add to our judgment of this man?

Spin-offs for writing

1. Write an argument in which you prove that Albert Speer was an evil henchman of Hitler and deserved his prison sentence like all of the other war criminals.

Or

Write an essay arguing that Albert Speer deserved special consideration because of his attitude and because of the good things he did for Germany, such as developing synthetic fuel and designing some beautiful buildings. (See also question 1, on page 269.)

2. Write an essay in which you argue that power is one of the most corruptive forces in society. State your proposition clearly and provide solid evidence for its support.

MARIO M. CUOMO

Mario M. Cuomo (b. 1932) is an American lawyer who held numerous political jobs, including the governorship of New York State. The son of Italian immigrants, he was graduated cum laude from St. John's University in 1956. An outstanding athlete, he considered a career in sports and for some time played Major League baseball for the Pittsburgh Pirates. Eventually he gave up professional baseball to serve in the United States District Court in New York and the United States Court of Appeals. From 1958 to 1975, he worked as an associate and then as a partner in the law firm of Corner, Cuomo, and Charles. From 1963 to 1973 he served on the faculty of St. John's University School of Law. Extremely popular in his home state of New York, he was elected Secretary of State in 1975, Lieutenant Governor in 1979, and Governor in 1983. During his public offices, he wrote many political essays and also authored two books: Forest Hill Diary: The Crisis of Low-Income Housing *(1974) and* Diaries of Mario M. Cuomo, Campaign for Governor *(1983), from which the following entries were excerpted.*

Cuomo's diary makes clear that running for office in the political world is not conducive to serenity or inner peace for someone who looks at life from an ethical and philosophical point of view. During his heated campaign for Governor of New York, Mario Cuomo has moments of agonized soul searching which remind us that the world's acclaim is just as phantasmagoric as the world's condemnation. In the ensuing entries we are allowed to witness the honest thoughts of a politician glancing into his own heart.

Saturday, November 22, 1990, 6:00 A.M.

Still dark out the window of the 10th floor of the Wellington, muffled sounds of auto engines revving up in the background. A car going by occasionally. Andrew's parrot—or whatever—silent, standing perched on a lamp in the second bedroom. Andrew asleep. A good time to think.

Approaching 50. You will die as you must. Maybe today. If you believe in nothing, you are not sure you would want not to. So you try desperately to believe in "An eternity of peace that's earned." But you don't understand eternity and you're afraid you have not earned it in any event. "A full and happy life for what's left of it." But what is there that I would want to "fill" it with? Achievement? Has anything ever been so useless as the momentary acclaim of a world that does not know you, no matter how "public"? Glory? The fear of shame and rejection is much more powerful a force than the desire for glory. Why? The world's condemnation should be as irrelevant as the world's acclaim. Then why? Why guilt over satisfaction?

3   Think:

4   How you reach a point of review and retrospection. I hope the Lord grades me easily. How you are troubled to think that even being troubled is cause for guilt. Because it's selfish.

5   "Selfish." That's the word. As long as you think about what *you* need, *you* want, *you* feel—as long as you are selfish—you are doomed to frustration. "Me" is a bottomless pit which cannot be filled no matter how much in achievement, glory, acclaim, you try shoveling into it. If only we were good enough to *do* perfectly what we know would work perfectly. But we can't.

6   Why not? When I say "I can't" am I saying it too soon? Am I saying it because I don't want to have to try? Because being required to love denies me too many of the delights of being loved or liked or applauded or smiled upon? And if that *is* the case, then aren't you silly—as Matilda[1] would say—because you know those delights don't last. You've tried them. You've had them. They don't work. A world filled with wisdom and stupidity came before you. And all that was wise told you that those "satisfactions" weren't really satisfactions—except in a terribly transitory way.

7   For God's sake, you know the truth! The truth is that the only way to make anything of your life is to be what you know you're supposed to be. You're kidding yourself if you prefer not to know. And you're kidding yourself if, in trying to be what you know you should be, you fail from time to time and use that failure as an excuse to abandon trying. You know—because it's the only logic—that the test is Timothy's: "to fight the good fight. To finish the race, to keep the faith."

8   I haven't. I've fought a thousand fights but not enough the good fight. I've been in the race but too often running in the wrong direction. I've not—truly enough—kept the faith. I've hurt people by bad example, even my own family. I have too often permitted people to know what I believed was right then witnessed my violation of my own truth. That is the truth and it is part of the pain in my chest.

9   Yes, I do know the truth. And way down deep I even feel the truth. But somewhere before the feeling reaches and marries with my knowing, another feeling intervenes: the imperfect feelings I know are wrong. The desire for the transitory.

10 So all that is left is to try again to *do* what I know I should do. And beginning this moment I will make the effort as I have not made it before because I have never been as old as I am now, and I have

---

[1] Cuomo's wife

never known as much as I do now and I have never had as much to undo as I do now and I have never had as much to compensate for as I do now and I have never had less time than I do now.

7:00 P.M.

Another frustrating day in the Senate. Negotiations all day on various pieces of special session legislation. Bank bill passed us before 6 P.M.[2] Assembly is still arguing it at 7 P.M. It will almost certainly be over tonight.

I'm left with the possibility of running for Governor or stepping aside. That's the case as of this moment, and things are sure to change, maybe even dramatically, but I mustn't do nothing while I'm waiting for all the facts. What I will do now is go forward even faster and harder with all preparations for the race. Things may change—let them. If I run, I will be a long shot, but so were Momma and Poppa.

Sunday, January 3, 1982

The new year begins. A year closer to the end. A chance to begin again the time that's left. A looking back—almost always in regret because of what I have failed to do or did poorly. A new resolve: to remember the purpose; to be what I am supposed to be; to show the love—to live it.

Matilda is exhausted after having spent herself entertaining, shopping, putting up with me and the kids. I must do more to make it easier for her.

Maria[3] will be going back to Iona and we won't see much of her for a while. I'll miss her.

Madeline[4] gets closer to her decision on college.

Chris[5]—still a bit supercharged—is a delight. I must try harder to do more for him. He is bright and sensitive. His sensitivity permits him to enjoy . . . and to suffer. I must be more gentle with it.

Andrew[6] is ensconced in his apartment in Albany pursuing his own life, trying to help here at the same time. I must do everything I can

---

[2] That is, passed the state senate, over which I presided as lieutenant governor. The bill didn't pass the other branch of the state legislature, the assembly, until later that night.
[3] Cuomo's daughter
[4] Cuomo's other daughter
[5] Cuomo's son
[6] Cuomo's son, who helped in the campaign

to make sure he gets past this last six months in school and then the Bar.

19 I did my weekly Sunday night call-in show on WMCA. Matilda is right: it takes a great deal out of our weekend. And though the reviews have been good for all the time I've done it, I've never been satisfied. I'm constantly uneasy about not having all the detailed information I need to answer each question on hand, immediately. I'm also struck by the difficulty of offering solutions to most of the issues that are raised. Sometimes it is—or seems to be—nothing more than an exercise in futility. So many of the problems—crime, unemployment, the homeless, the disabled, a chaotic tax structure—seem totally beyond our capacity to solve at the state level, or at any level of government. The temptation is to turn away, to give up the effort.

20 It's clear that this lack of confidence, even disdain for what government can do, is helping push the population of the city and state dramatically to the right. It's not just capital punishment and toughness on the poor. It's a general rejection of anything perceived as "liberal," unless the one offering the opinion is the immediate recipient of the benefit of the program. A welfare mother will be liberal on welfare. A prisoner will be liberal on penal reform. But even a welfare mother and a prisoner will be less than liberal on the programs that don't affect them. The senior citizens who are not rich are conservative on everything except Social Security and programs for the elderly.

21 Of course these are not universal truths, but they are dominant trends, more clearly pronounced than any opinions I've yet observed since I have been measuring public opinion.

22 Almost always the tendency is to see things from a narrow self-interest without the embarrassment that used to accompany the admission that one was self-seeking. It's now recognized, understood, accepted that the name of the game is taking care of one's self.

23 That leaves the politician with choices. Go along with the dominant trend and try to give the people all that they want to assure yourself popularity, enough to win the chance to serve. Then continue to behave that way in order to continue to earn the right to continue to serve. That's "good politics": it wins.

24 Another choice is to try to lead—at least in opinion—by pointing to what you think is a better way. This requires disagreeing with the people's dominant opinions from time to time and trying to convince them they are wrong. This is risky politics, and today it does not appear to succeed often, but it's the only kind of politics I'm comfortable with.

What is clear is that it is not just risky but suicidal, politically, to disagree with prevailing opinion and not to offer alternatives. Too often I am perceived as doing that.

I will have to take greater pains to be sure that when I disagree I show the alternatives.

Tonight, Chris asked why I stay in this political life. A good question.

I've never been totally satisfied with having to deal publicly. I tell myself I do it because public service is "good," but then I doubt I would be so selfless about it. So I continue to inquire.

I've always preferred privacy. Loneliness has never been the threat to me that the world has been. The more deeply I have become involved in opening myself, revealing myself, discussing myself, the more vulnerable I have felt. Nor do I see this life as proving any kind of personal success. My mind tells me the "success" is little more than good luck attached to efforts you make that aren't much different from the efforts of many others who don't get touched by the good luck. Why, then, am I in politics at all? I take power too seriously to be totally comfortable with it. It's not the notoriety: I'm reasonable enough not to attach significance to that. Indeed, on those occasions when acclaim does come, when the applause is loudest, I am the most uncomfortable, because at those times I judge myself so much more harshly than others do. When the rejection comes—the defeat, the disdain, the inattention—I feel it. But I am not allowed even the luxury of feeling sorry for myself, because quickly the intellect reminds me that however "natural" the hurt is, it is inconsistent with the truth as I know it, which is that the ultimate virtuous condition is selflessness.

Always, the feeling is one of being out of place. Not enjoying fully the things I most enjoy, not even being allowed the consolation of self-pity. Always, the nagging truth is that I should be something else—a person who gives only to give, who works only to provide, who speaks only to soothe or persuade for the good, who strives only for others. And always there is the depressing reality that I fail utterly at that truth, that my emotions are at war with it—or at least are too strong to surrender to it.

In the end, I am a man who knows what to do but knows even more sharply that he has failed by his own standards to do it as well as it can be done.

I am now in the midst of a campaign I cannot win. If I am successful at the polls, I will challenge the motivation that drove me to it, and wonder about the life it then requires. If I am not successful, I will feel again the sharp pain of rejection and "humiliation" and will dislike myself for feeling it. But I am in the midst of it. For however long it lasts, it is here. The anticipation, the frenetic work, the perpetual motion, the frustration of a thousand tasks to perform without the time to perform them; the concern about the public appearance, the debates, acceptance by the editorial boards, trying to win the favor of a union or a contributor or an important leader without losing your soul; the exhilaration of the contest, the waiting for a hundred verdicts, the victories, the coups, the soaring prospects, the defeats, the losses, the betrayals, the depths, the fear of slander, the bitterness, the embarrassment, the tears, the satisfaction, the pride, the happiness. The campaign is on, and I will be part of every part of it—and I will always be out of place.

Tuesday, March 30, 1982

33 Again today I was reminded that perhaps the greatest danger of all in a campaign like this one is forgetting why you are doing it—or at least why you should be doing it. The temptation is to measure everything as though victory is more than the most important thing—it is the only thing. A bad day in the press, an important rejection, a slumping poll—and the spirits sag, frustration, depression, sometimes even anger set in . . . because we forget that what is really important is the effort: doing it well, trying it well, living it well.

34 I don't like hearing from people: "You're a fighter; very competitive; everything is a challenge to you; you just win for the sake of winning. I think Andrew is like you." I hope he's not! And I hope I'm not. The political power one wins is good for the good it can do. The acceptance is good for the political power it gives. The joy of winning is the joy of having an opportunity to do the good. Losing, not having the acceptance that gives the political power, is being denied the chance to do good. But trying for it—for the right reason—is a good by itself. I'm so sure this is true that it's hard to live with the reality of my departure from it.

Speculations

1. What is your reaction to the author's insistence that the only worthwhile purpose is to "fight the good fight, to finish the race, to keep the faith"? Where did this idea originate? What is its meaning?

2. Is Cuomo right in saying that the fear of shame and rejection is a much more powerful force than the desire for glory? Use present-day politicians as your standard for answering the question.

3. In paragraph 7 Cuomo gives a recipe for success in life. What is it and how does one follow it? Offer your own process for doing what Cuomo suggests.

4. Cuomo's argument is highly personal—really a debate with himself. What kinds of evidence does he use to convince himself. How well has he convinced you?

5. According to paragraph 20, disdain for what government can do is pushing New Yorkers dramatically to the right. What does Cuomo mean? Do you see this same trend in your home state? Why or why not?

Spin-offs for writing

1. Using the following quotation, taken from Mario Cuomo's diary, write an essay in which you use evidence from your own experience and that of others to support the quotation:

    "The world's condemnation should be as irrelevant as the world's acclaim." (See paragraph 2.)

2. Argue against the trend, described by Cuomo in paragraph 22, that today "the name of the game is taking care of one's self." In other words, argue for a society in which people are compassionate and interested in the "greater good" rather than in me, me, me. Use experience, expert testimony, and facts to create solid evidence to support your proposition.

Student Journal—Argument

David Beckham

Wednesday, Nov. 28, 1990
Paris, 7:50 AM

It is beginning to be light outside.

I was up at 5:15 for a while, thinking about the concepts regarding workable and impossible relationships that were raised in my conversation last night with David. When I awoke again from a dream it was 7:15. I had been trying, in the dream, to reassemble a primitive drum that I had owned, but which had somehow been left in an intersection surrounded by traffic.

When I sat up on the side of the bed, I thought what an unlikely prophet I make, but I feel as if that has become my mission in life, and that perhaps I am called on to reform the world. My experience with Yorgos (George, in English) is, of course, what has prompted this bizarre conviction. Without that I would not be changed. Something happens between two men (or rather can, perhaps infrequently, happen) that seems to lead to a great unfolding and opening of the spirit of each. Yorgos contended that we are born alone and die alone, and even on those rare occasions when we feel we are one with someone else, the experience is an illusion of not being alone. But I disagree with him. This experience transcends separateness, and we are not alone. And after this experience, the condition of not being alone continues (for how long I don't know). The road to this condition seems to lead through passion (is it the only road?) but the passion is something it goes through—it is not the end point of the road. I don't know what the end point of the road is, perhaps it does not have an end, or perhaps that road leads where the poem I wrote about our first night implies.

Deity

> Are you not, then, because I worship you,
> A god? This rite, then, is it not, a sacrament?
> This bed not, then, an altar, where I make
> Oblation, receive communion, sacrifice?
> Have I not, then, prayed, and studied
> Doctrines of the past, and learned
> Entreaties to invite this visitation?
> Long abstinence, rites to purify, and
> Longing witness to the quests of other
> Pilgrims brought me, humble, to this night.
> Will you not, then, know yourself a god
> Because I worship you? Will you not,
> Then, attend the services I organize
> On your behalf, preside, reveal
> The mysteries that only gods
> Can show to mortal men. May we not,
> Together then, discover all the rituals
> Proper to the elevation of a god so new
> To godhead? Will you not, then,
> Elevate me, too?

I do know that it seems possible that human relations of a romantic nature may well be founded on completely false data. If the isolation of people is something that *can be overcome*, then most of what we have been taught is nonsense. The twentieth century basis for homosexual relations is false, and so is the heterosexual model on which it is loosely based and which it often corrupts. *If* to break out of the isolation of self is, in some way, actually possible, then that seems likely to be what man seeks. If that breaking out of isolation is not done at the cost of self, but at the expansion of self, it would seem to shake the whole foundation of modern human relations. If the introduction to this state comes from intimate contact with another member of one's own sex, leads through that to a state of consciousness that admits to a co-existence of spiritual beings that is conscious and aware and can be perceived, then the whole nature of human relations is changed. The world again becomes an organism in which man fits. The world is, in fact, reformed. What an exciting and mind-boggling concept. If people are capable of breaking out of their seemingly fundamental isolation, then fear is ended. Respect and love take its place, because if this is possible, it answers man's most fundamental hunger.

The questions then present themselves: Is my experience with my personal Greek unique to me or does almost everyone else have something comparable? Is it exclusive to homosexual relations or is the same experience possible to those with a heterosexual orientation? Does it mean that since I have had this experience with a man and not with a woman, that my orientation is really homosexual?

Certainly it would be the height of arrogance to assume that Yorgos and I are the only two people ever to experience this sense of being one person. The concept pervades literature from the 1200s onward, and every woman and man I have been seriously involved with has talked of it. These clues alone would seem to prove that it is not a unique experience. Still, from the descriptions that I have heard from friends, I think this experience was rare. Perhaps it is not excessive to conclude that not everyone has had a comparable experience.

I don't know how it would be possible to determine whether this particular kind of experience is exclusive to homosexual relations. Plato, in *The Symposium*, talks about levels or types of love, and the assumption is that the love discussed is homosexual, since that was the norm of the time. Aristophanes, one of the characters at the dinner, tells the tale that once people were actually composed of two individuals, and the gods were angered by their pride and separated them. There were three groupings possible in these composite beings: man/man, man/woman, and woman/woman. While this is obviously not a scientifically defensible analysis of the human condition, there is some kernel of plausibility in it that offers an explanation for differing sexual orientations. If we are each engaged in an obsessive search for our other half, why are some of us looking for the same sex partner and some looking for the opposite? Some of the romantic literature describing great heterosexual couples might be talking about the same kind of experience I enjoyed, but the things that make it unique seem to be missing in the descriptions. There is comparatively little contemporary homosexual literature, so it is hard to say if everyone else involved in a gay relationship is experiencing anything comparable.

Whether my having this experience with a man and not with a woman means that my orientation is truly homosexual depends on where it goes from here. If, as Socrates tells us in *The Symposium*, love progresses through stages (love of the beautiful *one*, love of *all* the beautiful ones, and love of beauty in the abstract) and this experience leads to further expansion along that line, then perhaps it does not signal an exclusive orientation. If it leads only to further search for my other (also male) half, then perhaps that is what it means to be gay. Time will tell if this experience best described as being one with another was a door into my personal being, or a door into the future of my species. That it was a door I have no doubt. That it opened into a realm of experience I had never dreamed existed, I am certain. What I don't yet know is where the path beyond the door will lead.

Index

Anonymous, 122–27
Argument, 251–82
  definition of an, 252
  goal of an, 252
  rules for evaluation of evidence in an, 253–54
  student example of an, 278–82
  tactics for waging a successful, 252–53
Arzumanian, Karineh J., 160–62
Ashurst, Henry Fountain, 201–02

Babayan, Saro, 73–74
Barbellion, W. N. P., 198–200
Beckham, David, 278–82
Boswell, James, 215–25
Brainstorming, 6
Byrd, William, 61–62

Camus, Albert, 64–66
Causal Analysis, 75–101
  antecedents and consequences in a, 76
  definition of a, 75
  student example of a, 100–01
  using words that indicate causation in a, 78
Comparison/Contrast, 191–210
  definition of a, 192
  practical strategies for writing the, 192–93
  student example of a, 208–10
  transitions in a, 193
Cotton, Jon, 137–39
Coward, Noel, 128–31
Cuomo, Mario M., 271–76
Curtis, Rebecca, 100–01

Definition, 163–91
  categorizing words in writing a, 164–65
  common errors to avoid in writing a, 165
  definition of a, 164
  student example of a, 188–91

Description, 51–54
  definition of a, 51
  dominant impression in a, 53
  focus in a, 53
  how to write a, 53–54
  memorable language in a, 53
  student example of a, 73–74
  vivid images and colorful words in a, 53
Division and Classification, 141–62
  definition of a, 142
  ideals to follow in writing a, 142–43
  student example of a, 160–62

Evelyn, John, 54–60
Examples, 211–50
  definition of, 212
  mistakes in writing, 212–13
  rhetorical modes in, 213
  student example of, 246–50

Frank, Anne, 204–07

Gide, André, 82–86
Grimke, Charlotte Forten, 68–71

Haley, John, 158–59
Hillesum, Etty, 94–99
Horner, Joyce Mary, 236–44

Journal, 1–7
  coherency in writing a, 6
  faithfulness and regularity in writing a, 5
  honesty in writing a, 4
  how to keep a, 4–7
  privacy of a, 5
  reasons to keep a, 2–3
  rhetorical patterns in a, 7

Kemble, Fanny, 151–53
Knight, Amelia Stewart, 106–20

Leconte, Emma Florence, 34–42
Lewis, C. S., 176–81

Lewis, Meriwether, 144–49
Lindbergh, Anne Morrow, 172–75

Maclane, Mary, 166–71
Mancia, Pimo, 208–10
Martin, Martha, 11–19
Matthiessen, Peter, 183–87

Narration, 9–50
   definition of a, 10
   how to write a, 10
   student example of a, 48–50
Nin, Anaïs, 88–92

Oli, Jo. J, 188–91

Pepys, Samuel, 44–47
Process, 103–39
   definition of, 104
   rules for writing the, 104–05
   student journal of, 137–39

Santamaria, Frances Karlen, 133–34
Sassoon, Siegfried, 231–34
Shirer, William, 260–65
Speer, Albert, 267–69
Stendhal, 227–29

Thoreau, Henry David, 194–97
Tolstoy, Sophia, 256–58
Tourtillot, Jane Gould, 21–32

Unterman, Katie, 246–50

Vanian, Lara, 48–50

Wagner, Cosima, 79–81
Woolf, Virginia, 154–57

Copyright Acknowlegments

Boswell, James. From BOSWELL ON THE GRAND TOUR 1756–1766 edited by Frank Brady & Frederick A. Pottle. Reprinted by permission of Edinburgh University Press and the Yale editions of the Private Papers of James Boswell.

Camus, Albert. "Death of an Old Actor," from NOTEBOOKS 1942–1951 by Albert Camus, trans, J. O'Brien. Copyright © 1965 by Alfred A. Knopf, Inc. Reprinted by permission of the publisher.

Cuomo, Mario M. From DIARIES OF MARIO M. CUOMO by Mario M. Cuomo. Copyright © 1984 by Mario M. Cuomo. Reprinted by permission of Random House, Inc.

Coward, Noel. From THE NOEL COWARD DIARIES edited by Graham Payn and Sheridan Morley. Reprinted by permission of George Weidenfeld & Nicolson Limited.

Englemann, Bernt. "The Battle of Stalingrad," from IN HITLER'S GERMANY. English translation copyright © 1986 by Random House, Inc. Reprinted by permission of Pantheon Books, a division of Random House, Inc.

Frank, Anne. From THE DIARY OF ANNE FRANK: THE CRITICAL EDITION by Anne Frank. Copyright © 1986 by Anne Frank-Fonds, Basle/Switzerland, for all texts of Anne Frank. Used by permission of Doubleday, a division of Bantam Doubleday Dell Publishing Group, Inc.

Gide, André. From THE JOURNALS OF ANDRE GIDE, VOL. II: 1914–1927 by André Gide. Copyright 1948 by Alfred A. Knopf, Inc. Reprinted by permission of Alfred A. Knopf, Inc.

Grimke, Charlotte Forten. Excerpt from THE JOURNALS OF CHARLOTTE FORTEN GRIMKE. Reprinted by permission of the Francis Grimke Papers, Moorland-Spingarn Research Center, Howard University.

Hillesum, Etty. Excerpt from AN INTERRUPTED LIFE by Etty Hillesum. English translation copyright © 1983 by Jonathan Cape Ltd. Reprinted by permission of Pantheon Books, a division of Random House, Inc.

Horner, Joyce. Reprinted from THAT TIME OF YEAR: A CHRONICLE OF LIFE IN A NURSING HOME, by Joyce Horner (Amherst: University of Massachusetts Press, 1982), copyright © 1982 by the University of Massachusetts Press.

LeConte, Emma Florence. "Poor Old Columbia" Reprinted with the permission of Macmillan Publishing Company from HEROINES OF DIXIE:

Confederate Women Tell Their Story of the War by Katharine M. Jones, editor, reissued by Mockingbird Books, 1990. Copyright © 1955 by the Bobbs-Merrill Company, Inc., renewed © 1983 by Jacqueline Jones.

Lewis, C. S. Excerpts from A GRIEF OBSERVED by C. S. Lewis. Copyright © 1961 by N. W. Clerk. Reprinted by permission of HarperCollins Publishers.

Lindberg, Anne Morrow. Excerpt from WAR WITHIN AND WITHOUT: DIARIES AND LETTERS 1939–1944, copyright © 1980 by Anne Morrow Lindberg, reprinted by permission of Harcourt Brace & Company.

Martin, Martha. Excerpt from O RUGGED LAND OF GOLD. Reprinted with the permission of Macmillan Publishing Company from O RUGGED LAND OF GOLD by Martha Martin. Copyright 1952, 1953 by Macmillan Publishing Company, renewed © 1980, 1981 by Christina H. Niemi.

Matthiessen, Peter. From NINE HEADED DRAGON RIVER, by Peter Matthiessen. © 1985 by Zen Community of New York. Reprinted by arrangement with Shambhala Publications, Inc., 300 Massachusetts Ave., Boston, MA 02115.

Mavor, Elizabeth. Excerpt from "Butler Island: Early-mid January, 1839," from FANNY KEMBLE: THE AMERICAN JOURNALS by Elizabeth Mavor. Reprinted by permission of Weidenfeld & Nicholson, 1990.

Nin, Anaïs. Excerpts from HENRY & JUNE: FROM THE UNEXPURGATED DIARY OF ANAÏS NIN, copyright © 1986 by Anaïs Nin, reprinted by permission of Harcourt Brace & Company.

Sage, Robert. From THE PRIVATE DIARIES OF STENDAHL by Robert Sage. Copyright © 1958 by Robert Sage. Used by permission of Doubleday, a division of Bantam Doubleday Dell Publishing Group, Inc.

Santamaria, Frances Karlen. From JOSHUA FIRSTBORN by Frances Karlen Santamaria. Copyright © 1970 by Frances Karlen Santamaria. Used by permission of Doubleday, a division of Bantam Doubleday Dell Publishing Group, Inc.

Sassoon, Siegfried. From SIEGFRIED SASSOON DIARIES, 1920–1922, edited by Rupert Hart-Davis 1981. Reprinted by permission of Faber & Faber Ltd.

Schlissel, Lillian. From WOMEN'S DIARIES OF THE WESTWARD JOURNEY by Lillian Schissel. Copyright © 1983 by Schocken Books, Inc. Reprinted by permission of Schocken Books, published by Pantheon Books, a division of Random House, Inc.

Shepard, Odell and Paul Spencer Wood. Excerpt from "John Evelyn's Diaries," from ENGLISH PROSE AND POETRY, 1660–1800. Copyright © 1934 by Houghton Mifflin Company.

Shirer, William L. From BERLIN DIARY: THE JOURNAL OF A FOREIGN CORRESPONDENT 1934–1941 by William L. Shirer. Copyright 1940, 1941 by William L. Shirer. By permission of Little, Brown and Company.

Silliker, Ruth J. From THE REBEL YELL AND THE YANKEE HURRAH by Ruth J. Silliker, Editor. Down East books, 1985.

Sparks, George. From A MANY COLORED TOGA: THE DIARY OF HENRY FOUNTAIN ASHURST, edited by George Sparks. Copyright 1962, The University of Arizona Press. Reprinted by permission of the publisher.

Speer, Albert. Reprinted by permission of Macmillan Publishing Company from SPANDAU: The Secret Diaries of Albert Speer by Albert Speer, translated from the German by Richard and Clara Winston. Copyright © English Translation © 1976 by Macmillan Publishing Company.

Tolstoy, Sofia. From THE DIARIES OF SOFIA TOLSTOY by Sophia Tolstoy, translated by Cathy Porter. Translation copyright © 1985 by Cathy Porter. Reprinted by permission of Random House, Inc.

Wagner, Cosima. "Friday, January 1" from Cosima Wagner's Diaries, Volume I, 1869–1877 translated by Geoffrey Skelton, copyright © 1976 by R. Piper & Co. Verlag, English translation copyright © 1978, 1977 by Geoffrey Skelton and Harcourt Brace & Company, reprinted by permission of Harcourt Brace & Company.

Woolf, Virginia. Excerpt from A PASSIONATE APPRENTICE: THE EARLY JOURNALS OF VIRGINIA WOOLF, 1897–1909 edited by Mitchell A. Leaska, copyright © 1990 by Quentin Bell and Angelica Garnett, reprinted by permission of Harcourt Brace & Company.